Keto Instant Vortex Air Fryer Oven Cookbook

600 Effortless, Delicious & Easy Recipes for Beginners and Advanced Users (Heal Your Body & Help You Lose Weight)

Koutan Jannes

© Copyright 2020 Koutan Jannes - All Rights Reserved.

In no way is it legal to reproduce, duplicate, or transmit any part of this document by either electronic means or in printed format. Recording of this publication is strictly prohibited, and any storage of this material is not allowed unless with written permission from the publisher. All rights reserved.

The information provided herein is stated to be truthful and consistent, in that any liability, regarding inattention or otherwise, by any usage or abuse of any policies, processes, or directions contained within is the solitary and complete responsibility of the recipient reader. Under no circumstances will any legal liability or blame be held against the publisher for any reparation, damages, or monetary loss due to the information herein, either directly or indirectly.

Respective authors own all copyrights not held by the publisher.

Legal Notice:

This book is copyright protected. This is only for personal use. You cannot amend, distribute, sell, use, quote or paraphrase any part of the content within this book without the consent of the author or copyright owner. Legal action will be pursued if this is breached.

Disclaimer Notice:

Please note the information contained within this document is for educational and entertainment purposes only. Every attempt has been made to provide accurate, up-to-date and reliable, complete information. No warranties of any kind are expressed or implied. Readers acknowledge that the author is not engaging in the rendering of legal, financial, medical or professional advice.

By reading this document, the reader agrees that under no circumstances are we responsible for any losses, direct or indirect, which are incurred as a result of the use of information contained within this document, including, but not limited to, errors, omissions, or inaccuracies.

Table of Contents

Introduction 8
Chapter 1: Keto Instant Vortex Air Fryer Oven Basics 9
    Instant Vortex Air Fryer Oven 9
    How Instant Vortex Air Fryer Oven Works? 9
    Buttons and Functions of Instant Vortex Air Fryer Oven 9
    Benefits of Vortex Air Fryer Oven 10
    Understanding Ketogenic Diet 11
Chapter 2: Breakfast & Brunch Recipes ... 12
    Spinach Egg Muffins 12
    Cheese Egg Bites 12
    Ham Egg Muffins 12
    Cheesy Egg Bites 13
    Healthy Zucchini Muffins 13
    Spinach Zucchini Egg Casserole 13
    Mushroom Cheese Quiche 14
    Sausage Omelet 14
    Bacon Egg Muffins 15
    Breakfast Egg Bake 15
    Artichoke Spinach Egg Bake 16
    Italian Egg Muffins 16
    Omelet Egg Cups 17
    Jalapeno Bacon Egg Cups 17
    Veggie Cheese Egg Bake 17
    Broccoli Egg Muffins 18
    Ham Egg Casserole 18
    Fluffy Egg Bake 19
    Baked Eggs 19
    Tomato Basil Egg Bake 19
    Healthy Asparagus Quiche 20
    Zucchini Breakfast Quiche 20
    Broccoli Egg Cups 20
    Broccoli Cheese Frittata 21
    Healthy Kale Egg Cups 21
    Italian Pesto Casserole 22
    Easy Egg Muffins 22
    Fresh Herb Egg Muffins 22
    Mexican Baked Omelet 23
    Spinach Bacon Egg Cups 23
    Roasted Pepper Frittata 24
    Healthy Tomato Spinach Frittata 24
    Sun-Dried Tomato Kale Egg Cups 24
    Breakfast Chicken Egg Cups 25
    Tomato Spinach Pepper Egg Cups 25
    Spicy Bacon Jalapeno Egg Cups 26
    Delicious Mexican Frittata 26
    Cream Cheese Muffins 26
    Coconut Breakfast Bread 27
    Banana Almond Bread Loaf 27
    Peanut Butter Bread Loaf 28
    Zucchini Breakfast Bread Loaf 28
    Almond Butter Bread 28
    Blueberry Breakfast Muffins 29
    Veggie Cheese Quiche 29
    Feta Mushroom Frittata 30
    Cheese Breakfast Quiche 30
    Delicious Artichoke Quiche 30
    Tasty Cappuccino Muffins 31
    Cauliflower Hash Browns 31
    Cheddar Jalapeno Breakfast Biscuits ... 32
    Healthy Spinach Pie 32
    Almond Pumpkin Muffins 32
    Pecan Breakfast Muffins 33
    Delicious Breakfast Casserole 33
    Zucchini Gratin 34
    Poppyseed Breakfast Muffins 34
    Chili Olive Breakfast Casserole 34
    Squash Casserole 35
Chapter 3: Poultry Recipes 36
    Delicious Turkey Cutlets 36
    Spinach Turkey Meatballs 36
    Baked Parmesan Chicken Breasts 36
    Juicy & Crispy Chicken Drumsticks ... 37
    Breaded Chicken Tenders 37
    Crispy Chicken Thighs 38
    Lemon Thyme Chicken 38
    Zucchini Turkey Meatballs 38
    Simple Baked Chicken Breasts 39
    Perfect Chicken Wings 39
    Greek Chicken Breasts 39
    Baked Chicken Thighs 40
    Spicy Chicken Meatballs 40
    Southwest Chicken 41
    Cheesy Ranch Chicken Breasts 41
    Spicy Chicken Breasts 41
    Pesto Chicken Thighs 42
    Delicious Chicken Fajitas 42
    Cheesy Tomato Baked Chicken 42
    Cajun Chicken 43
    Crunchy Chicken Tenders 43
    Zucchini Chicken Nuggets 43
    Asian Chicken Wings 44
    Easy Chicken Tenders 44
    Lemon Pepper Chicken 45

Delicious Chicken Casserole 45
Flavorful Chicken Fajita Casserole 45
Chicken Zucchini Casserole 46
Garlic Chicken 46
Meatloaf 47
Herb Chicken Drumsticks 47
Meatloaf 47
Flavorful Chicken Skewers 48
Sriracha Chicken 48
Cajun Chicken Drumsticks 49
Asian Chicken Skewers 49
Curried Chicken Thighs 49
Tandoori Chicken 50
Delicious Chicken Kabab 50
Simple Buffalo Wings 50
Crisp Crusted Chicken Breasts 51
Yummy Chicken Fajita 51
Dijon Chicken Breasts 52
Flavorful Chicken Thighs 52
Lemon Pepper Chicken Breasts 53
Hassel Back Chicken 53
Air Fryer Turkey Breast 53
Chicken with Broccoli 54
Ranch Chicken with Broccoli 54
Simple Chicken Thighs 54
BBQ Chicken Wings 55
Turkey Tenderloin 55
Pesto Chicken 55
Lemon Pepper Chicken Breasts 56
Baked Chicken with Tomato Mushrooms
.... 56
Meatloaf 57
Greek Chicken 57
Spicy Chicken Wings 57
Flavorful Chicken Drumsticks 58
Tasty Chicken Nuggets 58
Ranch Chicken Wings 58
Chicken Veggie Fritters 59
Healthy Chicken Patties 59
Parmesan Chicken Fritters 59
Marinated Greek Chicken 60
Simple Baked Chicken Breasts 60
Tasty Jerk Chicken Wings 61
Spiced Chicken Tenders 61
Herb Chicken Breast 61
Feta Turkey Patties 62

Chapter 4: Meat Recipes 63
Flavorful Baked Pork Chops 63
Cheesy Pork Chops 63
Juicy & Tender Pork Chops 63

Flavorful Bone-in Pork Chops 64
Super Delicious Ranch Pork Chops 64
Parmesan Pork Chops 64
Swiss Pork Chops 65
Lemon Garlic Pork Chops 65
Juicy Pork Tenderloin 66
Meatballs 66
Flavorful Lamb Chops 66
Spicy Jalapeno Sliders 67
Flavorful Cheese Casserole 67
Simple Herbed Beef Tips 67
Delicious Blackend Pork Tenderloin ... 68
Juicy Air Fryer Steak 68
Savory Lamb Chops 69
Ribeye Steaks 69
Mushroom Broccoli Steak Bites 69
Juicy Lime Jalapeno Steak 70
Steak Tips with Mushrooms 70
Cajun Pork Chops 71
Crispy Crusted Pork Chops 71
Garlic Herb Pork Chops 71
Pecan Crust Pork Chops 72
Ranch Pork Chops 72
Feta Lamb Patties 73
Meatballs 73
Rosemary Thyme Lamb Chops 73
Meatballs 74
Air Fryer Pork Ribs 74
Spicy Pork Chops 74
Marinated Pork Chops 75
Flavorful Lamb Steak 75
Asian Pork Shoulder 76
Meatloaf 76
Meatballs 76
Baked Beef with Broccoli 77
Meatballs 77
Burger Patties 78
Spicy Lamb Chunks 78
Thyme Lamb Chops 78
Marinated Lamb Chops 79
Dash Pork Chops 79
Meatballs 79
Coconut Pork Chops 80
Meatballs 80
Parmesan Crusted Pork Chops 81
Crispy Crusted Pork Chops 81
Meatballs 81
Lemon Pepper Pork Chops 82
Pork Burger Patties 82
Stuffed Pork Chops 82

Meatballs	83
Dill Beef Roast	83
Jamaican Pork Butt	84
Meatballs	84
Sirloin Steak	84
Delicious Kebab	85
Meatloaf	85
Montreal Steak	85
Basil Pesto Pork Chops	86
Creole Cheese Pork Chops	86
Garlic & Onion Pork Chops	86
Meatballs	87
Delicious Beef Satay	87
Easy Steak Fajita	88
Flavorful Beef Fajitas	88
Tasty Stuffed Peppers	88
Delicious Steak Kebab	89

Chapter 5: Vegetable Recipes 90

Perfect Roasted Brussels Sprouts	90
Zucchini Tomato Bake	90
Parmesan Yellow Squash	90
Tasty Baked Cabbage	91
Healthy Cauliflower Roast	91
Simple Roasted Beets	91
Flavorful Baked Okra	92
Baked Parmesan Fennel	92
Air Fryer Mushrooms	92
Air Fryer Asparagus	93
Spicy Garlic Cauliflower	93
Roasted Carrots Slices	94
Air Fry Garlic Broccoli	94
Curried Cauliflower	94
Buffalo Cauliflower	95
Lemon Garlic Roasted Eggplant	95
Radish Hash Browns	95
Air Fry Green Beans	96
Thyme Tomatoes	96
Chili Herb Tomatoes	96
Baked Artichoke Hearts	97
Lemon Broccoli & Tomatoes	97
Roasted Vegetables	97
Parmesan Zucchini	98
Air Fryer Tofu	98
Baked Zucchini Patties	99
Roasted Asparagus	99
Healthy Broccoli Fritters	99
Zucchini Casserole	100
Baked Cherry Tomatoes & Zucchini	100
Cauliflower Mac and Cheese	100
Baked Cheesy Eggplant Zucchini	101

Stuffed Bell Pepper	101
Mushrooms & Beans	102
Brussels Sprouts with Garlic	102
Lemon Cauliflower	103
Asparagus Quiche	103
Baked Parmesan Tomato	103
Zucchini Gratin	104
Baked Rutabaga Noodles	104
Feta Cheese Stuffed Peppers	105
Lemon Parmesan Broccoli	105
Cauliflower Rice	105
Cheesy Squash Noodles	106
Cauliflower Couscous	106
Cheesy Broccoli Casserole	107
Delicious Cheese Cutlet	107
Roasted Squash	107
Baked Broccoli	108
Roasted Ranch Broccoli	108
Spinach Stuffed Peppers	109
Alfredo Brussels Sprouts	109
Cheesy Butternut Squash	110
Baked Zucchini Noodles	110
Parmesan Green Bean Casserole	110
Basil Pesto Spaghetti Squash	111
Healthy Eggplant Salad	111
Eggplant Zucchini Casserole	112
Roasted Radishes	112
Broccoli Coconut Loaf	112

Chapter 6: Snacks & Appetizers 114

Delicious Broccoli Tots	114
Savory Jalapeno Poppers	114
Cheese Balls	114
Crab Stuffed Mushrooms	115
Cheesy Pesto Chicken Dip	115
Crisp Asparagus Fries	116
Healthy Zucchini Chips	116
Chicken Stuffed Mushrooms	116
Cheesy Stuffed Mini Peppers	117
Meatballs	117
Crispy Baked Broccoli	118
Parmesan Artichoke Hearts	118
Perfect Ricotta Cheese Dip	118
Tuna Muffins	119
Healthy Zucchini Patties	119
Garlicky Mushrooms	120
Sausage Balls	120
Spinach Ranch Dip	120
Tasty Buffalo Chicken Dip	121
Easy Artichoke Dip	121
Creamy Mexican Cheese Dip	122

Creamy Spinach Dip 122
Turkey Meatballs 122
Cauliflower Popcorn 123
Tasty Cauliflower Bites 123
Air Fryer Herb Mushrooms 123
Tasty Brussels Sprouts 124
Cheesy Spinach Dip 124
Cheese Dip 124
Ricotta Dip 125
Cheesy Onion Dip 125
Air Fryer Walnuts 126
Spicy Almonds 126
Easy Brussels Sprouts Chips 126
Crispy Onion Rings 127
Cinnamon Cashews 127
Broccoli Nuggets 127
Healthy Carrot Fries 128
Crispy Bacon 128
Salsa Jalapeno Poppers 128
Chestnuts Spinach Dip 129
Zucchini Fries 129
Chicken Dip 129
Delicious Jalapeno Poppers 130
Baked Eggplant Chips 130
Salmon Bites 131
Flavors Turkey Dip 131
Air Fryer Mushrooms 131
Creamy Shrimp Dip 132
Roasted Pecans 132
Cajun Zucchini Slices 132
Ranch Chicken Wings 133
Meatballs 133
Tasty Parmesan Carrot Fries 133
Broccoli Cheese Balls 134
Basil Pesto Poppers 134
Meatballs 135
Meatballs 135
Tasty Cauliflower Hummus 135
Tasty Cauliflower Tots 136

Chapter 7: Seafood Recipes 137
Delicious Baked Tilapia 137
Lemon Butter Tilapia 137
Baked Catfish 137
Easy Parmesan Tilapia 138
Garlic Butter Cod 138
Easy Baked Tilapia 139
Baked Parmesan Cod 139
Delicious Baked Cod 139
Lemon Parmesan Cod 140
Garlic Herb Cod 140

Lemon Pepper Sea Bass 140
Lemon Butter Shrimp 141
Shrimp with Cherry Tomatoes 141
Greek Shrimp 141
Flavorful Baked Shrimp 142
Italian Shrimp 142
Lemon Dill White Fish Fillets 143
Herb Salmon 143
Flavorful Crab Cakes 143
Lemon Garlic Scallops 144
Broiled Tilapia 144
Salmon with Tomato Salsa 144
Delicious Tuna Patties 145
Feta Tuna Patties 145
Salmon with Spread 146
Rosemary Salmon 146
Basil Tomato Salmon 146
Lemon Herb Tilapia 147
Italian Baked Cod 147
Air Fryer Catfish 148
Shrimp & Vegetables 148
Garlic Lemon Shrimp 148
Air Fryer Shrimp Scampi 149
Spicy Shrimp 149
Air Fryer Mackerel 149
Air Fryer Hot Shrimp 150
Creole Seasoned Shrimp 150
Shrimp with Cherry Tomatoes 150
Spicy Lemon Garlic Shrimp 151
Flavorful Crab Cakes 151
Lemon Pepper Tilapia 151
Easy Salmon Patties 152
Herb Butter Salmon 152
Lemon Herb Tilapia 152
Greek Salmon 153
Orange Chili Salmon 153
Parmesan Walnut Salmon 154
Taco Shrimp Fajitas 154
Chipotle Shrimp 154
Lime Shrimp Kababs 155
Curried Cod Fillets 155
Air Fryer Cajun Scallops 156
Tender Cod Fillets 156
Dill Salmon Patties 156
Lemon Garlic Cod 156
Salmon with Creamy Sauce 157
BBQ Parmesan Salmon 157
Delicious Parmesan Halibut 158
Ginger Garlic Fish Fillet 158
Chili Prawns 158

Chapter 8: Desserts Recipes 160
- Zesty Lemon Muffins 160
- Chocolate Chip Muffins 160
- Fudgey Flourless Chocolate Cake 160
- Chocolate Cookies 161
- Pumpkin Blondies 161
- Almond Butter Blondie's 162
- Healthy Chia Muffins 162
- Easy Choco Brownies 162
- Moist Cinnamon Muffins 163
- Cinnamon Strawberry Muffins 163
- Vanilla Pecan Muffins 164
- Almond Blueberry Muffins 164
- Coconut Pumpkin Muffins 164
- Lemon Blueberry Muffins 165
- Moist Chocolate Muffins 165
- Cranberry Bread Loaf 166
- Banana Almond Butter Bread 166
- Zucchini Chocolate Bread 166
- Delicious Mug Brownie 167
- Chocolate Cookies 167
- Vanilla Cinnamon Mug Cake 168
- Tasty Chocolate Brownies 168
- Coconut Muffins 168
- Vanilla Coconut Pie 169
- Tasty Brownie Muffins 169
- Raspberry Almond Muffins 169
- Cinnamon Apple Bars 170
- Moist Chocolate Cake 170
- Delicious Vanilla Cake 170
- Berry Cobbler 171
- Coffee Cookies 171
- Spiced Apples 172
- Chocolate Macaroon 172
- Pumpkin Pie 172
- Hazelnut Cookies 173
- Pumpkin Butter Cookies 173
- Almond Butter Coconut Cookies 173
- Almond Flaxseed Muffins 174
- Delicious Apple Muffins 174
- Choco Chip Peanut Butter Muffins .. 175

Chapter 9: Dehydrated Recipes 176
- Crisp Green Bean Chips 176
- Zucchini Chips 176
- Healthy Cashew Almond Crackers ... 176
- Walnut Crackers 177
- Parmesan Zucchini Chips 177
- Delicious BBQ Zucchini Chips 177
- Spicy Cucumber Chips 178
- Dehydrated Sweet Peppers 178
- Dehydrated Strawberries 178
- Healthy Beet Chips 179
- Broccoli Chips 179
- Dried Cauliflower 179
- Pork Jerky 180
- Beef Jerky 180
- Easy Chicken Jerky 180
- Spicy Pork Jerky 181
- Lamb Jerky 181
- Simple Tofu Jerky 182
- Eggplant Chips 182
- Squash Chips 182
- Avocado Chips 183
- Dehydrated Almonds 183
- Snap Pea Chips 183
- Mushroom Chips 183
- Marinated Eggplant Slices 184
- Easy Kale Chips 184
- Parsnips Chips 184
- Turkey Jerky 185
- Lemon Slices 185
- Dehydrated Bell Peppers 185

Chapter 10: 30-Day Meal Plan 187
Conclusion 189

Introduction

There are various advanced and smart cooking appliances are available in the market which helps to make your daily cooking easy in a smart way. In this cookbook, we have used such a smart cooking kitchen appliance popularly known as the Instant vortex air fryer oven. It is one of the versatile cooking appliances that use hot air circulation technology for making your daily cooking simple and easy. It works similarly to a convection oven in which very hot air is circulating into the cooking chamber with the help of a convection fan. The fan automatically adjusts the speed and maintains the desire internal temperature of the cooking chamber. It allows you to consume fewer calories compared to the deep-frying method. It cooks your food into very less oil, so the food cooked into instant vortex air fryer is healthier and low-calorie food. If you are one of the people who like fried food most and worried about extra calories. Then the vortex air fryer oven is one of the best choices for you. It fries a bowl of French fries into less than a tablespoon of oil and maintains the taste and texture of food like deep-fried food.

The instant vortex air fryer oven is a multi-tasking cooking appliance that helps you for grilling, roasting, baking, broiling, reheating your leftover food, and dehydrating food vegetables and meat. To do all these tasks you never need to buy separate appliances. Your instant vortex air fryer oven is capable to handle all these tasks. This will make your cooking simple, easy, and smart way.

In this book, we have used a unique combination of a healthy cooking appliance known as a vortex air fryer oven and a healthy diet plan known as the keto diet. Most of the peoples follow the keto diet for weight loss purpose. Keto diet changes your daily eating habit towards healthy eating food. The diet comes with long term health benefits. The book contains healthy keto recipes from breakfast to desserts. All the healthy and delicious recipes are done into an instant vortex air fryer oven. The recipes written in this book are unique and written into an easily understandable form. All the recipes are written in this book comes with their exact preparation and cooking time with their nutritional values. The nutritional values help you to keep the track of your daily calories and carb consumption.

My goal here is to introduce you with a unique combination of advanced healthy cooking gadgets and a healthy diet. There are various books available in the market on this topic thanks for choosing my book. I hope the book will help you during your keto journey and you love the recipes from this book.

Chapter 1: Keto Instant Vortex Air Fryer Oven Basics

Instant Vortex Air Fryer Oven

The instant vortex air fryer oven is one of the most advanced multi cooking appliances available in the market now. The biggest advantage of the vortex air fryer oven is that its large 10-quart capacity. It is capable to cook a large number of foods at once. Instant vortex air fryer oven is 7-in-1 multipurpose smart cooking appliances run on advanced microprocessor technology. It not only saves your kitchen space but also performs various cooking tasks into a single appliance. The smart programs are preset and design to get a perfect cooking result every time. Using these programs, you can easily air-fry crispy French fries, bake your favorite cakes and cookies, roast whole chicken at a time, broil fish or meat, reheat your leftover food and also dehydrate your favorite veggies and fruit slices. It is one of the best replacement options for your microwave, oven, dehydrator, and toaster.

The instant vortex air fryer oven comes with a user-friendly control system easily operates by anyone. No special skill requires operating your vortex air fryer oven. Just follow the instruction manual and cook healthy and delicious dishes at home. It cooks your food by circulating very hot air into the cooking chamber with the help of a convection fan. This will give you faster and even cooking results. It deep-fries your food into very less oil without compromising the taste and texture of deep-fried food. This will help to reduce your daily calorie consumption and make healthier and tasty dishes easily.

How Instant Vortex Air Fryer Oven Works?

The instant vortex air fryer requires 1500-watt energy and it is capable to produce a high temperature of 400° F. It works similarly as the convection oven technology. It uses hot air circulation technology in which very hot dry heats are circulating with the help of a convection fan around the food basket to cook your food fast and evenly from all the sides.

The instant vortex air fryer comes with 6 different accessories which help to make your daily cooking process easy. These accessories are 2 no's of Cooking Tray, Drip Pan, Rotisserie Basket, Rotisserie split with settings screw, 2 no's of rotisserie fork, and rotisserie lift. Before starting the actual cooking, process makes sure your instant vortex air fryer is kept on a flat surface.

- If preheat is require then preheat your vortex air fryer oven before placing the food inside. It takes approximately 3 to 4 minutes to preheat the air fryer oven.
- When the oven reaches the target temperature then the display indicates **Add Food**. Use hand protection gloves while placing your food into the cooking tray carefully and close the door.
- As per recipe requirements if the display indicates **turn Food** then turn, flip and shake the food.
- After finishing the cooking process display indicates **End** which means that the current running smart program has ended.

Buttons and Functions of Instant Vortex Air Fryer Oven

The vortex air fryer oven has various smart functions and buttons which makes your daily cooking simple and easy.

Touch Panel Display

The instant vortex air fryer oven comes with a big touch panel display. The display panel is equipped with automatic smart function and manual settings. The display helps to know the currently running programs, cooking time, cooking temperature, remainders, and error messages. When the air fryer oven is on standby mode then the display reads *OFF*.

Smart Functions

The vortex air fryer oven has equipped with smart functions, these functions are loaded with preset settings. While using these smart functions you never worry about time and temperature settings.

- **Air Fry:** Using this function you can air fry your favorite fried food into very less oil. A bowl of French fries requires just a tablespoon of oil to fry into an air fryer oven. It makes your French fries crispy from outside and tender from inside.
- **Roast:** Using rotisserie accessories you can roast your favorite meat, chicken, and beef under this function. Due to the 10-quart size, you can easily roast a whole chicken at a time.
- **Broil:** This function works similarly as grilling it helps to brown or toasting your food under direct radiant heat.
- **Bake:** This function is used to bake your favorite cakes, cookies, and desserts.
- **Reheat:** Using this function you can reheat pastries, frozen, and leftover food again.
- **Dehydrate:** This function allows you to dehydrate lots of food at once. It allows you to dehydrate your favorite fruits, vegetables, and meat slices.

Temp (+/-)

This function is used to adjust the temperature setting manually as per your recipe needs by pressing (+/-).

Time (+/-)

This function is used to adjust the time setting manually as per your recipe needs by processing (+/-).

Rotate

Once the cooking process is running you can use the rotate function to on and off the rotation of the rotisserie. This function is used while roasting your food.

Light

Using this function, you can see your food while cooking. Touching this function will ON and OFF the oven light. The light is automatically off after 2 minutes.

Cancel

Using this button, you can stop the current running program. While pressing this button the display reads OFF and the oven automatically goes into standby mode.

Start

This button is used to start the actual cooking process.

Benefits of Vortex Air Fryer Oven

The instant vortex air fryer has magical multi-cooking appliances that come with various benefits. These benefits include

1. Requires less oil to cook your food

   Compare to the traditional deep-frying method vortex air fryer requires very little oil to fry your food. It requires 85 % less oil compared with another deep-frying method. It fries your French fries within a tablespoon of oil without changing the taste and texture like deep-fried food. It makes your French fries crisp from outside and tender from inside.

2. Saves cooking time

Instant vortex air fryer oven is cooking your food by circulating very hot air into the cooking chamber. It blows 400° F hot air to cook your food very fast and it helps to save you cooking time. If you are one of the people who have a busy schedule, then the vortex air fryer oven is the best kitchen gadget for you. It cooks food faster and gives even cooking results within very less time.

3. Multi-cooking appliance

Vortex air fryer is one of the multi cooking appliances and the best replacement for microwave, oven, toaster, and dehydrator. It performs the task of the different appliances into a single cooking appliance. Due to this it not only saves your kitchen countertop space but also saves your money.

4. Smart cooking programs

Instant vortex air fryer loaded with smart cooking functions. It includes Air fry, Roast, Dehydrate, Reheat, Bake, and Broil. All these functions are pre-programmed, and you can use these functions without worrying about time and temperature settings.

5. Safe appliance to use

The vortex air fryer oven has come with a built-in protection feature against overheating. If the oven temperature exceeds over 450° F then the appliance is automatically shut off and the display reads error message E2.

Understanding Ketogenic Diet

A Keto diet is a LCHF (low carb high fat) diet plan. It is one of the most famous diet plans followed by many celebrities and sports persons to maintain their body weight and stamina. Many people face the overweight problem and follow various diet plans to reduce their weight. Some people take weight loss pills, doing hard exercise, workout in gyms but never get better results. A Keto diet is one of the natural and safest ways to reduce your excess body weight by just following a healthy diet plan. A Keto diet is one of the most effective diet plans which helps to reduce your body weight rapidly. It gives you long term weight loss benefits without any side effects. Normally our body uses glucose (carbohydrates) as a primary source for energy. While you are on a keto diet your body uses ketones as a primary source of energy instead of glucose. These ketones are produced when your body breaks down fats for energy. These ketones are one kind of acid production during the fat breaking process when your body doesn't get enough glucose. Your body shifts itself into the state of ketosis.

Ketosis is one of the metabolic states where your body doesn't get enough glucose for energy. It breaks down fats for energy instead of glucose. This will help to reduce your body weight effectively and ketones provide an endless source of energy for your body. It also helps to improve your both physical and mental health. Ketones not only provide energy to your body but also help to improve your heart functions. Due to antioxidant properties ketones helps to protect blood vessel lining and improves your blood circulation into the body. It improves your heart efficiency by 30 % and also improves blood flow by 75 %.

Compare to other diet plan keto diet is one of the most effective diets which helps to treat various medical conditions like Alzheimer's, Parkinson's disease, type-2 diabetes, high blood pressure, metabolic syndromes, and epilepsy conditions. During the keto diet, ketones are produced and used for energy. These ketones are one of the best sources of energy and it provides near about 70 % of your daily brain energy needs. It also improves your focus, learning and attention, and other memory functions.

Chapter 2: Breakfast & Brunch Recipes

Spinach Egg Muffins

Preparation Time: 10 minutes; Cooking Time: 12 minutes; Serve: 6

Ingredients:
- 4 eggs
- 6 tbsp cheddar cheese, shredded
- 2 tbsp heavy cream
- 1/4 cup fresh baby spinach, chopped
- 4 bacon slices, cooked chopped
- Pepper
- Salt

Directions:
1. Divide spinach and bacon evenly into the 6 silicone muffin molds.
2. In a bowl, whisk eggs with cheddar cheese, heavy cream, pepper, and salt.
3. Pour egg mixture over spinach and bacon.
4. Select BAKE mode, then set the temperature to 380 F and the time to 12 minutes, then press start.
5. When the display shows Add Food then place silicone muffin molds on the cooking tray and place in the vortex plus air fryer oven.
6. Serve and enjoy.

Nutritional Value (Amount per Serving):
Calories 157; Fat 12.4 g; Carbohydrates 0.7 g; Sugar 0.3 g; Protein 10.3 g; Cholesterol 137 mg

Cheese Egg Bites

Preparation Time: 10 minutes; Cooking Time: 15 minutes; Serve: 4

Ingredients:
- 4 eggs
- 1/2 tsp baking powder
- 1/3 cup almond flour
- 1 1/4 cups cheddar cheese, shredded
- 5 bacon slices, cooked & chopped
- 2 oz cream cheese, softened

Directions:
1. Add all ingredients into the mixing bowl and mix until well combined and let it sit for 10 minutes.
2. Pour mixture into the silicone muffin pan.
3. Select BAKE mode, then set the temperature to 350 F and the time to 15 minutes, then press start.
4. When the display shows Add Food then place the silicone muffin pan on the cooking tray and place it in the vortex plus air fryer oven.
5. Serve and enjoy.

Nutritional Value (Amount per Serving):
Calories 397; Fat 32.1 g; Carbohydrates 2.3 g; Sugar 0.6 g; Protein 24.7 g; Cholesterol 242 mg

Ham Egg Muffins

Preparation Time: 10 minutes; Cooking Time: 18 minutes; Serve: 12

Ingredients:
- 6 eggs
- 1 cup cheddar cheese, shredded
- 3/4 cup ham, chopped
- 1/2 tsp baking powder
- 1/4 cup heavy cream
- 1/4 tsp pepper
- 1/2 tsp salt

Directions:
1. In a bowl, whisk eggs with baking powder, cream, pepper, and salt. Stir in ham and cheese.
2. Pour egg mixture into the 12 silicone muffin molds.

3. Select BAKE mode, then set the temperature to 380 F and the time to 18 minutes, then press start.
4. When the display shows Add Food then place silicone muffin molds on the cooking tray and place in the vortex plus air fryer oven.
5. Serve and enjoy.

Nutritional Value (Amount per Serving):
Calories 92; Fat 7 g; Carbohydrates 0.8 g; Sugar 0.2 g; Protein 6.6 g; Cholesterol 100 mg

Cheesy Egg Bites

Preparation Time: 10 minutes; Cooking Time: 20 minutes; Serve: 4
Ingredients:
- 3 eggs, lightly beaten
- 1 1/2 cups cheddar cheese
- 1/2 tsp baking powder
- 1/3 cup coconut flour
- 4 oz cream cheese, softened
- 2 cups ham, chopped
- 1/2 tsp garlic powder
- Pepper
- Salt

Directions:
1. Add all ingredients into the mixing bowl and mix until well combined then place in the refrigerator for 10-15 minutes.
2. Drop mixture onto the parchment-lined cooking tray using a cookie scoop.
3. Select BAKE mode, then set the temperature to 350 F and the time to 20 minutes, then press start.
4. When the display shows Add Food then place the cooking tray and place in the vortex plus air fryer oven.
5. Serve and enjoy.

Nutritional Value (Amount per Serving):
Calories 434; Fat 33.2 g; Carbohydrates 5.4 g; Sugar 0.7 g; Protein 28.3 g; Cholesterol 237 mg

Healthy Zucchini Muffins

Preparation Time: 10 minutes; Cooking Time: 25 minutes; Serve: 12
Ingredients:
- 6 eggs
- 1/2 cup walnuts, chopped
- 1 1/2 cups shredded zucchini, squeeze out all liquid
- 1/2 tsp ground cinnamon
- 1/4 tsp baking soda
- 3 1/2 tbsp Truvia
- 1/2 cup coconut flour
- 1/3 cup coconut oil, melted
- 1/2 tsp salt

Directions:
1. In a bowl, whisk eggs with oil, coconut flour, Truvia, baking soda, cinnamon, and salt.
2. Stir in walnuts and shredded zucchini.
3. Pour egg mixture into the 12 silicone muffin molds.
4. Select BAKE mode, then set the temperature to 350 F and the time to 25 minutes, then press start.
5. When the display shows Add Food then place silicone muffin molds on the cooking tray and place in the vortex plus air fryer oven.
6. Serve and enjoy.

Nutritional Value (Amount per Serving):
Calories 121; Fat 11.4 g; Carbohydrates 2.9 g; Sugar 1.9 g; Protein 4.3 g; Cholesterol 82 mg

Spinach Zucchini Egg Casserole

Preparation Time: 10 minutes; Cooking Time: 30 minutes; Serve: 8

Ingredients:
- 10 eggs
- 1/4 cup goat cheese, crumbled
- 4 cherry tomatoes, cut in half
- 1/3 cup cheddar cheese, grated
- 1/3 cup ham, chopped
- 1 small zucchini, sliced
- 1/2 cup baby spinach, chopped
- 2/3 cup heavy cream
- Pepper
- Salt

Directions:
1. In a bowl, whisk eggs with pepper and salt. Stir in cheddar cheese, zucchini, ham, and spinach.
2. Pour egg mixture into the greased baking pan. Top with crumbled goat cheese, cheddar cheese, and tomatoes.
3. Select BAKE mode, then set the temperature to 350 F and the time to 30 minutes, and then presses start.
4. When the display shows Add Food then place the baking pan in the vortex plus air fryer oven.
5. Serve and enjoy.

Nutritional Value (Amount per Serving):
Calories 171; Fat 12.6 g; Carbohydrates 4 g; Sugar 2.4 g; Protein 11.1 g; Cholesterol 230 mg

Mushroom Cheese Quiche

Preparation Time: 10 minutes; Cooking Time: 40 minutes; Serve: 6

Ingredients:
- 6 eggs
- 1 cup mozzarella cheese, shredded
- 1/2 tsp garlic powder
- 1/3 cup parmesan cheese, shredded
- 1/2 cup water
- 1/2 cup heavy cream
- 2 cheese slices, cut into pieces
- 8 oz can mushroom, sliced
- 10 oz frozen spinach, thawed & drained
- Pepper
- Salt

Directions:
1. Spread spinach and mushrooms into the greased baking pan. Arrange cheese pieces on top of mushrooms and spinach.
2. In a bowl, whisk eggs with heavy cream, garlic powder, parmesan cheese, water, pepper, and salt.
3. Pour egg mixture over spinach and mushroom mixture. Sprinkle mozzarella cheese on top.
4. Select BAKE mode, then set the temperature to 350 F and the time to 40 minutes, then press start.
5. When the display shows Add Food then place the baking pan in the vortex plus air fryer oven.
6. Serve and enjoy.

Nutritional Value (Amount per Serving):
Calories 187; Fat 13.2 g; Carbohydrates 4.8 g; Sugar 0.7 g; Protein 13.3 g; Cholesterol 193 mg

Sausage Omelet

Preparation Time: 10 minutes; Cooking Time: 25 minutes; Serve: 12

Ingredients:
- 7 eggs
- 1 lb breakfast sausage
- 1 tsp mustard
- 2 cups cheddar cheese, shredded
- 3/4 cup heavy cream
- 1/4 onion, chopped
- 1/2 bell pepper, chopped
- 1/4 tsp pepper
- 1/2 tsp salt

Directions:
1. Brown the sausage in a pan until brown. Add bell pepper and onion and cook for 2 minutes more.
2. Transfer sausage mixture into the baking dish.
3. In a bowl, whisk eggs with mustard, 1 3/4 cup cheese, heavy cream, pepper, and salt.
4. Pour egg mixture over sausage mixture. Sprinkle remaining cheese on top.
5. Select BAKE mode, then set the temperature to 350 F and the time to 20 minutes, then press start.
6. When the display shows Add Food then place the baking dish in the vortex plus air fryer oven.
7. Serve and enjoy.

Nutritional Value (Amount per Serving):
Calories 271; Fat 22.4 g; Carbohydrates 1.4 g; Sugar 0.7 g; Protein 15.6 g; Cholesterol 157 mg

Bacon Egg Muffins

Preparation Time: 10 minutes; Cooking Time: 30 minutes; Serve: 12

Ingredients:
- 5 eggs, lightly beaten
- 1/2 cup cheddar cheese, shredded
- 3 bacon slices, cooked and chopped
- 3 tbsp water
- 1 tsp baking powder
- 3/4 cup almond flour
- 1/2 cup parmesan cheese, grated
- 2/3 cup cottage cheese
- 1/2 tsp salt

Directions:
1. In a bowl, whisk eggs with baking powder, water, almond flour, and salt.
2. Add remaining ingredients and mix until well combined.
3. Pour egg mixture into the 12 silicone muffin molds.
4. Select BAKE mode, then set the temperature to 400 F and the time to 25-30 minutes, then press start.
5. When the display shows Add Food then place silicone muffin molds on the cooking tray and place in the vortex plus air fryer oven.
6. Serve and enjoy.

Nutritional Value (Amount per Serving):
Calories 135; Fat 9.9 g; Carbohydrates 2.6 g; Sugar 0.5 g; Protein 9.7 g; Cholesterol 82 mg

Breakfast Egg Bake

Preparation Time: 10 minutes; Cooking Time: 20 minutes; Serve: 12

Ingredients:
- 7 eggs
- 2 cups cheddar cheese, shredded
- 3/4 cup heavy cream
- 2 tbsp butter
- 1 lb ham, chopped
- 1/2 bell pepper, chopped
- 1/4 tsp pepper
- 1/2 tsp salt

Directions:
1. Melt butter in a pan over medium heat.
2. Add bell peppers and ham in a pan and saute until peppers are softened and ham is browned.
3. In a bowl, whisk eggs with heavy cream, pepper, and salt. Stir in sauteed bell pepper and ham.
4. Pour egg mixture into the greased baking dish.
5. Select BAKE mode, then set the temperature to 350 F and the time to 20 minutes, then press start.

6. When the display shows Add Food then place the baking dish in the vortex plus air fryer oven.
7. Serve and enjoy.

Nutritional Value (Amount per Serving):
Calories 219; Fat 16.8 g; Carbohydrates 2.5 g; Sugar 0.6 g; Protein 14.4 g; Cholesterol 152 mg

Artichoke Spinach Egg Bake

Preparation Time: 10 minutes; Cooking Time: 35 minutes; Serve: 8
Ingredients:
- 8 eggs
- 4 egg whites
- 1/2 cup artichoke hearts, drained & chopped
- 10 oz frozen spinach, thawed and squeezed out all liquid
- 1/2 cup feta cheese, crumbled
- 1/4 tsp black pepper
- 2 tbsp parmesan cheese, grated
- 1/4 cup unsweetened almond milk
- 1 tbsp dill, chopped
- 1/2 tsp garlic, minced
- 1/3 cup bell pepper, diced
- 1/2 cup green onions, chopped
- 1 1/4 tsp kosher salt

Directions:
1. In a baking dish, mix together spinach, dill, garlic, bell pepper, artichoke, and green onions and spread evenly.
2. In a bowl, whisk eggs with egg whites, parmesan cheese, milk, pepper, and salt. Stir in feta cheese.
3. Pour egg mixture over vegetables.
4. Select BAKE mode, then set the temperature to 375 F and the time to 35 minutes, then press start.
5. When the display shows Add Food then place the baking dish in the vortex plus air fryer oven.
6. Serve and enjoy.

Nutritional Value (Amount per Serving):
Calories 119; Fat 7 g; Carbohydrates 173 g; Sugar 1.5 g; Protein 10.7 g; Cholesterol 173 mg

Italian Egg Muffins

Preparation Time: 10 minutes; Cooking Time: 20 minutes; Serve: 12
Ingredients:
- 8 eggs
- 1/3 cup feta cheese, crumbled
- 1/4 cup unsweetened almond milk
- 4 basil leaves, chopped
- 1/2 onion, diced
- 1 cup spinach, diced
- 1/2 cup sun-dried tomatoes, sliced
- Pepper
- Salt

Directions:
1. Divide spinach, feta cheese, onion, and sun-dried tomatoes evenly into the 12 silicone muffin molds.
2. In a bowl, whisk eggs with milk, basil, pepper, and salt.
3. Pour egg mixture over vegetable mixture.
4. Select BAKE mode, then set the temperature to 350 F and the time to 20 minutes, then press start.
5. When the display shows Add Food then place silicone muffin molds on the cooking tray and place in the vortex plus air fryer oven.
6. Serve and enjoy.

Nutritional Value (Amount per Serving):

Calories 58; Fat 3.9 g; Carbohydrates 1.3 g; Sugar 0.8 g; Protein 4.5 g; Cholesterol 113 mg

Omelet Egg Cups

Preparation Time: 10 minutes; Cooking Time: 20 minutes; Serve: 6

Ingredients:
- 9 eggs
- 2 oz cheddar cheese, shredded
- 1/2 bell pepper, diced
- 3 tbsp onion, diced
- 3 tbsp tomatoes, diced
- 3 tbsp spinach, chopped
- 3 bacon slices, cooked & chopped
- Pepper
- Salt

Directions:
1. In a bowl, whisk eggs with pepper and salt.
2. Add remaining ingredients and mix well.
3. Pour egg mixture into the 6 silicone muffin molds.
4. Select BAKE mode, then set the temperature to 350 F and the time to 20 minutes, then press start.
5. When the display shows Add Food then place silicone muffin molds on the cooking tray and place in the vortex plus air fryer oven.
6. Serve and enjoy.

Nutritional Value (Amount per Serving):
Calories 190; Fat 13.7 g; Carbohydrates 2.3 g; Sugar 1.4 g; Protein 14.4 g; Cholesterol 266 mg

Jalapeno Bacon Egg Cups

Preparation Time: 10 minutes; Cooking Time: 15 minutes; Serve: 12

Ingredients:
- 10 eggs
- 1/3 cup bacon, cooked & crumbled
- 1/2 cup cheddar cheese, grated
- 1/3 cup cream cheese, softened
- 3 jalapeno peppers, remove seeds & chopped
- 1/2 tsp onion powder
- 1/2 tsp garlic powder
- 1/4 tsp pepper
- 1 1/2 tsp sea salt

Directions:
1. In a bowl, whisk eggs with onion powder, garlic powder, cream cheese, pepper, and salt.
2. Add remaining ingredients and mix well.
3. Pour egg mixture into the 12 silicone muffin molds.
4. Select BAKE mode, then set the temperature to 400 F and the time to 15 minutes, then press start.
5. When the display shows Add Food then place silicone muffin molds on the cooking tray and place in the vortex plus air fryer oven.
6. Serve and enjoy.

Nutritional Value (Amount per Serving):
Calories 99; Fat 7.7 g; Carbohydrates 1 g; Sugar 0.5 g; Protein 6.6 g; Cholesterol 149 mg

Veggie Cheese Egg Bake

Preparation Time: 10 minutes; Cooking Time: 30 minutes; Serve: 8

Ingredients:
- 8 eggs, lightly beaten
- 2 cups mozzarella cheese, shredded
- 1/2 cup half and half
- 1 small onion, chopped
- 10 cherry tomatoes, sliced in half
- 8 asparagus, chopped
- Pepper
- Salt

Directions:
1. In a baking dish, mix together asparagus, cherry tomatoes, onion, and mozzarella cheese and spread evenly.
2. In a bowl, whisk eggs with half and half, pepper, and salt.
3. Pour egg mixture over vegetable mixture.
4. Select BAKE mode, then set the temperature to 350 F and the time to 30 minutes, then press start.
5. When the display shows Add Food then place the baking dish in the vortex plus air fryer oven.
6. Serve and enjoy.

Nutritional Value (Amount per Serving):
Calories 137; Fat 7.7 g; Carbohydrates 8.7 g; Sugar 5.1 g; Protein 9.8 g; Cholesterol 173 mg

Broccoli Egg Muffins

Preparation Time: 10 minutes; Cooking Time: 15 minutes; Serve: 6
Ingredients:
- 4 eggs
- 1/2 cup mozzarella cheese, shredded
- 1 cup broccoli, chopped and steamed
- Pepper
- Salt

Directions:
1. In a bowl, whisk eggs with pepper and salt. Stir in cheese and broccoli.
2. Pour egg mixture into the 6 silicone muffin molds.
3. Select BAKE mode, then set the temperature to 375 F and the time to 15 minutes, then press start.
4. When the display shows Add Food then place silicone muffin molds on the cooking tray and place in the vortex plus air fryer oven.
5. Serve and enjoy.

Nutritional Value (Amount per Serving):
Calories 54; Fat 3.4 g; Carbohydrates 1.3 g; Sugar 0.5 g; Protein 4.8 g; Cholesterol 110 mg

Ham Egg Casserole

Preparation Time: 10 minutes; Cooking Time: 30 minutes; Serve: 6
Ingredients:
- 9 eggs
- 1/2 cup bell pepper, chopped
- 1 1/3 cup ham, diced
- 1 cup cheddar cheese, shredded
- 1 tbsp butter
- 1 onion, diced
- 1/2 cup heavy cream
- Pepper
- Salt

Directions:
1. Melt butter in a pan over medium heat.
2. Add onion to the pan and saute until softened.
3. In a bowl, whisk eggs with heavy cream, pepper, and salt. Stir in sauteed onion, bell pepper, ham, and cheese.
4. Pour egg mixture into the greased baking dish.
5. Select BAKE mode, then set the temperature to 400 F and the time to 30 minutes, then press start.
6. When the display shows Add Food then place the baking dish in the vortex plus air fryer oven.
7. Serve and enjoy.

Nutritional Value (Amount per Serving):

Calories 281; Fat 21 g; Carbohydrates 4.7 g; Sugar 1.9 g; Protein 18.5 g; Cholesterol 301 mg

Fluffy Egg Bake

Preparation Time: 10 minutes; Cooking Time: 35 minutes; Serve: 6

Ingredients:
- 12 eggs
- 1/4 cup butter, melted
- 1 tsp baking powder
- 2 tbsp almond flour
- Pepper
- Salt

Directions:
1. In a bowl, whisk eggs until frothy. Add remaining ingredients and whisk until just combined.
2. Pour egg mixture into the greased baking dish.
3. Select BAKE mode, then set the temperature to 350 F and the time to 35 minutes, then press start.
4. When the display shows Add Food then place the baking dish in the vortex plus air fryer oven.
5. Serve and enjoy.

Nutritional Value (Amount per Serving):
Calories 208; Fat 17.6 g; Carbohydrates 1.6 g; Sugar 0.8 g; Protein 11.7 g; Cholesterol 348 mg

Baked Eggs

Preparation Time: 10 minutes; Cooking Time: 15 minutes; Serve: 2

Ingredients:
- 4 eggs
- 2 tbsp cheddar cheese, shredded
- 4 tbsp butter, melted

Directions:
1. Divide melted butter into the two ramekins.
2. Drop 2 eggs into each ramekin and top with 1 tbsp cheddar cheese.
3. Select BAKE mode, then set the temperature to 350 F and the time to 15 minutes, then press start.
4. When the display shows Add Food then place ramekins on the cooking tray and place in the vortex plus air fryer oven.
5. Serve and enjoy.

Nutritional Value (Amount per Serving):
Calories 358; Fat 34.1 g; Carbohydrates 0.8 g; Sugar 0.7 g; Protein 13.1 g; Cholesterol 369 mg

Tomato Basil Egg Bake

Preparation Time: 10 minutes; Cooking Time: 35 minutes; Serve: 6

Ingredients:
- 12 eggs
- 1/4 cup butter, melted
- 1/2 cup tomato basil sauce
- 8 oz mozzarella cheese
- Pepper
- Salt

Directions:
1. In a bowl, whisk eggs with melted butter, tomato basil sauce, cheese, pepper, and salt.
2. Pour egg mixture into the greased baking dish.
3. Select BAKE mode, then set the temperature to 350 F and the time to 35 minutes, then press start.
4. When the display shows Add Food then place the baking dish in the vortex plus air fryer oven.
5. Serve and enjoy.

Nutritional Value (Amount per Serving):
Calories 305; Fat 23.2 g; Carbohydrates 2.8 g; Sugar 1.3 g; Protein 22 g; Cholesterol 368 mg

Healthy Asparagus Quiche

Preparation Time: 10 minutes; Cooking Time: 45 minutes; Serve: 8

Ingredients:
- 10 eggs
- 2 lbs asparagus, trimmed and cut the ends
- 2 tbsp olive oil
- 1/4 tsp garlic powder
- 1/4 tsp pepper
- 1 tsp salt

Directions:
1. Arrange asparagus on a cooking tray.
2. Select ROAST mode, then set the temperature to 350 F and the time to 15 minutes, then press start.
3. When the display shows Add Food then place cooking in the vortex plus air fryer oven.
4. Meanwhile, in a bowl, whisk together eggs, oil, garlic powder, pepper, and salt.
5. Arrange roasted asparagus in a greased baking dish, pour egg mixture over asparagus.
6. Select BAKE mode, then set the temperature to 400 F and the time to 30 minutes, then press start.
7. When the display shows Add Food then place the baking dish in the vortex plus air fryer oven.
8. Serve and enjoy.

Nutritional Value (Amount per Serving):
Calories 132; Fat 9.1 g; Carbohydrates 4.9 g; Sugar 2.6 g; Protein 9.4 g; Cholesterol 205 mg

Zucchini Breakfast Quiche

Preparation Time: 10 minutes; Cooking Time: 40 minutes; Serve: 6

Ingredients:
- 8 eggs
- 1 cup zucchini, shredded and squeeze out all liquid
- 1/2 cup heavy cream
- 1 cup cheddar cheese, shredded
- 1/2 cup ham, cooked and diced
- 1/2 tsp dry mustard
- Pepper
- Salt

Directions:
1. Mix together zucchini, cheddar cheese, and ham in a greased baking dish.
2. In a bowl, whisk together eggs, heavy cream, mustard, pepper, and salt. Pour egg mixture over the zucchini mixture.
3. Select BAKE mode, then set the temperature to 375 F and the time to 40 minutes, then press start.
4. When the display shows Add Food then place the baking dish in the vortex plus air fryer oven.
5. Serve and enjoy.

Nutritional Value (Amount per Serving):
Calories 217; Fat 16.9 g; Carbohydrates 2.1 g; Sugar 0.9 g; Protein 14.5 g; Cholesterol 258 mg

Broccoli Egg Cups

Preparation Time: 10 minutes; Cooking Time: 30 minutes; Serve: 6

Ingredients:
- 4 eggs
- 4 oz broccoli, chopped
- 4 oz cheddar cheese, grated
- 2 tbsp butter, melted

- 1/3 cup unsweetened almond milk
- 1 3/4 cup almond flour
- 1 tbsp vinegar
- 1/4 tsp garlic powder
- 1 tsp parsley
- 1 1/2 tsp oregano
- 1/4 tsp baking soda
- 1/2 tsp baking powder
- 1/4 tsp black pepper
- 1/2 tsp salt

Directions:
1. In a large bowl, mix vinegar and milk and let sit for 5 minutes. Add butter and eggs and whisk well.
2. In a separate bowl, mix together all dry ingredients.
3. Pour wet ingredients to the dry ingredients and mix well.
4. Add cheddar cheese and chopped broccoli and mix well.
5. Pour mixture into the 6 silicone muffin molds.
6. Select BAKE mode, then set the temperature to 400 F and the time to 30 minutes, then press start.
7. When the display shows Add Food then place muffin molds on the cooking tray and place in the vortex plus air fryer oven.
8. Serve and enjoy.

Nutritional Value (Amount per Serving):
Calories 163; Fat 29.7 g; Carbohydrates 9.5 g; Sugar 1.9 g; Protein 16.1 g; Cholesterol 139 mg

Broccoli Cheese Frittata

Preparation Time: 10 minutes; Cooking Time: 25 minutes; Serve: 4

Ingredients:
- 10 eggs
- 2 cups broccoli, chopped
- 1/2 red bell pepper, diced
- 2 oz feta cheese, crumbled
- 2 tbsp olive oil
- 1 tsp black pepper
- 1 tsp salt

Directions:
1. In a bowl, whisk eggs with oil, pepper, and salt. Stir in broccoli, bell pepper, and feta cheese.
2. Pour egg mixture into the greased baking dish.
3. Select BAKE mode, then set the temperature to 400 F and the time to 25-30 minutes, then press start.
4. When the display shows Add Food then place the baking dish in the vortex plus air fryer oven.
5. Serve and enjoy.

Nutritional Value (Amount per Serving):
Calories 276; Fat 5.9 g; Carbohydrates 5.9 g; Sugar 3 g; Protein 17.3 g; Cholesterol 422 mg

Healthy Kale Egg Cups

Preparation Time: 10 minutes; Cooking Time: 30 minutes; Serve: 8

Ingredients:
- 6 eggs
- 1 cup kale, chopped
- 1/2 cup unsweetened almond milk
- 1/4 tsp garlic powder
- Pepper
- Salt

Directions:
1. Whisk eggs with garlic powder, pepper, milk, and salt in a mixing bowl. Stir in kale.
2. Pour mixture into the 8 silicone muffin molds.
3. Select BAKE mode, then set the temperature to 350 F and the time to 30 minutes, then press start.

4. When the display shows Add Food then place muffin molds on the cooking tray and place in the vortex plus air fryer oven.
   5. Serve and enjoy.

Nutritional Value (Amount per Serving):
Calories 54; Fat 3.5 g; Carbohydrates 1.3 g; Sugar 0.3 g; Protein 4.5 g; Cholesterol 123 mg

Italian Pesto Casserole

Preparation Time: 10 minutes; Cooking Time: 35 minutes; Serve: 4

Ingredients:
- 2 eggs
- 4 egg whites
- 1 lb Italian sausage
- 1/4 cup roasted pepper, sliced
- 1/4 cup basil pesto
- 3 oz parmesan cheese, grated
- 2/3 cup unsweetened almond milk
- Pepper
- Salt

Directions:
1. Brown the sausage in a pan over medium heat.
2. Spread sausage in 8-inch greased baking dish.
3. In a bowl, whisk together eggs, egg whites, parmesan cheese, milk, pepper, pesto, and salt. Stir in roasted pepper.
4. Pour egg mixture over sausage.
5. Select BAKE mode, then set the temperature to 400 F and the time to 35 minutes, then press start.
6. When the display shows Add Food then place the baking dish in the vortex plus air fryer oven.
7. Serve and enjoy.

Nutritional Value (Amount per Serving):
Calories 511; Fat 39.6 g; Carbohydrates 2.3 g; Sugar 0.9 g; Protein 35.6 g; Cholesterol 192 mg

Easy Egg Muffins

Preparation Time: 10 minutes; Cooking Time: 30 minutes; Serve: 12

Ingredients:
- 6 eggs
- 1 red bell pepper, chopped
- 1 1/2 tsp dried oregano
- 1/3 cup unsweetened almond milk
- 1 tomato, chopped
- 1/2 cup feta cheese, crumbled
- 1/4 tsp pepper
- 1/8 tsp salt

Directions:
1. In a bowl, whisk eggs with milk, oregano, pepper, and salt.
2. Divide cheese, tomato, and bell pepper evenly in 12 silicone muffin molds.
3. Pour egg mixture over cheese vegetable mixture.
4. Select BAKE mode, then set the temperature to 350 F and the time to 25-30 minutes, then press start.
5. When the display shows Add Food then place muffin molds on the cooking tray and place in the vortex plus air fryer oven.
6. Serve and enjoy.

Nutritional Value (Amount per Serving):
Calories 54; Fat 3.7 g; Carbohydrates 1.6 g; Sugar 1.1 g; Protein 3.9 g; Cholesterol 87 mg

Fresh Herb Egg Muffins

Preparation Time: 10 minutes; Cooking Time: 30 minutes; Serve: 12

Ingredients:

- 12 eggs
- 1 garlic clove, minced
- 1 1/2 tbsp fresh mixed herbs, chopped
- 1 small onion, chopped
- 3 tbsp olive oil
- Pepper
- Salt

Directions:
1. In a large bowl, whisk eggs with mixed herbs, pepper, and salt.
2. Heat oil in a pan over medium-high heat. Add onion and sauté for 4-5 minutes. Add garlic and sauté for 1 minute.
3. Add sauteed onion and garlic in the egg mixture.
4. Pour egg mixture into the 12 silicone muffin molds.
5. Select BAKE mode, then set the temperature to 350 F and the time to 25-30 minutes, then press start.
6. When the display shows Add Food then place muffin molds on the cooking tray and place in the vortex plus air fryer oven.
7. Serve and enjoy.

Nutritional Value (Amount per Serving):
Calories 96; Fat 7.9 g; Carbohydrates 1.1 g; Sugar 0.6 g; Protein 5.6 g; Cholesterol 164 mg

Mexican Baked Omelet

Preparation Time: 10 minutes; Cooking Time: 45 minutes; Serve: 8

Ingredients:
- 16 eggs
- 1 lb ground breakfast sausage
- 1 cup cheddar cheese, shredded
- 1 cup mozzarella cheese, shredded
- 1 1/2 cups unsweetened almond milk
- 1/2 cup salsa
- Pepper
- Salt

Directions:
1. Brown the sausage in a pan over medium heat.
2. In a large bowl, whisk eggs with milk, pepper, and salt. Stir in cheese, cooked sausage, and salsa.
3. Pour omelet mixture into the greased baking dish.
4. Select BAKE mode, then set the temperature to 350 F and the time to 40-45 minutes, then press start.
5. When the display shows Add Food then place the baking dish in the vortex plus air fryer oven.
6. Serve and enjoy.

Nutritional Value (Amount per Serving):
Calories 303; Fat 20.8 g; Carbohydrates 2.4 g; Sugar 1.3 g; Protein 26 g; Cholesterol 388 mg

Spinach Bacon Egg Cups

Preparation Time: 10 minutes; Cooking Time: 20 minutes; Serve: 12

Ingredients:
- 12 large eggs
- 4 bacon slices, cooked & chopped
- 1 tsp paprika
- 1/4 tsp garlic powder
- 2 cups fresh spinach, chopped
- 1 cup cheddar cheese, shredded
- Pepper
- Salt

Directions:
1. In a bowl, whisk eggs with paprika, garlic powder, pepper, and salt. Stir in bacon, spinach, and cheese.
2. Pour egg mixture into the 12 silicone muffin molds.

3. Select BAKE mode, then set the temperature to 350 F and the time to 20 minutes, then press start.
4. When the display shows Add Food then place muffin molds on the cooking tray and place in the vortex plus air fryer oven.
5. Serve and enjoy.

Nutritional Value (Amount per Serving):
Calories 146; Fat 10.8 g; Carbohydrates 0.9 g; Sugar 0.5 g; Protein 11.2 g; Cholesterol 203 mg

Roasted Pepper Frittata

Preparation Time: 10 minutes; Cooking Time: 45 minutes; Serve: 4
Ingredients:
- 2 cups egg whites
- 1/2 cup roasted red peppers, sliced
- 1/2 cup mozzarella cheese, shredded
- 1/4 cup fresh basil, sliced
- 1 cup cottage cheese, fat-free and crumbled
- 1/4 tsp garlic powder
- Pepper
- Salt

Directions:
1. In a bowl, whisk egg whites with garlic powder, pepper, and salt. Stir in roasted red pepper, mozzarella cheese, basil, and cottage cheese.
2. Pour egg mixture into the greased baking dish.
3. Select BAKE mode, then set the temperature to 375 F and the time to 45 minutes, then press start.
4. When the display shows Add Food then place the baking dish in the vortex plus air fryer oven.
5. Serve and enjoy.

Nutritional Value (Amount per Serving):
Calories 131; Fat 2 g; Carbohydrates 4.7 g; Sugar 2.1 g; Protein 22.3 g; Cholesterol 6 mg

Healthy Tomato Spinach Frittata

Preparation Time: 10 minutes; Cooking Time: 20 minutes; Serve: 8
Ingredients:
- 12 eggs
- 2 cups baby spinach, shredded
- 1/4 cup sun-dried tomatoes, sliced
- 1/4 cup parmesan cheese, grated
- 1 tsp dried basil
- Pepper
- Salt

Directions:
1. Whisk eggs in a large bowl with pepper and salt.
2. Add remaining ingredients and stir well to combine.
3. Pour egg mixture into the greased baking dish.
4. Select BAKE mode, then set the temperature to 400 F and the time to 15-20 minutes, then press start.
5. When the display shows Add Food then place the baking dish in the vortex plus air fryer oven.
6. Serve and enjoy.

Nutritional Value (Amount per Serving):
Calories 106; Fat 7.2 g; Carbohydrates 1.1 g; Sugar 0.7 g; Protein 9.5 g; Cholesterol 248 mg

Sun-Dried Tomato Kale Egg Cups

Preparation Time: 10 minutes; Cooking Time: 35 minutes; Serve: 12
Ingredients:

- 10 eggs
- 1 cup unsweetened almond milk
- 1/4 cup sausage, sliced
- 1/4 cup kale, chopped
- 1/4 cup sun-dried tomatoes, chopped
- Pepper
- Salt

Directions:
1. In a large bowl, whisk eggs with milk, pepper, and salt. Stir in sausage, and kale.
2. Pour egg mixture into the 12 silicone muffin molds.
3. Select BAKE mode, then set the temperature to 350 F and the time to 30-35 minutes, then press start.
4. When the display shows Add Food then place muffin molds on the cooking tray and place in the vortex plus air fryer oven.
5. Serve and enjoy.

Nutritional Value (Amount per Serving):
Calories 59; Fat 4.1 g; Carbohydrates 0.8 g; Sugar 0.4 g; Protein 4.9 g; Cholesterol 137 mg

Breakfast Chicken Egg Cups

Preparation Time: 10 minutes; Cooking Time: 15 minutes; Serve: 12

Ingredients:
- 10 eggs
- 1/3 cup green onions, chopped
- 1 cup cooked chicken, chopped
- 1/4 tsp garlic powder
- 1/4 tsp pepper
- 1 tsp sea salt

Directions:
1. In a large bowl, whisk eggs with garlic powder, pepper, and salt. Add remaining ingredients and stir well.
2. Pour egg mixture into the 12 silicone muffin molds.
3. Select BAKE mode, then set the temperature to 400 F and the time to 15 minutes, then press start.
4. When the display shows Add Food then place muffin molds on the cooking tray and place in the vortex plus air fryer oven.
5. Serve and enjoy.

Nutritional Value (Amount per Serving):
Calories 71; Fat 4 g; Carbohydrates 0.6 g; Sugar 0.4 g; Protein 8.1 g; Cholesterol 145 mg

Tomato Spinach Pepper Egg Cups

Preparation Time: 10 minutes; Cooking Time: 20 minutes; Serve: 12

Ingredients:
- 12 eggs
- 1 cup fresh spinach, chopped
- 1/2 cup red bell pepper, chopped
- 1/2 cup tomatoes, chopped
- 4 tbsp water
- 1 tsp Italian seasoning
- 1/2 tsp pepper
- 1/4 tsp salt

Directions:
1. In a bowl, whisk eggs with water, Italian seasoning, pepper, and salt. Stir in spinach, bell pepper, and tomatoes.
2. Pour egg mixture into the 12 silicone muffin molds.
3. Select BAKE mode, then set the temperature to 350 F and the time to 20 minutes, then press start.
4. When the display shows Add Food then place muffin molds on the cooking tray and place in the vortex plus air fryer oven.
5. Serve and enjoy.

Nutritional Value (Amount per Serving):

Calories 68; Fat 4.5 g; Carbohydrates 1.2 g; Sugar 0.8 g; Protein 5.7 g; Cholesterol 164 mg

Spicy Bacon Jalapeno Egg Cups

Preparation Time: 10 minutes; Cooking Time: 20 minutes; Serve: 12

Ingredients:
- 9 eggs
- 1 1/2 jalapeno pepper, sliced
- 8 oz cheddar cheese, shredded
- 4 bacon slices, cooked and chopped
- 3/4 cup heavy cream
- Pepper
- Salt

Directions:
1. In a large bowl, whisk eggs with cheese, heavy cream, pepper, and salt.
2. Divide bacon and jalapeno pepper evenly in 12 silicone muffin molds.
3. Pour egg mixture into the prepared muffin molds.
4. Select BAKE mode, then set the temperature to 350 F and the time to 20 minutes, then press start.
5. When the display shows Add Food then place muffin molds on the cooking tray and place in the vortex plus air fryer oven.
6. Serve and enjoy.

Nutritional Value (Amount per Serving):
Calories 184; Fat 15 g; Carbohydrates 0.9 g; Sugar 0.4 g; Protein 11.4 g; Cholesterol 160 mg

Delicious Mexican Frittata

Preparation Time: 10 minutes; Cooking Time: 25 minutes; Serve: 6

Ingredients:
- 8 eggs
- 1/2 cup cheddar cheese, grated
- 2 tbsp green onion, chopped
- 1/3 lb tomatoes, sliced
- 1 small green pepper, chopped
- 1 tbsp olive oil
- 1/2 cup salsa
- 2 tsp taco seasoning
- 1/2 lb ground beef
- 1/4 tsp salt

Directions:
1. Heat oil in a pan over medium heat. Add beef and sauté until browned.
2. Add salsa and taco seasoning and stir well.
3. Transfer meat from the pan and place on a plate.
4. Add green pepper to the same pan and cook for a few minutes.
5. Return meat to the pan with green onion and tomato.
6. Transfer meat mixture into the greased baking dish.
7. In a bowl, whisk eggs with cheddar cheese.
8. Pour egg mixture on top of meat mixture.
9. Select BAKE mode, then set the temperature to 375 F and the time to 20-25 minutes, then press start.
10. When the display shows Add Food then place the baking dish in the vortex plus air fryer oven.
11. Serve and enjoy.

Nutritional Value (Amount per Serving):
Calories 232; Fat 14.1 g; Carbohydrates 4.1 g; Sugar 2.2 g; Protein 22.3 g; Cholesterol 263 mg

Cream Cheese Muffins

Preparation Time: 10 minutes; Cooking Time: 25 minutes; Serve: 6

Ingredients:
- 4 eggs
- 4 oz cream cheese

- 1 scoop vanilla protein powder
- 2 tbsp butter, melted
- 1/2 tsp vanilla extract

Directions:
1. Add cream cheese and butter in a microwave-safe bowl and microwave until cheese is melted.
2. Add eggs, vanilla, and protein powder and beat until well combined.
3. Pour egg mixture into the 6 silicone muffin molds.
4. Select BAKE mode, then set the temperature to 350 F and the time to 25 minutes, then press start.
5. When the display shows Add Food then place muffin molds on the cooking tray and place in the vortex plus air fryer oven.
6. Serve and enjoy.

Nutritional Value (Amount per Serving):
Calories 161; Fat 13.4 g; Carbohydrates 0.9 g; Sugar 0.4 g; Protein 9.7 g; Cholesterol 140 mg

Coconut Breakfast Bread

Preparation Time: 10 minutes; Cooking Time: 40 minutes; Serve: 12
Ingredients:
- 5 eggs
- 1 1/4 cups almond flour
- 1/2 cup coconut flour
- 1/2 tsp baking soda
- 1 tbsp vinegar
- 4 tbsp coconut oil, melted
- 4 tbsp ground chia seeds
- 1/4 tsp sea salt

Directions:
1. In a bowl, mix together baking soda, chia seeds, almond flour, coconut flour, and sea salt.
2. In a separate bowl beat eggs with vinegar and coconut oil.
3. Add dry ingredients mixture into the egg mixture and mix until just combined.
4. Pour batter into the greased loaf pan.
5. Select BAKE mode, then set the temperature to 350 F and the time to 40 minutes, then press start.
6. When the display shows Add Food then place the loaf pan in the vortex plus air fryer oven.
7. Slice and serve.

Nutritional Value (Amount per Serving):
Calories 140; Fat 12.7 g; Carbohydrates 3.5 g; Sugar 0.6 g; Protein 5.2 g; Cholesterol 68 mg

Banana Almond Bread Loaf

Preparation Time: 10 minutes; Cooking Time: 50 minutes; Serve: 10
Ingredients:
- 3 eggs
- 3 bananas
- 1 tsp baking soda
- 2 cups almond flour
- 4 tbsp olive oil
- 1/2 cup walnuts, chopped

Directions:
1. Add all ingredients into the food processor and process until just combined.
2. Pour batter into the greased loaf pan.
3. Select BAKE mode, then set the temperature to 350 F and the time to 50 minutes, then press start.
4. When the display shows Add Food then place the loaf pan in the vortex plus air fryer oven.
5. Slice and serve.

Nutritional Value (Amount per Serving):

Calories 265; Fat 21.9 g; Carbohydrates 13.6 g; Sugar 5.3 g; Protein 8.5 g; Cholesterol 49 mg

Peanut Butter Bread Loaf

Preparation Time: 10 minutes; Cooking Time: 25 minutes; Serve: 8

Ingredients:
- 3 eggs
- 1 tbsp vinegar
- 1 cup peanut butter
- 1 tsp liquid stevia
- 1/2 tsp baking soda

Directions:
1. In a bowl, mix together all ingredients and until well combined.
2. Pour batter into the greased loaf pan.
3. Select BAKE mode, then set the temperature to 350 F and the time to 25 minutes, then press start.
4. When the display shows Add Food then place the loaf pan in the vortex plus air fryer oven.
5. Slice and serve.

Nutritional Value (Amount per Serving):
Calories 213; Fat 17.9 g; Carbohydrates 6.5 g; Sugar 3.2 g; Protein 10.1 g; Cholesterol 61 mg

Zucchini Breakfast Bread Loaf

Preparation Time: 10 minutes; Cooking Time: 45 minutes; Serve: 12

Ingredients:
- 4 eggs
- 1 cup zucchini, shredded and squeeze out all liquid
- 3/4 tsp baking soda
- 1/2 cup coconut flour
- 1 tbsp coconut oil
- 1 banana, mashed
- 1/2 cup walnuts, chopped
- 1 tsp vinegar
- 1/2 tsp nutmeg
- 1 tbsp cinnamon
- 1 tsp liquid stevia
- 1/2 tsp salt

Directions:
1. In a large bowl, mix together egg, banana, oil, and stevia.
2. Add all dry ingredients, vinegar, and zucchini and stir until smooth. Add walnuts and stir well.
3. Pour batter into the greased loaf pan.
4. Select BAKE mode, then set the temperature to 350 F and the time to 45 minutes, then press start.
5. When the display shows Add Food then place the loaf pan in the vortex plus air fryer oven.
6. Slice and serve.

Nutritional Value (Amount per Serving):
Calories 78; Fat 5.8 g; Carbohydrates 4 g; Sugar 1.6 g; Protein 3.4 g; Cholesterol 55 mg

Almond Butter Bread

Preparation Time: 10 minutes; Cooking Time: 45 minutes; Serve: 10

Ingredients:
- 3 eggs
- 1/4 cup butter, melted
- 3 1/2 cups almond flour
- 1 cup yogurt
- 1 tsp baking soda
- 1/4 tsp salt

Directions:
1. Add all ingredients into the large bowl and mix until well combined.

2. Pour batter into the greased loaf pan.
3. Select BAKE mode, then set the temperature to 350 F and the time to 45 minutes, then press start.
4. When the display shows Add Food then place the loaf pan in the vortex plus air fryer oven.
5. Slice and serve.

Nutritional Value (Amount per Serving):
Calories 301; Fat 25.8 g; Carbohydrates 10.2 g; Sugar 3.2 g; Protein 11.5 g; Cholesterol 63 mg

Blueberry Breakfast Muffins

Preparation Time: 10 minutes; Cooking Time: 25 minutes; Serve: 12
Ingredients:
- 2 eggs
- 1/2 cup fresh blueberries
- 1 tsp baking powder
- 6 drops stevia
- 1/4 cup butter, melted
- 1 cup heavy cream
- 2 cups almond flour
- 1/4 tsp lemon zest
- 1/2 tsp lemon extract

Directions:
1. In a mixing bowl, whisk eggs. Add remaining ingredients and mix until well combined.
2. Pour egg mixture into the 12 silicone muffin molds.
3. Select BAKE mode, then set the temperature to 350 F and the time to 25 minutes, then press start.
4. When the display shows Add Food then place muffin molds on the cooking tray and place in the vortex plus air fryer oven.
5. Serve and enjoy.

Nutritional Value (Amount per Serving):
Calories 190; Fat 17.6 g; Carbohydrates 5.4 g; Sugar 1.4 g; Protein 5.2 g; Cholesterol 51 mg

Veggie Cheese Quiche

Preparation Time: 10 minutes; Cooking Time: 40 minutes; Serve: 6
Ingredients:
- 8 egg whites
- 1/4 cup onion, diced
- 1 garlic clove, minced
- 1/2 cup unsweetened almond milk
- 1/4 cup roasted red peppers, sliced
- 1/2 cup cherry tomatoes, halved
- 1 cup cheddar cheese, shredded
- 2 cups steamed spinach, squeeze out all liquid
- 1 tsp olive oil
- Pepper
- Salt

Directions:
1. Heat oil in a pan over medium-high heat.
2. Add garlic and onion and sauté until onion softened.
3. In a bowl, whisk egg whites with cheese, and milk.
4. Add sautéed onion and garlic into the egg mixture and stir well.
5. Arrange tomatoes, roasted peppers, and spinach in a greased baking dish.
6. Pour egg mixture over the vegetables.
7. Select BAKE mode, then set the temperature to 350 F and the time to 40 minutes, then press start.
8. When the display shows Add Food then place the baking dish in the vortex plus air fryer oven.
9. Serve and enjoy.

Nutritional Value (Amount per Serving):

Calories 118; Fat 7.5 g; Carbohydrates 2.8 g; Sugar 1.4 g; Protein 10.1 g; Cholesterol 20 mg

Feta Mushroom Frittata

Preparation Time: 10 minutes; Cooking Time: 20 minutes; Serve: 2

Ingredients:
- 6 eggs
- 5 oz mushrooms, sliced
- 2 oz scallions, chopped
- 3 oz fresh spinach, chopped
- 4 oz feta cheese, crumbled
- 2 oz butter
- Pepper
- Salt

Directions:
1. In a bowl, whisk eggs, cheese, pepper, and salt.
2. Melt butter in a pan over medium heat. Add mushrooms and scallions and sauté for 5-10 minutes.
3. Add spinach and sauté for 2-3 minutes.
4. Pour egg mixture into the greased baking dish.
5. Select BAKE mode, then set the temperature to 350 F and the time to 20 minutes, then press start.
6. When the display shows Add Food then place the baking dish in the vortex plus air fryer oven.
7. Serve and enjoy.

Nutritional Value (Amount per Serving):
Calories 576; Fat 48.6 g; Carbohydrates 9.3 g; Sugar 5.4 g; Protein 28.9 g; Cholesterol 602 mg

Cheese Breakfast Quiche

Preparation Time: 10 minutes; Cooking Time: 45 minutes; Serve: 8

Ingredients:
- 12 eggs
- 4 oz cream cheese, softened
- 8 oz cheddar cheese, grated
- 3/4 cup butter
- Pepper
- Salt

Directions:
1. Add half cup cheddar cheese in greased baking dish.
2. Add eggs, cream cheese, and butter into the blender and blend until just combined.
3. Pour egg mixture over cheese in baking dish. Top with remaining cheddar cheese.
4. Select BAKE mode, then set the temperature to 325 F and the time to 45 minutes, then press start.
5. When the display shows Add Food then place the baking dish in the vortex plus air fryer oven.
6. Serve and enjoy.

Nutritional Value (Amount per Serving):
Calories 411; Fat 38.2 g; Carbohydrates 1.3 g; Sugar 0.7 g; Protein 16.6 g; Cholesterol 337 mg

Delicious Artichoke Quiche

Preparation Time: 10 minutes; Cooking Time: 40 minutes; Serve: 4

Ingredients:
- 3 eggs
- 1 cup artichoke hearts, chopped
- 1 cup mushrooms, sliced
- 1/2 cup cottage cheese
- 10 oz spinach
- 1/2 tsp olive oil
- 1 small onion, chopped
- 3 garlic cloves, minced
- Pepper
- Salt

Directions:

1. Heat oil in a pan over medium heat. Add onion, mushrooms, garlic, and spinach, and sauté for 2-3 minutes.
2. In a mixing bowl, whisk eggs with pepper and salt. Stir in cheese and artichoke hearts. Add sautéed vegetable mixture and mix well.
3. Pour egg and vegetable mixture into the greased baking dish.
4. Select BAKE mode, then set the temperature to 350 F and the time to 40 minutes, then press start.
5. When the display shows Add Food then place the baking dish in the vortex plus air fryer oven.
6. Serve and enjoy.

Nutritional Value (Amount per Serving):
Calories 123; Fat 4.8 g; Carbohydrates 10.2 g; Sugar 2 g; Protein 12 g; Cholesterol 125 mg

Tasty Cappuccino Muffins

Preparation Time: 10 minutes; Cooking Time: 25 minutes; Serve: 12
Ingredients:
- 4 eggs
- 2 cups almond flour
- 1/2 tsp vanilla
- 1 tsp espresso powder
- 1/2 cup sour cream
- 1 tsp cinnamon
- 2 tsp baking powder
- 1/4 cup coconut flour
- 1/2 cup Swerve
- Pinch of salt

Directions:
1. In a bowl, whisk eggs, sour cream, vanilla, and espresso powder.
2. Add almond flour, cinnamon, baking powder, coconut flour, Swerve, and salt and mix until well combined.
3. Pour egg mixture into the 12 silicone muffin molds.
4. Select BAKE mode, then set the temperature to 350 F and the time to 25 minutes, then press start.
5. When the display shows Add Food then place muffin molds on the cooking tray and place in the vortex plus air fryer oven.
6. Serve and enjoy.

Nutritional Value (Amount per Serving):
Calories 134; Fat 11 g; Carbohydrates 5.1 g; Sugar 0.9 g; Protein 6 g; Cholesterol 55 mg

Cauliflower Hash Browns

Preparation Time: 10 minutes; Cooking Time: 20 minutes; Serve: 12
Ingredients:
- 3 eggs
- 1 lb cauliflower, grated
- 1/2 cup almond flour
- 1 1/2 tsp lemon pepper
- 1/2 tsp baking powder
- 1/2 cup parmesan cheese, grated
- 3 oz onion, chopped
- 1 tsp salt

Directions:
1. Add all ingredients into the large bowl and mix until well combined.
2. Make small patties from mixture and place onto the parchment-lined cooking tray.
3. Select BAKE mode, then set the temperature to 400 F and the time to 20 minutes, then press start.
4. When the display shows Add Food then place the cooking tray and place in the vortex plus air fryer oven.
5. Turn hash browns halfway through.
6. Serve and enjoy.

Nutritional Value (Amount per Serving):
Calories 68; Fat 4.3 g; Carbohydrates 4.1 g; Sugar 1.5 g; Protein 4.5 g; Cholesterol 44 mg

Cheddar Jalapeno Breakfast Biscuits

Preparation Time: 10 minutes; Cooking Time: 20 minutes; Serve: 8
Ingredients:
- 1 egg
- 1 1/4 cups almond flour
- 1/4 tsp onion powder
- 1/4 tsp garlic powder
- 1/4 tsp Italian seasoning
- 3 garlic cloves, minced
- 1 1/2 cups cheddar cheese, shredded
- 4 oz cream cheese, softened
- 1/4 cup pickled jalapeno, chopped
- 1/4 cup water
- 1/4 cup heavy cream

Directions:
1. In a bowl, beat egg and cream cheese until well combined.
2. Add cheddar cheese, onion powder, garlic powder, Italian seasoning, and garlic and mix well.
3. Stir in almond flour, jalapeno, water, and heavy cream.
4. Pour egg mixture into the 8 silicone muffin molds.
5. Select BAKE mode, then set the temperature to 350 F and the time to 20 minutes, then press start.
6. When the display shows Add Food then place muffin molds on the cooking tray and place in the vortex plus air fryer oven.
7. Serve and enjoy.

Nutritional Value (Amount per Serving):
Calories 262; Fat 22.9 g; Carbohydrates 5.3 g; Sugar 1.1 g; Protein 11.1 g; Cholesterol 64 mg

Healthy Spinach Pie

Preparation Time: 10 minutes; Cooking Time: 30 minutes; Serve: 6
Ingredients:
- 5 eggs
- 10 oz frozen spinach, thawed, squeezed, and drained
- 2 1/2 cups cheddar cheese, grated
- 1/4 tsp garlic powder
- 1/4 tsp onion powder
- Pepper
- Salt

Directions:
1. Add all ingredients into the large bowl and mix until well combined.
2. Pour mixture into the greased baking dish.
3. Select BAKE mode, then set the temperature to 375 F and the time to 30 minutes, then press start.
4. When the display shows Add Food then place the baking dish in the vortex plus air fryer oven.
5. Serve and enjoy.

Nutritional Value (Amount per Serving):
Calories 254; Fat 19.4 g; Carbohydrates 2.8 g; Sugar 0.8 g; Protein 17.7 g; Cholesterol 186 mg

Almond Pumpkin Muffins

Preparation Time: 10 minutes; Cooking Time: 25 minutes; Serve: 8
Ingredients:
- 4 eggs
- 1 tsp vanilla
- 1/2 cup pumpkin puree
- 1 tbsp pumpkin pie spice
- 1 tbsp baking powder
- 2/3 cup erythritol

- 1/3 cup coconut oil, melted
- 1 cup almond flour
- 1/2 tsp sea salt

Directions:
1. In a large bowl, mix together pumpkin pie spice, baking powder, erythritol, almond flour, and sea salt.
2. Stir in eggs, vanilla, coconut oil, and pumpkin puree until well combined.
3. Pour egg mixture into the 8 silicone muffin molds.
4. Select BAKE mode, then set the temperature to 350 F and the time to 25 minutes, then press start.
5. When the display shows Add Food then place muffin molds on the cooking tray and place in the vortex plus air fryer oven.
6. Serve and enjoy.

Nutritional Value (Amount per Serving):
Calories 201; Fat 18.4 g; Carbohydrates 5.8 g; Sugar 1.3 g; Protein 6 g; Cholesterol 82 mg

Pecan Breakfast Muffins

Preparation Time: 10 minutes; Cooking Time: 20 minutes; Serve: 12
Ingredients:
- 4 eggs
- 1 1/2 cups almond flour
- 1/2 cup pecans, chopped
- 1/4 cup unsweetened almond milk
- 2 tbsp butter, melted
- 1/2 cup swerve
- 1 tsp psyllium husk
- 1 tbsp baking powder
- 1/2 tsp ground cinnamon
- 2 tsp allspice
- 1 tsp vanilla

Directions:
1. In a bowl, whisk eggs, almond milk, vanilla, sweetener, and butter until smooth.
2. Add remaining ingredients and mix until just combined.
3. Pour egg mixture into the 12 silicone muffin molds.
4. Select BAKE mode, then set the temperature to 400 F and the time to 15-20 minutes, then press start.
5. When the display shows Add Food then place muffin molds on the cooking tray and place in the vortex plus air fryer oven.
6. Serve and enjoy.

Nutritional Value (Amount per Serving):
Calories 145; Fat 12.6 g; Carbohydrates 5.5 g; Sugar 0.8 g; Protein 5.2 g; Cholesterol 60 mg

Delicious Breakfast Casserole

Preparation Time: 10 minutes; Cooking Time: 35 minutes; Serve: 4
Ingredients:
- 2 eggs
- 4 egg whites
- 2/3 cup parmesan cheese, grated
- 2/3 cup chicken broth
- 1 lb Italian sausage
- 1/4 cup roasted red pepper, sliced
- 1/4 cup pesto sauce
- 1/8 tsp black pepper
- 1/4 tsp sea salt

Directions:
1. Brown sausage in a pan over medium heat.
2. Transfer sausage in greased baking dish.
3. Whisk remaining ingredients in a mixing bowl and pour over sausage.
4. Select BAKE mode, then set the temperature to 400 F and the time to 35 minutes, then press start.

5. When the display shows Add Food then place the baking dish in the vortex plus air fryer oven.
6. Serve and enjoy.

Nutritional Value (Amount per Serving):
Calories 558; Fat 44.3 g; Carbohydrates 2.8 g; Sugar 2 g; Protein 35.6 g; Cholesterol 191 mg

Zucchini Gratin

Preparation Time: 10 minutes; Cooking Time: 25 minutes; Serve: 4

Ingredients:
- 1 egg, lightly beaten
- 1 1/4 cup unsweetened almond milk
- 3 medium zucchinis, sliced
- 1 tbsp Dijon mustard
- 1/2 cup nutritional yeast
- 1 tsp sea salt

Directions:
1. Arrange zucchini slices in the greased baking dish.
2. In a small saucepan, heat milk over low heat and stir in Dijon mustard, nutritional yeast, and sea salt.
3. Add beaten egg and whisk well.
4. Pour sauce over zucchini slices.
5. Select BAKE mode, then set the temperature to 400 F and the time to 25-30 minutes, then press start.
6. When the display shows Add Food then place the baking dish in the vortex plus air fryer oven.
7. Serve and enjoy.

Nutritional Value (Amount per Serving):
Calories 125; Fat 3.7 g; Carbohydrates 15 g; Sugar 2.7 g; Protein 12.8 g; Cholesterol 41 mg

Poppyseed Breakfast Muffins

Preparation Time: 10 minutes; Cooking Time: 40 minutes; Serve: 12

Ingredients:
- 3 eggs
- 2 tbsp poppy seeds
- 1/4 cup coconut oil
- 1/4 cup ricotta cheese
- 1 cup almond flour
- 1 tsp lemon extract
- 1/4 cup heavy cream
- 4 true lemon packets
- 1 tsp baking powder
- 1/3 cup Truvia

Directions:
1. Add all ingredients into the large bowl and beat until fluffy.
2. Pour egg mixture into the 12 silicone muffin molds.
3. Select BAKE mode, then set the temperature to 350 F and the time to 40 minutes, then press start.
4. When the display shows Add Food then place muffin molds on the cooking tray and place in the vortex plus air fryer oven.
5. Serve and enjoy.

Nutritional Value (Amount per Serving):
Calories 133; Fat 12.3 g; Carbohydrates 2.9 g; Sugar 0.8 g; Protein 4.3 g; Cholesterol 46 mg

Chili Olive Breakfast Casserole

Preparation Time: 10 minutes; Cooking Time: 35 minutes; Serve: 8

Ingredients:
- 12 eggs
- 4 oz green chilies, diced
- 2 cups cheddar cheese, grated

- 2 cups cottage cheese, rinsed and drained
- 6 oz olives, pitted and sliced
- 1/4 cup green onions, sliced
- Pepper
- Salt

Directions:
1. Add cottage cheese, cheddar cheese, green chilies, green onion, and olives in the greased baking dish.
2. Whisk beaten eggs and pour over cheese mixture. Season with pepper and salt.
3. Select BAKE mode, then set the temperature to 375 F and the time to 35 minutes, then press start.
4. When the display shows Add Food then place the baking dish in the vortex plus air fryer oven.
5. Serve and enjoy.

Nutritional Value (Amount per Serving):
Calories 232; Fat 13.1 g; Carbohydrates 14.4 g; Sugar 6.1 g; Protein 16.2 g; Cholesterol 40 mg

Squash Casserole

Preparation Time: 10 minutes; Cooking Time: 25 minutes; Serve: 6

Ingredients:
- 12 eggs
- 2 cups spaghetti squash, cooked
- 1 cup cheddar cheese, shredded
- 1 cup heavy cream
- 4 tbsp butter, melted
- 1/2 cup bell pepper, diced
- Pepper
- Salt

Directions:
1. In a large bowl, add all ingredients and mix well until combine.
2. Pour mixture into the greased baking dish.
3. Select BAKE mode, then set the temperature to 350 F and the time to 25 minutes, then press start.
4. When the display shows Add Food then place the baking dish in the vortex plus air fryer oven.
5. Serve and enjoy.

Nutritional Value (Amount per Serving):
Calories 352; Fat 30.3 g; Carbohydrates 4.6 g; Sugar 1.3 g; Protein 16.6 g; Cholesterol 395 mg

Chapter 3: Poultry Recipes

Delicious Turkey Cutlets

Preparation Time: 10 minutes; Cooking Time: 25 minutes; Serve: 4

Ingredients:
- 1 egg
- 1 1/2 lbs turkey cutlets
- 1/2 tsp garlic powder
- 1/2 tsp onion powder
- 1/2 tsp dried parsley
- 1/4 cup parmesan cheese, grated
- 1/2 cup almond flour
- Pepper
- Salt

Directions:
1. Season turkey cutlets with pepper and salt.
2. Add eggs into the small bowl and whisk well.
3. In a shallow dish, mix together parmesan cheese, garlic powder, onion powder, parsley, and almond flour.
4. Dip each turkey cutlet into the egg then coat with parmesan cheese mixture.
5. Place coated turkey cutlets onto the parchment-lined cooking tray.
6. Select BAKE mode, then set the temperature to 350 F and the time to 25 minutes, then press start.
7. When the display shows Add Food then place the cooking tray in the vortex plus air fryer oven.
8. Turn cutlet halfway through.
9. Serve and enjoy.

Nutritional Value (Amount per Serving):
Calories 405; Fat 17.8 g; Carbohydrates 3.8 g; Sugar 0.8 g; Protein 56.1 g; Cholesterol 174 mg

Spinach Turkey Meatballs

Preparation Time: 10 minutes; Cooking Time: 25 minutes; Serve: 6

Ingredients:
- 1 egg
- 2 lbs ground turkey
- 1/2 tsp garlic, minced
- 1 small onion, minced
- 10 oz frozen spinach, thawed, drained & chopped
- 1/4 tsp pepper
- 1 1/2 tsp salt

Directions:
1. Add all ingredients into the bowl and mix until well combined.
2. Make small balls from meat mixture and place onto the parchment-lined cooking tray.
3. Select BAKE mode, then set the temperature to 400 F and the time to 25 minutes, then press start.
4. When the display shows Add Food then place the cooking tray in the vortex plus air fryer oven.
5. Serve and enjoy.

Nutritional Value (Amount per Serving):
Calories 322; Fat 17.5 g; Carbohydrates 3 g; Sugar 0.8 g; Protein 43.8 g; Cholesterol 181 mg

Baked Parmesan Chicken Breasts

Preparation Time: 10 minutes; Cooking Time: 45 minutes; Serve: 4

Ingredients:
- 4 chicken breasts, skinless & boneless
- 5 Plain Greek yogurts
- 1 tsp garlic powder
- 1/2 cup parmesan cheese, grated
- 1/2 tsp pepper
- 1 tsp salt

Directions:
1. Season chicken breasts with pepper and salt and place into the baking dish.
2. Mix together yogurt, garlic powder, and parmesan cheese and pour over chicken breasts. Cover dish with foil.
3. Select BAKE mode, then set the temperature to 375 F and the time to 45 minutes, then press start.
4. When the display shows Add Food then place the baking dish in the vortex plus air fryer oven.
5. Serve and enjoy.

Nutritional Value (Amount per Serving):
Calories 347; Fat 13.3 g; Carbohydrates 5.1 g; Sugar 3.9 g; Protein 49.3 g; Cholesterol 139 mg

Juicy & Crispy Chicken Drumsticks

Preparation Time: 10 minutes; Cooking Time: 45 minutes; Serve: 6
Ingredients:
- 2 lbs chicken drumsticks
- 1 tsp parsley, chopped
- 1 tsp onion powder
- 1 tsp garlic powder
- 1 tsp paprika
- 2 tbsp olive oil
- 1/2 tsp pepper
- 1/2 tsp salt

Directions:
1. Add chicken drumsticks and remaining ingredients into the zip-lock bag, seal bag and shake well to coat.
2. Arrange chicken drumsticks onto the cooking tray.
3. Select BAKE mode, then set the temperature to 400 F and the time to 40-45 minutes, then press start.
4. When the display shows Add Food then place the cooking tray in the vortex plus air fryer oven.
5. Serve and enjoy.

Nutritional Value (Amount per Serving):
Calories 300; Fat 13.4 g; Carbohydrates 1 g; Sugar 0.3 g; Protein 41.8 g; Cholesterol 133 mg

Breaded Chicken Tenders

Preparation Time: 10 minutes; Cooking Time: 20 minutes; Serve: 4
Ingredients:
- 3 chicken breasts, cut into strips
- 2 tsp Italian seasoning
- 1/2 cup pork rinds, crushed
- 1/2 cup parmesan cheese, grated
- 1/2 cup mayonnaise

Directions:
1. In a small bowl, add mayonnaise.
2. In a shallow dish, mix together pork rinds, parmesan cheese, and Italian seasoning.
3. Dip the chicken strip into the mayonnaise then coats with pork rind mixture.
4. Place coated chicken strips onto the parchment-lined cooking tray.
5. Select BAKE mode, then set the temperature to 350 F and the time to 20 minutes, then press start.
6. When the display shows Add Food then place the cooking tray in the vortex plus air fryer oven.
7. Serve and enjoy.

Nutritional Value (Amount per Serving):
Calories 376; Fat 21.7 g; Carbohydrates 7.7 g; Sugar 2.1 g; Protein 36.7 g; Cholesterol 117 mg

Crispy Chicken Thighs

Preparation Time: 10 minutes; Cooking Time: 45 minutes; Serve: 4
Ingredients:
- 1 1/2 lbs chicken thighs, bone-in
- 1/4 tsp pepper
- 1/2 tsp onion powder
- 1/2 tsp garlic powder
- 1/2 tsp paprika
- 1 tbsp olive oil
- 1/2 tsp salt

Directions:
1. Add chicken thighs into the zip-lock bag, add remaining ingredients over chicken, seal bag and shake well to coat.
2. Arrange chicken thighs onto the cooking tray.
3. Select BAKE mode, then set the temperature to 400 F and the time to 34-45 minutes, then press start.
4. When the display shows Add Food then place the cooking tray in the vortex plus air fryer oven.
5. Serve and enjoy.

Nutritional Value (Amount per Serving):
Calories 356; Fat 16.1 g; Carbohydrates 0.7 g; Sugar 0.2 g; Protein 49.4 g; Cholesterol 151 mg

Lemon Thyme Chicken

Preparation Time: 10 minutes; Cooking Time: 30 minutes; Serve: 2
Ingredients:
- 2 chicken breasts, boneless & skinless
- 1 lemon juice
- 2 tbsp olive oil
- 2 sprigs thyme
- Pepper
- Salt

Directions:
1. Place chicken breasts into the baking dish then pour the remaining ingredients over the chicken.
2. Select BAKE mode, then set the temperature to 400 F and the time to 30 minutes, then press start.
3. When the display shows Add Food then place the baking dish in the vortex plus air fryer oven.
4. Slice and serve.

Nutritional (Amount per Serving):
Calories 415; Fat 25.3 g; Carbohydrates 3.3 g; Sugar 0.6 g; Protein 42.8 g; Cholesterol 130 mg

Zucchini Turkey Meatballs

Preparation Time: 10 minutes; Cooking Time: 18 minutes; Serve: 6
Ingredients:
- 2 eggs, lightly beaten
- 1 medium zucchini, grated
- 1 lb ground turkey
- 1 tsp cumin
- 1 tbsp dried onion flakes
- 1 tbsp basil, chopped
- 2 tbsp fresh oregano, chopped
- 1 tbsp garlic, minced
- 1 tbsp nutritional yeast
- 1/3 cup coconut flour
- 1/2 tsp salt

Directions:
1. Add all ingredients into the bowl and mix until well combined.
2. Make small balls from meat mixture and place onto the parchment-lined cooking tray.
3. Select BAKE mode, then set the temperature to 400 F and the time to 18 minutes, then press start.

4. When the display shows Add Food then place the cooking tray in the vortex plus air fryer oven.
5. Serve and enjoy.

Nutritional Value (Amount per Serving):
Calories 194; Fat 10.3 g; Carbohydrates 4.7 g; Sugar 1.1 g; Protein 24.2 g; Cholesterol 132 mg

Simple Baked Chicken Breasts

Preparation Time: 10 minutes; Cooking Time: 22 minutes; Serve: 6

Ingredients:
- 6 chicken breasts, boneless & skinless
- 1/4 tsp paprika
- 1 tsp Italian seasoning
- 2 tbsp olive oil
- 1/4 tsp pepper
- 1/2 tsp salt

Directions:
1. In a small bowl, mix together paprika, Italian seasoning, pepper, and salt.
2. Brush chicken breasts with oil and rub with spice mixture.
3. Place chicken breasts onto the cooking tray.
4. Select BAKE mode, then set the temperature to 400 F and the time to 22 minutes, then press start.
5. When the display shows Add Food then place the cooking tray in the vortex plus air fryer oven.
6. Serve and enjoy.

Nutritional Value (Amount per Serving):
Calories 320; Fat 15.7 g; Carbohydrates 0.2 g; Sugar 0.1 g; Protein 42.3 g; Cholesterol 130 mg

Perfect Chicken Wings

Preparation Time: 10 minutes; Cooking Time: 40 minutes; Serve: 4

Ingredients:
- 2 lbs chicken wings
- 1/8 tsp cayenne pepper
- 1/4 tsp pepper
- 1 tsp garlic powder
- 1 tsp onion powder
- 2 tbsp butter, melted
- 1 tsp sea salt

Directions:
1. In a small bowl, mix together cayenne pepper, pepper, garlic powder, onion powder, and salt.
2. Brush chicken wings with melted butter and rub with spice mixture.
3. Place chicken wings onto the cooking tray.
4. Select BAKE mode, then set the temperature to 400 F and the time to 40 minutes, then press start.
5. When the display shows Add Food then place the cooking tray in the vortex plus air fryer oven.
6. Serve and enjoy.

Nutritional Value (Amount per Serving):
Calories 487; Fat 22.6 g; Carbohydrates 1.1 g; Sugar 0.4 g; Protein 65.9 g; Cholesterol 217 mg

Greek Chicken Breasts

Preparation Time: 10 minutes; Cooking Time: 30 minutes; Serve: 4

Ingredients:
- 1 1/2 lbs chicken breasts, skinless & boneless
- 1 tbsp olive oil
- 1/2 tbsp dried oregano
- 2 garlic cloves, crushed
- 1 lemon zest, grated

- 1/4 tsp salt

Directions:
1. In a small bowl, mix together oil, oregano, garlic, lemon zest, and salt.
2. Rub oil mixture onto the chicken breasts. Place chicken breasts onto the cooking tray.
3. Select BAKE mode, then set the temperature to 350 F and the time to 30 minutes, then press start.
4. When the display shows Add Food then place the cooking tray in the vortex plus air fryer oven.
5. Serve and enjoy.

Nutritional Value (Amount per Serving):
Calories 358; Fat 16.2 g; Carbohydrates 1 g; Sugar 0.1 g; Protein 49.4 g; Cholesterol 151 mg

Baked Chicken Thighs

Preparation Time: 10 minutes; Cooking Time: 30 minutes; Serve: 4

Ingredients:
- 4 chicken thighs, pat dry with a paper towel
- 1 tsp dried parsley
- 1 tsp onion powder
- 1 tsp garlic powder
- Pepper
- Salt

Directions:
1. Mix together garlic powder, onion powder, dried parsley, pepper, and salt and rub all over chicken thighs.
2. Place chicken thighs onto the cooking tray.
3. Select BAKE mode, then set the temperature to 400 F and the time to 30 minutes, then press start.
4. When the display shows Add Food then place the cooking tray in the vortex plus air fryer oven.
5. Serve and enjoy.

Nutritional Value (Amount per Serving):
Calories 282; Fat 10.8 g; Carbohydrates 1 g; Sugar 0.4 g; Protein 42.4 g; Cholesterol 130 mg

Spicy Chicken Meatballs

Preparation Time: 10 minutes; Cooking Time: 25 minutes; Serve: 4

Ingredients:
- 1 lb ground chicken
- 1 tbsp vinegar
- 1/2 cup fresh cilantro, chopped
- 1 jalapeno pepper, minced
- 1 habanero pepper, minced
- 1 poblano chili pepper, minced
- 1 tsp salt

Directions:
1. Add all ingredients into the bowl and mix until well combined.
2. Make small balls from meat mixture and place onto the parchment-lined cooking tray.
3. Select BAKE mode, then set the temperature to 400 F and the time to 25 minutes, then press start.
4. When the display shows Add Food then place the cooking tray in the vortex plus air fryer oven.
5. Serve and enjoy.

Nutritional Value (Amount per Serving):
Calories 222; Fat 8.5 g; Carbohydrates 1.3 g; Sugar 0.8 g; Protein 33.1 g; Cholesterol 101 mg

Southwest Chicken

Preparation Time: 10 minutes; Cooking Time: 30 minutes; Serve: 4

Ingredients:
- 4 chicken breasts, boneless & skinless
- 1 cup cheddar cheese, shredded
- 1 cup of salsa
- 2 tbsp taco seasoning

Directions:
1. Rub chicken breasts with taco seasoning and place them into the baking dish. Pour salsa over chicken.
2. Select BAKE mode, then set the temperature to 350 F and the time to 25 minutes, then press start.
3. When the display shows Add Food then place the baking dish in the vortex plus air fryer oven.
4. Sprinkle cheese on top of the chicken and bake for 5 minutes more.
5. Serve and enjoy.

Nutritional Value (Amount per Serving):
Calories 419; Fat 20.8 g; Carbohydrates 5.1 g; Sugar 2.1 g; Protein 50.8 g; Cholesterol 161 mg

Cheesy Ranch Chicken Breasts

Preparation Time: 10 minutes; Cooking Time: 30 minutes; Serve: 4

Ingredients:
- 1 1/4 lbs chicken breasts, skinless & boneless
- 1/2 cup parmesan cheese, grated
- 1/2 cup cheddar cheese, shredded
- 1/4 cup ranch dressing

Directions:
1. Brush chicken breasts with ranch dressing and place onto the cooking tray.
2. Mix together parmesan cheese and cheddar cheese and place on top of chicken.
3. Select BAKE mode, then set the temperature to 350 F and the time to 30 minutes, then press start.
4. When the display shows Add Food then place the cooking tray in the vortex plus air fryer oven.
5. Serve and enjoy.

Nutritional Value (Amount per Serving):
Calories 367; Fat 17.6 g; Carbohydrates 1.4 g; Sugar 0.5 g; Protein 48.3 g; Cholesterol 149 mg

Spicy Chicken Breasts

Preparation Time: 10 minutes; Cooking Time: 45 minutes; Serve: 4

Ingredients:
- 4 chicken breasts
- 1 tbsp olive oil
- 2 tbsp Creole seasoning

Directions:
1. Brush chicken with oil and rub with Creole seasoning and place onto the cooking tray.
2. Select BAKE mode, then set the temperature to 400 F and the time to 40-45 minutes, then press start.
3. When the display shows Add Food then place the cooking tray in the vortex plus air fryer oven.
4. Serve and enjoy.

Nutritional Value (Amount per Serving):
Calories 307; Fat 14.3 g; Carbohydrates 0 g; Sugar 0 g; Protein 42.2 g; Cholesterol 130 mg

Pesto Chicken Thighs

Preparation Time: 10 minutes; Cooking Time: 30 minutes; Serve: 4
Ingredients:
- 2 lbs chicken thighs, bone-in
- 1/4 cup pesto
- 3 tbsp olive oil
- Pepper
- Salt

Directions:
1. Season chicken with pepper and salt and place into the bowl.
2. Mix together oil and pesto and pour over chicken. Coat chicken with pesto.
3. Arrange chicken onto the parchment-lined cooking tray.
4. Select BAKE mode, then set the temperature to 375 F and the time to 30 minutes, then press start.
5. When the display shows Add Food then place the cooking tray in the vortex plus air fryer oven.
6. Turn chicken after 20 minutes.
7. Serve and enjoy.

Nutritional Value (Amount per Serving):
Calories 589; Fat 33.8 g; Carbohydrates 1 g; Sugar 1 g; Protein 67.1 g; Cholesterol 206 mg

Delicious Chicken Fajitas

Preparation Time: 10 minutes; Cooking Time: 20 minutes; Serve: 6
Ingredients:
- 1 lb chicken breasts, skinless, boneless, & cut into strips
- 1/2 green bell pepper, cut into strips
- 1/2 red bell pepper, cut into strips
- 1 onion, sliced
- 1/2 tsp dried oregano
- 1 tsp garlic powder
- 1 1/2 tsp cumin
- 2 tsp chili powder
- 2 tbsp olive oil
- 1/2 tsp salt

Directions:
1. Add chicken and remaining ingredients into the zip-lock bag, seal bag shakes well and place in the refrigerator overnight.
2. Add marinated chicken mixture into the baking dish.
3. Select BAKE mode, then set the temperature to 400 F and the time to 20 minutes, then press start.
4. When the display shows Add Food then place the baking dish in the vortex plus air fryer oven.
5. Serve and enjoy.

Nutritional Value (Amount per Serving):
Calories 204; Fat 10.6 g; Carbohydrates 4.3 g; Sugar 2 g; Protein 22.6 g; Cholesterol 67 mg

Cheesy Tomato Baked Chicken

Preparation Time: 10 minutes; Cooking Time: 25 minutes; Serve: 4
Ingredients:
- 1 lb chicken breasts, skinless & boneless
- 1/2 cup Italian seasoning
- 1 cup mozzarella cheese, shredded
- 1 tbsp garlic, minced
- 1/4 cup butter, melted
- 14.5 oz can tomato, diced

Directions:
1. Season chicken with Italian seasoning.
2. Add tomatoes into the baking dish then place chicken breasts into the dish.

3. Add garlic and butter over chicken.
4. Select BAKE mode, then set the temperature to 400 F and the time to 20 minutes, then press start.
5. When the display shows Add Food then place the baking dish in the vortex plus air fryer oven.
6. Top with cheese and select BROIL mode then press start and broil until cheese is melted.
7. Serve and enjoy.

Nutritional Value (Amount per Serving):
Calories 448; Fat 29.5 g; Carbohydrates 9.3 g; Sugar 6 g; Protein 36.1 g; Cholesterol 155 mg

Cajun Chicken

Preparation Time: 10 minutes; Cooking Time: 45 minutes; Serve: 4

Ingredients:
- 2 lbs chicken wings
- 3 tbsp Cajun seasoning

Directions:
1. Add chicken wings into the mixing bowl. Sprinkle Cajun seasoning on top of the chicken and toss well.
2. Arrange chicken wings onto the cooking tray.
3. Select BAKE mode, then set the temperature to 400 F and the time to 45 minutes, then press start.
4. When the display shows Add Food then place the cooking tray in the vortex plus air fryer oven.
5. Serve and enjoy.

Nutritional Value (Amount per Serving):
Calories 86; Fat 3.4 g; Carbohydrates 0 g; Sugar 0 g; Protein 13.1 g; Cholesterol 40 mg

Crunchy Chicken Tenders

Preparation Time: 10 minutes; Cooking Time: 20 minutes; Serve: 6

Ingredients:
- 1 1/2 lbs chicken breasts, cut into strips
- 1 tbsp olive oil
- 2 egg whites, lightly beaten
- 1/2 cup pistachios, chopped
- 1 tbsp fresh thyme, chopped
- 1 tbsp fresh rosemary, chopped
- 1/2 tsp salt

Directions:
1. Add egg whites into the small bowl.
2. In a shallow dish, mix together pistachios, thyme, rosemary, and salt.
3. Dip each chicken strip into the egg whites then coat with pistachios mixture.
4. Place coated chicken strips onto the cooking tray and drizzle with olive oil.
5. Select BAKE mode, then set the temperature to 350 F and the time to 20 minutes, then press start.
6. When the display shows Add Food then place the cooking tray in the vortex plus air fryer oven.
7. Serve and enjoy.

Nutritional Value (Amount per Serving):
Calories 271; Fat 13.2 g; Carbohydrates 2.1 g; Sugar 0.4 g; Protein 35.1 g; Cholesterol 101 mg

Zucchini Chicken Nuggets

Preparation Time: 10 minutes; Cooking Time: 20 minutes; Serve: 4

Ingredients:
- 1 lb ground chicken
- 1 tsp dill, chopped

- 1 tsp onion powder
- 4 bacon slices, cooked and crumbled
- 1 zucchini, grated
- 1/2 tsp salt

Directions:
1. Add all ingredients into the mixing bowl and mix until well combined.
2. Make small patties from mixture and place onto the parchment-lined cooking tray.
3. Select BAKE mode, then set the temperature to 350 F and the time to 20 minutes, then press start.
4. When the display shows Add Food then place the cooking tray in the vortex plus air fryer oven.
5. Serve and enjoy.

Nutritional Value (Amount per Serving):
Calories 329; Fat 16.5 g; Carbohydrates 2.5 g; Sugar 1.1 g; Protein 40.6 g; Cholesterol 122 mg

Asian Chicken Wings

Preparation Time: 10 minutes; Cooking Time: 20 minutes; Serve: 4

Ingredients:
- 24 chicken wings
- 1 tsp pepper
- 2 tbsp soy sauce
- 2 tbsp Gochujang
- 2 tbsp canola oil
- 1 tbsp kosher salt

Directions:
1. Add chicken wings and remaining ingredients into the zip-lock bag, seal bag and shake well and place in the refrigerator overnight.
2. Arrange marinated chicken wings onto the parchment-lined cooking tray.
3. Select BAKE mode, then set the temperature to 350 F and the time to 20-30 minutes, then press start.
4. When the display shows Add Food then place the cooking tray in the vortex plus air fryer oven.
5. Serve and enjoy.

Nutritional Value (Amount per Serving):
Calories 307; Fat 16.4 g; Carbohydrates 1 g; Sugar 0.1 g; Protein 37 g; Cholesterol 112 mg

Easy Chicken Tenders

Preparation Time: 10 minutes; Cooking Time: 25 minutes; Serve: 5

Ingredients:
- 1 1/2 lb chicken tenders
- 1 tbsp olive oil
- 1/2 tbsp pepper
- 1 tbsp paprika
- 1 tbsp onion powder
- 1 tbsp garlic powder
- 1 tbsp kosher salt

Directions:
1. Add chicken tenders and remaining ingredients into the mixing bowl and toss well.
2. Arrange chicken tenders onto the cooking tray.
3. Select BAKE mode, then set the temperature to 375 F and the time to 25 minutes, then press start.
4. When the display shows Add Food then place the cooking tray in the vortex plus air fryer oven.
5. Serve and enjoy.

Nutritional Value (Amount per Serving):
Calories 299; Fat 13.1 g; Carbohydrates 3.5 g; Sugar 1 g; Protein 40.1 g; Cholesterol 121 mg

Lemon Pepper Chicken

Preparation Time: 10 minutes; Cooking Time: 30 minutes; Serve: 5
Ingredients:
- 2 lbs chicken tenderloins
- 1/2 tsp paprika
- 1/2 tsp garlic powder
- 1 tsp dried oregano
- 2 tsp lemon pepper
- 1 lemon juice
- 1 tbsp olive oil

Directions:
1. Brush chicken with oil and lemon juice. Mix together lemon pepper, oregano, garlic powder, and pepper and rub over chicken tenderloins.
2. Arrange chicken tenderloins onto the cooking tray.
3. Select BAKE mode, then set the temperature to 350 F and the time to 25-30 minutes, then press start.
4. When the display shows Add Food then place the cooking tray in the vortex plus air fryer oven.
5. Serve and enjoy.

Nutritional Value (Amount per Serving):
Calories 185; Fat 3.9 g; Carbohydrates 1.3 g; Sugar 0.3 g; Protein 37 g; Cholesterol 77 mg

Delicious Chicken Casserole

Preparation Time: 10 minutes; Cooking Time: 40 minutes; Serve: 8
Ingredients:
- 2 lbs cooked chicken, shredded
- 6 oz cream cheese, softened
- 4 oz butter, melted
- 5 oz ham, cut into small pieces
- 5 oz Swiss cheese slices
- 1 oz fresh lemon juice
- 1 tbsp Dijon mustard
- 1/2 tsp salt

Directions:
1. Add chicken in the greased baking dish then top with ham.
2. Add butter, lemon juice, mustard, cream cheese, and salt into the blender and blend until smooth.
3. Pour blended mixture on top of chicken and ham mixture.
4. Arrange Swiss cheese slices on top of sauce.
5. Select BAKE mode, then set the temperature to 350 F and the time to 40 minutes, then press start.
6. When the display shows Add Food then place the baking dish in the vortex plus air fryer oven.
7. Serve and enjoy.

Nutritional Value (Amount per Serving):
Calories 435; Fat 27.8 g; Carbohydrates 2.1 g; Sugar 0.8 g; Protein 42.7 g; Cholesterol 164 mg

Flavorful Chicken Fajita Casserole

Preparation Time: 10 minutes; Cooking Time: 15 minutes; Serve: 4
Ingredients:
- 1 lb cooked chicken, shredded
- 1 onion, sliced
- 1 bell pepper, sliced
- 1/3 cup mayonnaise
- 6 oz cream cheese
- 6 oz cheddar cheese, shredded
- 2 tbsp tex-mix seasoning
- Pepper
- Salt

Directions:
1. Mix all ingredients except 2 oz shredded cheddar cheese in a greased baking dish.

2. Spread remaining cheese on top.
3. Select BAKE mode, then set the temperature to 400 F and the time to 15 minutes, then press start.
4. When the display shows Add Food then place the baking dish in the vortex plus air fryer oven.
5. Serve and enjoy.

Nutritional Value (Amount per Serving):
Calories 476; Fat 26.3 g; Carbohydrates 12.6 g; Sugar 4.5 g; Protein 45 g; Cholesterol 142 mg

Chicken Zucchini Casserole

Preparation Time: 10 minutes; Cooking Time: 40 minutes; Serve: 8
Ingredients:
- 2 1/2 lbs chicken breasts, boneless and cubed
- 5 zucchinis, cut into cubes
- 12 oz roasted red peppers, drained and chopped
- 10 garlic cloves
- 2/3 cup mayonnaise
- 1 tsp xanthan gum
- 1 tbsp tomato paste
- 5 oz coconut cream
- 1 tsp salt

Directions:
1. Add zucchini and chicken in greased baking dish. Cover dish with foil.
2. Select BAKE mode, then set the temperature to 400 F and the time to 35 minutes, then press start.
3. When the display shows Add Food then place the baking dish in the vortex plus air fryer oven.
4. Meanwhile, in a bowl, stir together the remaining ingredients and pour over zucchini and chicken.
5. Select BROIL mode, then set the temperature to 350 F and the time to 5 minutes, then press start.
6. When the display shows Add Food then place the baking dish in the vortex plus air fryer oven.
7. Serve and enjoy.

Nutritional Value (Amount per Serving):
Calories 407; Fat 21.4 g; Carbohydrates 10.4 g; Sugar 4.2 g; Protein 42.4 g; Cholesterol 131 mg

Garlic Chicken

Preparation Time: 10 minutes; Cooking Time: 35 minutes; Serve: 4
Ingredients:
- 2 lbs chicken drumsticks
- 1 fresh lemon juice
- 10 garlic cloves, sliced
- 2 tbsp olive oil
- 4 tbsp butter
- 2 tbsp parsley, chopped
- Pepper
- Salt

Directions:
1. Season chicken with pepper and salt and place in greased baking dish.
2. Sprinkle the parsley and garlic over the chicken.
3. Drizzle lemon juice and olive oil on top of chicken.
4. Select BAKE mode, then set the temperature to 400 F and the time to 35-40 minutes, then press start.
5. When the display shows Add Food then place the baking dish in the vortex plus air fryer oven.
6. Serve and enjoy.

Nutritional Value (Amount per Serving):
Calories 560; Fat 31.6 g; Carbohydrates 2.9 g; Sugar 0.4 g; Protein 63.1 g; Cholesterol 230 mg

Meatloaf

Preparation Time: 10 minutes; Cooking Time: 30 minutes; Serve: 8
Ingredients:
- 1 egg
- 2 lbs ground turkey
- 1 tsp garlic powder
- 1 tsp garlic, minced
- 1 tbsp onion, minced
- 1 cup cheddar cheese, shredded
- 2 oz BBQ sauce, sugar-free
- 1 tsp ground mustard
- 1 tsp chili powder
- 1 tsp salt

Directions:
1. In a large bowl, mix together all ingredients then transfer to the greased loaf pan.
2. Select BAKE mode, then set the temperature to 400 F and the time to 30-35 minutes, then press start.
3. When the display shows Add Food then place the loaf pan in the vortex plus air fryer oven.
4. Serve and enjoy.

Nutritional Value (Amount per Serving):
Calories 302; Fat 17.9 g; Carbohydrates 3.6 g; Sugar 2.2 g; Protein 35.5 g; Cholesterol 151 mg

Herb Chicken Drumsticks

Preparation Time: 10 minutes; Cooking Time: 20 minutes; Serve: 4
Ingredients:
- 4 chicken drumsticks
- 1 tsp chili powder
- 1 1/2 tsp mixed herbs
- 1 tbsp lemon juice
- 1 tsp garlic salt

Directions:
1. In a small bowl, mix together garlic salt, chili powder, and mixed herbs.
2. Brush chicken with lemon juice and rub with garlic salt mixture.
3. Place chicken onto the cooking tray.
4. Select AIRFRY mode, then set the temperature to 350 F and the time to 15-20 minutes, then press start.
5. When the display shows Add Food then place the cooking tray in the vortex plus air fryer oven.
6. Turn chicken drumsticks halfway through.
7. Serve and enjoy.

Nutritional Value (Amount per Serving):
Calories 84; Fat 2.8 g; Carbohydrates 1.1 g; Sugar 0.3 g; Protein 40 g; Cholesterol 40 mg

Meatloaf

Preparation Time: 10 minutes; Cooking Time: 40 minutes; Serve: 6
Ingredients:
- 1 egg
- 1 lb ground chicken
- 3/4 cup spinach, chopped
- 1/2 cup onion, grated
- 1 tsp water
- 2 tbsp tomato paste
- 1/4 cup goat cheese, crumbled
- 1/2 cup sun-dried tomatoes, chopped
- 1/2 lemon zest
- 1/2 tsp dried dill
- 1/2 tsp pepper
- 1/2 tsp kosher salt

Directions:

1. In a mixing bowl, add all ingredients and mix until well combined.
2. Transfer meat mixture into the greased loaf pan.
3. Select BAKE mode, then set the temperature to 375 F and the time to 40 minutes, then press start.
4. When the display shows Add Food then place the loaf pan in the vortex plus air fryer oven.
5. Slice and serve.

Nutritional Value (Amount per Serving):
Calories 186; Fat 7.9 g; Carbohydrates 3 g; Sugar 1.6 g; Protein 24.7 g; Cholesterol 99 mg

Flavorful Chicken Skewers

Preparation Time: 10 minutes; Cooking Time: 20 minutes; Serve: 4
Ingredients:
- 1 1/2 lbs chicken breast, cut into 1-inch cubes

For marinade:
- 1/4 cup fresh mint leaves
- 4 garlic cloves
- 1/2 cup lemon juice
- 1/4 tsp cayenne
- 1 tbsp vinegar
- 1/2 cup yogurt
- 2 tbsp fresh rosemary, chopped
- 2 tbsp dried oregano
- 1 cup olive oil
- Pepper
- Salt

Directions:
1. Add all marinade ingredients into the blender and blend until smooth.
2. Pour blended mixture in a large bowl. Add chicken and coat well and place it in the refrigerator for 1 hour.
3. Slide marinated chicken onto the skewers. Place skewers onto the cooking tray.
4. Select BAKE mode, then set the temperature to 400 F and the time to 15-20 minutes, then press start.
5. When the display shows Add Food then place the cooking tray in the vortex plus air fryer oven.
6. Serve and enjoy.

Nutritional Value (Amount per Serving):
Calories 676; Fat 55.8 g; Carbohydrates 6.9 g; Sugar 3 g; Protein 38.8 g; Cholesterol 111 mg

Sriracha Chicken

Preparation Time: 10 minutes; Cooking Time: 33 minutes; Serve: 2
Ingredients:
- 1 lb chicken wings
- 2 tbsp sriracha sauce
- 1/2 lime juice
- 1 tbsp butter

Directions:
1. Arrange chicken wings onto the cooking tray.
2. Select AIRFRY mode, then set the temperature to 360 F and the time to 30 minutes, then press start.
3. When the display shows Add Food then place the cooking tray in the vortex plus air fryer oven.
4. Meanwhile, In a pan, add all remaining ingredients and cook for 3 minutes.
5. Toss chicken wings with sauce and serve.

Nutritional Value (Amount per Serving):
Calories 485; Fat 22.6 g; Carbohydrates 0.9 g; Sugar 0.2 g; Protein 65.7 g; Cholesterol 217 mg

Cajun Chicken Drumsticks

Preparation Time: 10 minutes; Cooking Time: 15 minutes; Serve: 2
Ingredients:
- 2 chicken drumsticks
- 2 tsp olive oil
- 1 tbsp Cajun seasoning

Directions:
1. Brush chicken drumsticks with oil and season with Cajun seasoning.
2. Place chicken drumsticks onto the cooking tray.
3. Select AIRFRY mode, then set the temperature to 400 F and the time to 15 minutes, then press start.
4. When the display shows Add Food then place the cooking tray in the vortex plus air fryer oven.
5. Serve and enjoy.

Nutritional Value (Amount per Serving):
Calories 118; Fat 7.3 g; Carbohydrates 0 g; Sugar 0 g; Protein 12.7 g; Cholesterol 40 mg

Asian Chicken Skewers

Preparation Time: 10 minutes; Cooking Time: 7 minutes; Serve: 4
Ingredients:
- 1 lb chicken tenders, boneless
- 4 garlic cloves, chopped
- 1/4 cup sesame oil
- 1/2 cup orange juice
- 2 tsp sesame seeds, toasted
- 1 tbsp ginger, grated
- 1 tbsp scallions, chopped
- Pepper
- Salt

Directions:
1. Slide chicken tenders on wooden skewers.
2. In a bowl, mix together the remaining ingredients. Add chicken skewers into the bowl and coat well and place it in the refrigerator for 1 hour.
3. Place marinated chicken skewers onto the cooking tray.
4. Select AIRFRY mode, then set the temperature to 390 F and the time to 5-7 minutes, then press start.
5. When the display shows Add Food then place the cooking tray in the vortex plus air fryer oven.
6. Serve and enjoy.

Nutritional Value (Amount per Serving):
Calories 368; Fat 22.9 g; Carbohydrates 5.7 g; Sugar 2.7 g; Protein 33.6 g; Cholesterol 101 mg

Curried Chicken Thighs

Preparation Time: 10 minutes; Cooking Time: 20 minutes; Serve: 4
Ingredients:
- 1 lb chicken thighs, boneless and skinless
- 1/2 cup coconut milk
- 2 tbsp curry paste
- 2 tsp ginger, minced
- 1 tbsp garlic, chopped

Directions:
1. Add all ingredients into the zip-lock bag, seal bag, and shake well and place it in the refrigerator overnight.
2. Add marinated chicken with sauce in baking dish.
3. Select AIRFRY mode, then set the temperature to 180 F and the time to 20 minutes, then press start.

4. When the display shows Add Food then place the baking dish in the vortex plus air fryer oven.
5. Serve and enjoy.

Nutritional Value (Amount per Serving):
Calories 341; Fat 20 g; Carbohydrates 5.1 g; Sugar 1.1 g; Protein 34.1 g; Cholesterol 101 mg

Tandoori Chicken

Preparation Time: 10 minutes; Cooking Time: 20 minutes; Serve: 4

Ingredients:
- 1 lb chicken tenders, cut each in half
- 1/4 cup parsley, chopped
- 1 tbsp garlic, minced
- 1 tbsp ginger, minced
- 1/4 cup lemon juice
- 1 tsp paprika
- 1 tsp garam masala
- 1/4 tsp turmeric
- 1 tsp cayenne pepper
- 1 tsp salt

Directions:
1. Add all ingredients into the large zip-lock bag, seal bag, and place in the refrigerator overnight.
2. Place marinated chicken tenders onto the cooking tray.
3. Select AIRFRY mode, then set the temperature to 350 F and the time to 20 minutes, then press start.
4. When the display shows Add Food then place the cooking tray in the vortex plus air fryer oven.
5. Turn chicken tenders halfway through.
6. Serve and enjoy.

Nutritional Value (Amount per Serving):
Calories 232; Fat 8.8 g; Carbohydrates 2.9 g; Sugar 0.5 g; Protein 33.4 g; Cholesterol 101 mg

Delicious Chicken Kabab

Preparation Time: 10 minutes; Cooking Time: 15 minutes; Serve: 4

Ingredients:
- 1 lb chicken thighs, skinless, boneless, and cut into 4 pieces
- 1 tbsp oil
- 1 tbsp tomato paste
- 1 tbsp garlic, minced
- 1/4 cup lemon juice
- 1/2 tsp cayenne pepper
- 1/2 tsp black pepper
- 1/2 tsp ground cinnamon
- 1 tsp paprika
- 1 tsp ground cumin
- 1 tsp salt

Directions:
1. Add all ingredients into the zip-lock bag, seal bag, and place in the refrigerator for 1 hour.
2. Arrange marinated chicken onto the cooking tray.
3. Select AIRFRY mode, then set the temperature to 370 F and the time to 15 minutes, then press start.
4. When the display shows Add Food then place the cooking tray in the vortex plus air fryer oven.
5. Turn chicken after 10 minutes.
6. Serve and enjoy.

Nutritional Value (Amount per Serving):
Calories 261; Fat 12.2 g; Carbohydrates 2.8 g; Sugar 0.9 g; Protein 33.5 g; Cholesterol 101 mg

Simple Buffalo Wings

Preparation Time: 10 minutes; Cooking Time: 12 minutes; Serve: 4

Ingredients:
- 2 lbs chicken wings
- 3 tbsp butter, melted
- 1/4 cup hot sauce
- Salt

Directions:
1. Add chicken wings, butter, hot sauce, and salt into the bowl, toss well and place in the refrigerator for 1-2 hours.
2. Place marinated chicken wings onto the cooking tray.
3. Select AIRFRY mode, then set the temperature to 400 F and the time to 12 minutes, then press start.
4. When the display shows Add Food then place the cooking tray in the vortex plus air fryer oven.
5. Turn chicken wings halfway through.
6. Serve and enjoy.

Nutritional Value (Amount per Serving):
Calories 509; Fat 25.5 g; Carbohydrates 0.3 g; Sugar 0.2 g; Protein 65.8 g; Cholesterol 225 mg

Crisp Crusted Chicken Breasts

Preparation Time: 10 minutes; Cooking Time: 10 minutes; Serve: 3

Ingredients:
- 12 oz chicken breasts, skinless and boneless
- 1/2 cup almond flour
- 1 egg, beaten
- 1/2 tsp black pepper
- 1/2 tsp salt

Directions:
1. In a bowl, add egg and whisk well.
2. In a shallow dish, mix almond flour, pepper, and salt.
3. Dip chicken breasts with egg and coat with almond flour mixture.
4. Place the coated chicken onto the cooking tray.
5. Select AIRFRY mode, then set the temperature to 330 F and the time to 10 minutes, then press start.
6. When the display shows Add Food then place the cooking tray in the vortex plus air fryer oven.
7. Serve and enjoy.

Nutritional Value (Amount per Serving):
Calories 344; Fat 19.2 g; Carbohydrates 4.3 g; Sugar 0.8 g; Protein 38.7 g; Cholesterol 156 mg

Yummy Chicken Fajita

Preparation Time: 10 minutes; Cooking Time: 20 minutes; Serve: 4

Ingredients:
- 1 lb chicken breast, boneless, skinless & sliced
- 2 tsp olive oil
- 1 onion, sliced
- 1 red bell pepper, sliced
- 1 yellow bell pepper, sliced
- 1/8 tsp cayenne
- 1 tsp cumin
- 2 tsp chili powder
- Pepper
- Salt

Directions:
1. Add chicken, onion, and sliced bell peppers into the bowl. Add cayenne, cumin, chili powder, oil, pepper, and salt and toss well.
2. Add chicken mixture onto the cooking tray.
3. Select AIRFRY mode, then set the temperature to 360 F and the time to 15-20 minutes, then press start.

4. When the display shows Add Food then place the cooking tray in the vortex plus air fryer oven.
5. Stir chicken mixture halfway through.
6. Serve and enjoy.

Nutritional Value (Amount per Serving):
Calories 186; Fat 5.7 g; Carbohydrates 8.1 g; Sugar 4.3 g; Protein 25.2 g; Cholesterol 73 mg

Dijon Chicken Breasts

Preparation Time: 10 minutes; Cooking Time: 15 minutes; Serve: 6

Ingredients:
- 1 1/2 lbs chicken breasts, boneless
- 1 tbsp fresh lemon juice
- 1 tbsp Dijon mustard
- 1/2 cup mayonnaise
- 1/4 tsp cayenne
- 1 tsp Italian seasoning
- 1 tbsp coconut aminos
- 1/2 tsp pepper
- 1 tsp sea salt

Directions:
1. In a small bowl, mix together mayonnaise, Italian seasoning, cayenne, coconut amino, lemon juice, mustard, pepper, and salt.
2. Add chicken and mayonnaise mixture into the zip-lock bag, seal bag, and place in the refrigerator overnight.
3. Seal the ziplock bag and place it in the refrigerator overnight.
4. Add marinated chicken onto the cooking tray.
5. Select AIRFRY mode, then set the temperature to 400 F and the time to 15 minutes, then press start.
6. When the display shows Add Food then place the cooking tray in the vortex plus air fryer oven.
7. Turn chicken halfway through.
8. Serve and enjoy.

Nutritional Value (Amount per Serving):
Calories 300; Fat 15.3 g; Carbohydrates 5.6 g; Sugar 1.4 g; Protein 33.2 g; Cholesterol 107 mg

Flavorful Chicken Thighs

Preparation Time: 10 minutes; Cooking Time: 22 minutes; Serve: 4

Ingredients:
- 4 chicken thighs, bone-in & skin-on
- 1 tsp paprika
- 1 tbsp olive oil
- 3/4 tsp onion powder
- 1/2 tsp oregano
- 3/4 tsp garlic powder
- 1/2 tsp kosher salt

Directions:
1. Preheat the cosori air fryer to 380 F.
2. Add chicken thighs and remaining ingredients into the large zip-lock bag, seal bag and shake well.
3. Add marinated chicken thighs onto the cooking tray.
4. Select AIRFRY mode, then set the temperature to 390 F and the time to 22 minutes, then press start.
5. When the display shows Add Food then place the cooking tray in the vortex plus air fryer oven.
6. Turn chicken thighs after 12 minutes.
7. Serve and enjoy.

Nutritional Value (Amount per Serving):

Calories 313; Fat 14.4 g; Carbohydrates 1.2 g; Sugar 0.4 g; Protein 42.5 g; Cholesterol 130 mg

Lemon Pepper Chicken Breasts

Preparation Time: 10 minutes; Cooking Time: 30 minutes; Serve: 4

Ingredients:
- 4 chicken breasts, boneless & skinless
- 1 tbsp lemon pepper seasoning
- 1 tsp granulated garlic
- 1 tsp salt

Directions:
1. Season chicken breasts with lemon pepper seasoning, granulated garlic, and salt and place onto the cooking tray.
2. Select AIRFRY mode, then set the temperature to 360 F and the time to 30 minutes, then press start.
3. When the display shows Add Food then place the cooking tray in the vortex plus air fryer oven.
4. Turn chicken breasts halfway through.
5. Serve and enjoy.

Nutritional Value (Amount per Serving):
Calories 284; Fat 10.9 g; Carbohydrates 1.6 g; Sugar 0.2 g; Protein 42.5 g; Cholesterol 130 mg

Hassel Back Chicken

Preparation Time: 10 minutes; Cooking Time: 15 minutes; Serve: 2

Ingredients:
- 2 chicken breasts, boneless and skinless
- 2 oz cream cheese, softened
- 4 bacon slices, cooked and crumbled
- 1/2 cup mozzarella cheese, shredded
- 4 tbsp pickled jalapenos, chopped

Directions:
1. Using a sharp knife cut 4-5 slits on top of chicken breasts.
2. In a bowl, mix together 1/2 mozzarella cheese, pickled jalapenos, cream cheese, and bacon.
3. Stuff mozzarella cheese mixture into the slits.
4. Place chicken onto the cooking tray.
5. Select AIRFRY mode, then set the temperature to 350 F and the time to 15 minutes, then press start.
6. When the display shows Add Food then place the cooking tray in the vortex plus air fryer oven.
7. Serve and enjoy.

Nutritional Value (Amount per Serving):
Calories 602; Fat 37.8 g; Carbohydrates 1.5 g; Sugar 0.1 g; Protein 60.5 g; Cholesterol 207 mg

Air Fryer Turkey Breast

Preparation Time: 10 minutes; Cooking Time: 60 minutes; Serve: 8

Ingredients:
- 4 lbs turkey breast, boneless
- 1 1/2 tsp paprika
- 1 1/2 tsp garlic powder
- 1 tbsp olive oil
- 1/2 tsp cinnamon
- 1/2 tsp pepper
- 2 tsp salt

Directions:
1. In a small bowl, mix together cinnamon, paprika, garlic powder, pepper, and salt.
2. Brush turkey breast with oil and rub with spice mixture and place onto the cooking tray.

3. Select AIRFRY mode, then set the temperature to 350 F and the time to 60 minutes, then press start.
4. When the display shows Add Food then place the cooking tray in the vortex plus air fryer oven.
5. Turn turkey breast after 25 minutes.
6. Slice and serve.

Nutritional Value (Amount per Serving):
Calories 254; Fat 5.6 g; Carbohydrates 10.4 g; Sugar 8.1 g; Protein 38.9 g; Cholesterol 98 mg

Chicken with Broccoli

Preparation Time: 10 minutes; Cooking Time: 20 minutes; Serve: 4

Ingredients:
- 1 lb chicken breast, boneless, skinless, & cut into bite-size pieces
- 2 tsp rice vinegar
- 1 tsp sesame oil
- 1 tbsp soy sauce
- 1 tsp garlic, minced
- 1/2 onion, sliced
- 2 cups broccoli florets
- 2 tbsp olive oil
- Pepper
- Salt

Directions:
1. In a large bowl, mix together olive oil, garlic, soy sauce, sesame oil, rice, vinegar, pepper, and salt.
2. Add chicken, onion, and broccoli and mix well and place in the refrigerator for 1 hour.
3. Place marinated chicken and vegetables onto the cooking tray.
4. Select AIRFRY mode, then set the temperature to 380 F and the time to 20 minutes, then press start.
5. When the display shows Add Food then place the cooking tray in the vortex plus air fryer oven.
6. Serve and enjoy.

Nutritional Value (Amount per Serving):
Calories 225; Fat 11.1 g; Carbohydrates 4.9 g; Sugar 1.4 g; Protein 25.8 g; Cholesterol 73 mg

Ranch Chicken with Broccoli

Preparation Time: 10 minutes; Cooking Time: 30 minutes; Serve: 4

Ingredients:
- 4 chicken breasts, skinless and boneless
- 1/2 cup ranch dressing
- 5 bacon slices, cooked and chopped
- 2 cups broccoli florets, blanched and chopped
- 1/3 cup mozzarella cheese, shredded
- 1 cup cheddar cheese, shredded

Directions:
1. Add chicken and broccoli into the baking dish and top with remaining ingredients.
2. Select BAKE mode, then set the temperature to 375 F and the time to 30 minutes, then press start.
3. When the display shows Add Food then place the baking dish in the vortex plus air fryer oven.
4. Serve and enjoy.

Nutritional Value (Amount per Serving):
Calories 551; Fat 30.8 g; Carbohydrates 5.4 g; Sugar 1.7 g; Protein 60.4 g; Cholesterol 187 mg

Simple Chicken Thighs

Preparation Time: 10 minutes; Cooking Time: 35 minutes; Serve: 6

Ingredients:
- 6 chicken thighs
- 2 tbsp olive oil
- 1 1/2 tsp poultry seasoning
- Pepper
- Salt

Directions:
1. Brush chicken with oil and season with poultry seasoning, pepper, and salt.
2. Arrange chicken onto the cooking tray.
3. Select BAKE mode, then set the temperature to 350 F and the time to 35-40 minutes, then press start.
4. When the display shows Add Food then place the cooking tray in the vortex plus air fryer oven.
5. Serve and enjoy.

Nutritional Value (Amount per Serving):
Calories 319; Fat 15.5 g; Carbohydrates 0.3 g; Sugar 0 g; Protein 42.3 g; Cholesterol 130 mg

BBQ Chicken Wings

Preparation Time: 10 minutes; Cooking Time: 45 minutes; Serve: 4

Ingredients:
- 1 1/2 lbs chicken wings
- 1/4 cup BBQ spice rub
- 1 tbsp olive oil

Directions:
1. Brush chicken wings with oil and season with BBQ spice rub and place onto the cooking tray.
2. Select BAKE mode, then set the temperature to 390 F and the time to 45 minutes, then press start.
3. When the display shows Add Food then place the cooking tray in the vortex plus air fryer oven.
4. Serve and enjoy.

Nutritional Value (Amount per Serving):
Calories 386; Fat 18 g; Carbohydrates 4.2 g; Sugar 0.5 g; Protein 49.7 g; Cholesterol 151 mg

Turkey Tenderloin

Preparation Time: 10 minutes; Cooking Time: 45 minutes; Serve: 4

Ingredients:
- 1 1/2 lbs turkey breast tenderloin
- 1 tsp Italian seasoning
- 1/2 tbsp olive oil
- 1/4 tsp pepper
- 1/2 tsp salt

Directions:
1. Brush turkey tenderloin with oil and season with Italian seasoning, pepper, and salt and place onto the cooking tray.
2. Select BAKE mode, then set the temperature to 390 F and the time to 45 minutes, then press start.
3. When the display shows Add Food then place the cooking tray in the vortex plus air fryer oven.
4. Serve and enjoy.

Nutritional Value (Amount per Serving):
Calories 200; Fat 4.3 g; Carbohydrates 0.2 g; Sugar 0.1 g; Protein 42.2 g; Cholesterol 69 mg

Pesto Chicken

Preparation Time: 10 minutes; Cooking Time: 25 minutes; Serve: 4

Ingredients:
- 4 chicken breasts, skinless & boneless
- 1/2 cup basil pesto
- 1/2 cup mozzarella cheese, shredded
- Pepper
- Salt

Directions:
1. Season chicken with pepper and salt and place into the baking dish and top with pesto and shredded cheese.
2. Select BAKE mode, then set the temperature to 390 F and the time to 25 minutes, then press start.
3. When the display shows Add Food then place the baking dish in the vortex plus air fryer oven.
4. Serve and enjoy.

Nutritional Value (Amount per Serving):
Calories 288; Fat 11.5 g; Carbohydrates 0.2 g; Sugar 0 g; Protein 43.3 g; Cholesterol 132 mg

Lemon Pepper Chicken Breasts

Preparation Time: 10 minutes; Cooking Time: 30 minutes; Serve: 4

Ingredients:
- 4 chicken breasts, skinless and boneless
- 1 tsp lemon pepper seasoning
- 4 tsp lemon juice
- 4 tsp butter, sliced
- 1/2 tsp paprika
- 1 tsp garlic powder
- Pepper
- Salt

Directions:
1. Season chicken with garlic powder, paprika, lemon pepper seasoning, pepper, and salt and place into the baking dish. Top with lemon juice and butter.
2. Select BAKE mode, then set the temperature to 350 F and the time to 30 minutes, then press start.
3. When the display shows Add Food then place the baking dish in the vortex plus air fryer oven.
4. Serve and enjoy.

Nutritional Value (Amount per Serving):
Calories 317; Fat 14.7 g; Carbohydrates 1.1 g; Sugar 0.3 g; Protein 45.5 g; Cholesterol 140 mg

Baked Chicken with Tomato Mushrooms

Preparation Time: 10 minutes; Cooking Time: 30 minutes; Serve: 4

Ingredients:
- 2 lbs chicken breasts, halved
- 1/3 cup sun-dried tomatoes
- 8 oz mushrooms, sliced
- 1/2 cup mayonnaise
- 1 tsp salt

Directions:
1. Season chicken with salt and place into the greased baking dish, top with remaining ingredients.
2. Select BAKE mode, then set the temperature to 390 F and the time to 30 minutes, then press start.
3. When the display shows Add Food then place the baking dish in the vortex plus air fryer oven.
4. Serve and enjoy.

Nutritional Value (Amount per Serving):
Calories 560; Fat 26.8 g; Carbohydrates 9.5 g; Sugar 3.2 g; Protein 67.8 g; Cholesterol 209 mg

Meatloaf

Preparation Time: 10 minutes; Cooking Time: 40 minutes; Serve: 8

Ingredients:
- 2 eggs
- 2 lbs ground turkey
- 2 tsp Italian seasoning
- 1/4 cup basil pesto
- 1/2 cup parmesan cheese, grated
- 1/2 cup marinara sauce, sugar-free
- 1 cup cottage cheese
- 1 lb mozzarella cheese, cut into cubes
- 1 tsp salt

Directions:
1. Add all ingredients into the large bowl and mix until well combined.
2. Transfer mixture into the greased loaf pan.
3. Select BAKE mode, then set the temperature to 390 F and the time to 40 minutes, then press start.
4. When the display shows Add Food then place the loaf pan in the vortex plus air fryer oven.
5. Serve and enjoy.

Nutritional Value (Amount per Serving):
Calories 308; Fat 16.7 g; Carbohydrates 3.7 g; Sugar 1.7 g; Protein 39.4 g; Cholesterol 166 mg

Greek Chicken

Preparation Time: 10 minutes; Cooking Time: 20 minutes; Serve: 4

Ingredients:
- 4 chicken breasts, boneless and halves
- 3 tbsp olive oil
- 2 tbsp capers, rinsed and drained
- 14 olives, pitted and halved
- 2 cups cherry tomatoes
- Pepper
- Salt

Directions:
1. Season chicken with pepper and salt and place into the baking dish. Drizzle with oil.
2. Pour remaining ingredients over chicken.
3. Select BAKE mode, then set the temperature to 390 F and the time to 20 minutes, then press start.
4. When the display shows Add Food then place the baking dish in the vortex plus air fryer oven.
5. Serve and enjoy.

Nutritional Value (Amount per Serving):
Calories 253; Fat 15.2 g; Carbohydrates 4.7 g; Sugar 2.4 g; Protein 24.8 g; Cholesterol 72 mg

Spicy Chicken Wings

Preparation Time: 10 minutes; Cooking Time: 25 minutes; Serve: 4

Ingredients:
- 2 lbs chicken wings
- 10 oz hot sauce
- 1 tsp Tabasco
- 5 tbsp butter, melted

Directions:
1. Place chicken with onto the cooking tray.
2. Select BAKE mode, then set the temperature to 380 F and the time to 25 minutes, then press start.
3. When the display shows Add Food then place the cooking tray in the vortex plus air fryer oven.
4. Meanwhile, in a bowl, mix together hot sauce, Tabasco, and butter.
5. Toss chicken wings with sauce and serve.

Nutritional Value (Amount per Serving):
Calories 566; Fat 31.5 g; Carbohydrates 1.3 g; Sugar 0.9 g; Protein 66.1 g; Cholesterol 240 mg

Flavorful Chicken Drumsticks

Preparation Time: 10 minutes; Cooking Time: 25 minutes; Serve: 6
Ingredients:
- 6 chicken drumsticks
- 1/2 tsp garlic powder
- 2 tbsp olive oil
- 1/2 tsp ground cumin
- 1 tsp paprika
- Pepper
- Salt

Directions:
1. Brush chicken drumsticks with oil and season with garlic powder, ground cumin, paprika, pepper, and salt.
2. Arrange chicken drumsticks onto the cooking tray.
3. Select BAKE mode, then set the temperature to 400 F and the time to 25 minutes, then press start.
4. When the display shows Add Food then place the cooking tray in the vortex plus air fryer oven.
5. Serve and enjoy.

Nutritional Value (Amount per Serving):
Calories 120; Fat 7.4 g; Carbohydrates 0.5 g; Sugar 0.1 g; Protein 12.8 g; Cholesterol 40 mg

Tasty Chicken Nuggets

Preparation Time: 10 minutes; Cooking Time: 25 minutes; Serve: 4
Ingredients:
- 1 1/2 lbs chicken breast, boneless & cut into chunks
- 1/4 cup parmesan cheese, shredded
- 1/4 cup mayonnaise
- 1/2 tsp garlic powder
- 1/4 tsp salt

Directions:
1. In a bowl, mix together mayonnaise, garlic powder, cheese, and salt. Add chicken chunks and toss until well coated.
2. Arrange chicken chunks onto the parchment-lined cooking tray.
3. Select BAKE mode, then set the temperature to 400 F and the time to 25 minutes, then press start.
4. When the display shows Add Food then place the cooking tray in the vortex plus air fryer oven.
5. Serve and enjoy.

Nutritional Value (Amount per Serving):
Calories 270; Fat 10.4 g; Carbohydrates 4 g; Sugar 1 g; Protein 38.1 g; Cholesterol 117 mg

Ranch Chicken Wings

Preparation Time: 10 minutes; Cooking Time: 20 minutes; Serve: 4
Ingredients:
- 1 lb chicken wings
- 2 tbsp ranch seasoning
- 1 tbsp garlic, minced
- 2 tbsp butter, melted

Directions:
1. Add chicken wings and remaining ingredients into the large bowl and toss well.
2. Arrange chicken wings onto the cooking tray.
3. Select BAKE mode, then set the temperature to 360 F and the time to 20 minutes, then press start.

4. When the display shows Add Food then place the cooking tray in the vortex plus air fryer oven.
5. Turn chicken wings halfway through.
6. Serve and enjoy.

Nutritional Value (Amount per Serving):
Calories 285; Fat 14.2 g; Carbohydrates 0.7 g; Sugar 0 g; Protein 33 g; Cholesterol 116 mg

Chicken Veggie Fritters

Preparation Time: 10 minutes; Cooking Time: 25 minutes; Serve: 4

Ingredients:
- 1 lb ground chicken
- 3/4 cup almond flour
- 1 egg, lightly beaten
- 1 garlic clove, minced
- 1 1/2 cup mozzarella cheese, shredded
- 1/2 cup shallots, chopped
- 2 cups broccoli, chopped
- Pepper
- Salt

Directions:
1. Add all ingredients into the large bowl and mix until well combined.
2. Make small patties from mixture and place onto the parchment-lined cooking tray.
3. Select BAKE mode, then set the temperature to 390 F and the time to 25 minutes, then press start.
4. When the display shows Add Food then place the cooking tray in the vortex plus air fryer oven.
5. Turn chicken patties halfway through.
6. Serve and enjoy.

Nutritional Value (Amount per Serving):
Calories 412; Fat 22.1 g; Carbohydrates 11.6 g; Sugar 1.6 g; Protein 43.5 g; Cholesterol 147 mg

Healthy Chicken Patties

Preparation Time: 10 minutes; Cooking Time: 25 minutes; Serve: 4

Ingredients:
- 1 lb ground chicken
- 1 egg, lightly beaten
- 1 cup Monterey jack cheese, grated
- 1 cup carrot, grated
- 1 cup cauliflower, grated
- 1/8 tsp red pepper flakes
- 2 garlic cloves, minced
- 1/2 cup onion, minced
- 3/4 cup almond flour
- Pepper
- Salt

Directions:
1. Add all ingredients into the large bowl and mix until well combined.
2. Make small patties from mixture and place onto the parchment-lined cooking tray.
3. Select BAKE mode, then set the temperature to 400 F and the time to 25 minutes, then press start.
4. When the display shows Add Food then place the cooking tray in the vortex plus air fryer oven.
5. Serve and enjoy.

Nutritional Value (Amount per Serving):
Calories 482; Fat 28.6 g; Carbohydrates 10.7 g; Sugar 3.6 g; Protein 46.6 g; Cholesterol 167 mg

Parmesan Chicken Fritters

Preparation Time: 10 minutes; Cooking Time: 10 minutes; Serve: 4

Ingredients:

- 1 lb ground chicken
- 1/2 cup parmesan cheese, shredded
- 1/2 tbsp dill, chopped
- 1/2 cup almond flour
- 2 tbsp green onions, chopped
- 1/2 tsp onion powder
- 1/2 tsp garlic powder
- Pepper
- Salt

Directions:
1. Add all ingredients into the large bowl and mix until well combined.
2. Make small patties from mixture and place onto the parchment-lined cooking tray.
3. Select AIRFRY mode, then set the temperature to 350 F and the time to 10 minutes, then press start.
4. When the display shows Add Food then place the cooking tray in the vortex plus air fryer oven.
5. Serve and enjoy.

Nutritional Value (Amount per Serving):
Calories 269; Fat 14.3 g; Carbohydrates 3.5 g; Sugar 0.6 g; Protein 31.7 g; Cholesterol 87 mg

Marinated Greek Chicken

Preparation Time: 10 minutes; Cooking Time: 30 minutes; Serve: 4

Ingredients:
- 1 lb chicken breasts, skinless & boneless

For marinade:
- 1/2 tsp dill
- 1 tsp onion powder
- 1/4 tsp basil
- 1/4 tsp oregano
- 3 garlic cloves, minced
- 1 tbsp lemon juice
- 3 tbsp olive oil
- 1/4 tsp pepper
- 1/2 tsp salt

Directions:
1. Add chicken and marinade ingredients into the mixing bowl and mix well and place it in the refrigerator overnight.
2. Arrange marinated chicken breasts onto the cooking tray.
3. Select BAKE mode, then set the temperature to 400 F and the time to 30 minutes, then press start.
4. When the display shows Add Food then place the cooking tray in the vortex plus air fryer oven.
5. Serve and enjoy.

Nutritional Value (Amount per Serving):
Calories 313; Fat 19 g; Carbohydrates 1.5 g; Sugar 0.3 g; Protein 33.1 g; Cholesterol 101 mg

Simple Baked Chicken Breasts

Preparation Time: 10 minutes; Cooking Time: 25 minutes; Serve: 6

Ingredients:
- 6 chicken breasts, skinless & boneless
- 1 tsp Italian seasoning
- 1/4 tsp paprika
- 2 tbsp olive oil
- 1/4 tsp pepper
- 1/2 tsp garlic salt

Directions:
1. Brush chicken with oil and season with Italian seasoning, paprika, pepper, and salt and place onto the cooking tray.
2. Select BAKE mode, then set the temperature to 400 F and the time to 25 minutes, then press start.

3. When the display shows Add Food then place the cooking tray in the vortex plus air fryer oven.
4. Serve and enjoy.

Nutritional Value (Amount per Serving):
Calories 321; Fat 15.7 g; Carbohydrates 0.4 g; Sugar 0.1 g; Protein 42.3 g; Cholesterol 130 mg

Tasty Jerk Chicken Wings

Preparation Time: 10 minutes; Cooking Time: 20 minutes; Serve: 2

Ingredients:
- 1 lb chicken wings
- 1 tsp olive oil
- 1 tbsp arrowroot
- 1 tbsp jerk seasoning
- Pepper
- Salt

Directions:
1. Add chicken wings and remaining ingredients into the mixing bowl and toss well.
2. Arrange chicken wings onto the cooking tray.
3. Select AIRFRY mode, then set the temperature to 380 F and the time to 20 minutes, then press start.
4. When the display shows Add Food then place the cooking tray in the vortex plus air fryer oven.
5. Turn chicken wings halfway through.
6. Serve and enjoy.

Nutritional Value (Amount per Serving):
Calories 453; Fat 19.2 g; Carbohydrates 0.5 g; Sugar 0 g; Protein 65.8 g; Cholesterol 202 mg

Spiced Chicken Tenders

Preparation Time: 10 minutes; Cooking Time: 16 minutes; Serve: 4

Ingredients:
- 1 lb chicken tenders

For rub:
- 1/2 tbsp dried thyme
- 1 tbsp garlic powder
- 1 tbsp paprika
- 1/2 tbsp onion powder
- 1/2 tsp cayenne pepper
- Pepper
- Salt

Directions:
1. Add chicken tenders into the mixing bowl, mix together rub ingredients and sprinkle over chicken tenders and toss to coat.
2. Arrange chicken tenders onto the cooking tray.
3. Select AIRFRY mode, then set the temperature to 370 F and the time to 16 minutes, then press start.
4. When the display shows Add Food then place the cooking tray in the vortex plus air fryer oven.
5. Turn chicken tender halfway through.
6. Serve and enjoy.

Nutritional Value (Amount per Serving):
Calories 232; Fat 8.7 g; Carbohydrates 3.6 g; Sugar 1 g; Protein 33.6 g; Cholesterol 101 mg

Herb Chicken Breast

Preparation Time: 10 minutes; Cooking Time: 25 minutes; Serve: 4

Ingredients:
- 4 chicken breasts, skinless & boneless
- 1 tbsp olive oil

For rub:
- 1 tsp oregano
- 1 tsp thyme
- 1 tsp parsley
- 1 tsp onion powder
- 1 tsp basil
- Pepper
- Salt

Directions:
1. In a small bowl mix together all rub ingredients.
2. Brush chicken with oil and rub with herb mixture.
3. Arrange chicken onto the cooking tray.
4. Select BAKE mode, then set the temperature to 390 F and the time to 25 minutes, then press start.
5. When the display shows Add Food then place the cooking tray in the vortex plus air fryer oven.
6. Turn chicken halfway through.
7. Serve and enjoy.

Nutritional Value (Amount per Serving):
Calories 312; Fat 14.4 g; Carbohydrates 0.9 g; Sugar 0.2 g; Protein 42.4 g; Cholesterol 130 mg

Feta Turkey Patties

Preparation Time: 10 minutes; Cooking Time: 22 minutes; Serve: 4

Ingredients:
- 1 lb ground turkey
- 4 oz feta cheese, crumbled
- 1 1/4 cup spinach, chopped
- 1 tsp Italian seasoning
- 1 tbsp olive oil
- 1 tbsp garlic paste
- Pepper
- Salt

Directions:
1. Add all ingredients into the bowl and mix until well combined.
2. Make four equal shapes of patties from the mixture and place them onto the cooking tray.
3. Select AIRFRY mode, then set the temperature to 390 F and the time to 22 minutes, then press start.
4. When the display shows Add Food then place the cooking tray in the vortex plus air fryer oven.
5. Turn chicken patties through.
6. Serve and enjoy.

Nutritional Value (Amount per Serving):
Calories 335; Fat 22.4 g; Carbohydrates 2.3 g; Sugar 1.3 g; Protein 35.5 g; Cholesterol 142 mg

Chapter 4: Meat Recipes

Flavorful Baked Pork Chops

Preparation Time: 10 minutes; Cooking Time: 18 minutes; Serve: 4

Ingredients:
- 4 pork chops, boneless
- 2 tbsp olive oil
- 1 tsp oregano
- 1 tsp onion powder
- 1 tsp garlic powder
- 1 tbsp paprika
- Pepper
- Salt

Directions:
1. Brush pork chops with 1 tablespoon of olive oil.
2. Mix together paprika, garlic powder, onion powder, oregano, pepper, and salt and rub all over pork chops.
3. Place pork chops onto the parchment-lined cooking tray. Drizzle remaining oil over pork chops.
4. Select BAKE mode, then set the temperature to 400 F and the time to 18 minutes, then press start.
5. When the display shows Add Food then place the cooking tray in the vortex plus air fryer oven.
6. Serve and enjoy.

Nutritional Value (Amount per Serving):
Calories 327; Fat 27.2 g; Carbohydrates 2.2 g; Sugar 0.6 g; Protein 18.5 g; Cholesterol 69 mg

Cheesy Pork Chops

Preparation Time: 10 minutes; Cooking Time: 35 minutes; Serve: 4

Ingredients:
- 1 lb pork chops, boneless
- 8 oz cheddar cheese, grated
- 1/4 cup mayonnaise
- 1 small onion, sliced
- Pepper
- Salt

Directions:
1. Season pork chops with pepper and salt and place into the baking dish.
2. Add sliced onion, mayonnaise, and cheese on top of pork chops.
3. Select BAKE mode, then set the temperature to 350 F and the time to 35 minutes, then press start.
4. When the display shows Add Food then place the baking dish in the vortex plus air fryer oven.
5. Serve and enjoy.

Nutritional Value (Amount per Serving):
Calories 656; Fat 51.9 g; Carbohydrates 5.9 g; Sugar 2 g; Protein 39.9 g; Cholesterol 161 mg

Juicy & Tender Pork Chops

Preparation Time: 10 minutes; Cooking Time: 15 minutes; Serve: 4

Ingredients:
- 4 pork chops, boneless
- 1 tsp onion powder
- 1 tsp smoked paprika
- 4 tbsp olive oil
- Pepper
- Salt

Directions:
1. Brush pork chops with oil and season with onion powder, paprika, pepper, and salt.
2. Place pork chops onto the cooking tray.

3. Select BAKE mode, then set the temperature to 400 F and the time to 15 minutes, then press start.
4. When the display shows Add Food then place the cooking tray in the vortex plus air fryer oven.
5. Serve and enjoy.

Nutritional Value (Amount per Serving):
Calories 380; Fat 34 g; Carbohydrates 0.8 g; Sugar 0.3 g; Protein 18.1 g; Cholesterol 69 mg

Flavorful Bone-in Pork Chops

Preparation Time: 10 minutes; Cooking Time: 20 minutes; Serve: 3

Ingredients:
- 1 1/2 lb pork chops, bone-in
- 1 tsp paprika
- 1/2 tsp onion powder
- 1/2 tsp pepper
- 4 tbsp olive oil
- 1 tsp salt

Directions:
1. In a small bowl, mix together paprika, onion powder, pepper, and salt.
2. Brush pork chops with oil and rub with spice mixture.
3. Place pork chops onto the cooking tray.
4. Select BAKE mode, then set the temperature to 400 F and the time to 15-20 minutes, then press start.
5. When the display shows Add Food then place the cooking tray in the vortex plus air fryer oven.
6. Serve and enjoy.

Nutritional Value (Amount per Serving):
Calories 890; Fat 75.1 g; Carbohydrates 0.9 g; Sugar 0.2 g; Protein 51.1 g; Cholesterol 195 mg

Super Delicious Ranch Pork Chops

Preparation Time: 10 minutes; Cooking Time: 20 minutes; Serve: 4

Ingredients:
- 2 lbs pork chops, bone-in
- 2 tbsp ranch seasoning
- 2 tbsp olive oil
- Pepper
- Salt

Directions:
1. Brush pork chops with oil and rub with ranch seasoning, pepper, and salt.
2. Place pork chops onto the cooking tray.
3. Select BAKE mode, then set the temperature to 400 F and the time to 20 minutes, then press start.
4. When the display shows Add Food then place the cooking tray in the vortex plus air fryer oven.
5. Serve and enjoy.

Nutritional Value (Amount per Serving):
Calories 801; Fat 63.4 g; Carbohydrates 0 g; Sugar 0 g; Protein 51 g; Cholesterol 195 mg

Parmesan Pork Chops

Preparation Time: 10 minutes; Cooking Time: 45 minutes; Serve: 4

Ingredients:
- 4 pork chops, boneless
- 2 tbsp olive oil
- 1 tsp garlic powder
- 1 cup parmesan cheese, grated
- 1 cup pork rinds, crushed
- 1 tsp black pepper

Directions:

1. In a shallow dish, mix together crushed pork rinds, black pepper, parmesan cheese, and garlic powder.
2. Brush pork chops with oil and coat with pork rind mixture.
3. Place coated pork chops onto the cooking tray.
4. Select BAKE mode, then set the temperature to 350 F and the time to 40-45 minutes, then press start.
5. When the display shows Add Food then place the cooking tray in the vortex plus air fryer oven.
6. Serve and enjoy.

Nutritional Value (Amount per Serving):
Calories 412; Fat 33 g; Carbohydrates 1.7 g; Sugar 0.2 g; Protein 27.6 g; Cholesterol 90 mg

Swiss Pork Chops

Preparation Time: 10 minutes; Cooking Time: 15 minutes; Serve: 6
Ingredients:
- 3 pork chops, bone-in
- 1/2 cup Swiss cheese, shredded
- 4 bacon slices, cut in half
- 1/2 tsp garlic, minced
- 1 tbsp olive oil
- Pepper
- Salt

Directions:
1. Season pork chops with pepper and salt.
2. In a small bowl, mix together oil and garlic. Brush pork chops with oil.
3. Place pork chops into the baking dish and top with bacon slices.
4. Select BAKE mode, then set the temperature to 400 F and the time to 12-15 minutes, then press start.
5. When the display shows Add Food then place the baking dish in the vortex plus air fryer oven.
6. Top with shredded cheese and let it sit for 5 minutes.
7. Serve and enjoy.

Nutritional Value (Amount per Serving):
Calories 251; Fat 20.1 g; Carbohydrates 0.8 g; Sugar 0.1 g; Protein 16.1 g; Cholesterol 57 mg

Lemon Garlic Pork Chops

Preparation Time: 10 minutes; Cooking Time: 20 minutes; Serve: 4
Ingredients:
- 4 pork chops
- 1 tbsp olive oil
- 1 tbsp garlic, minced
- 1 lemon juice
- Pepper
- Salt

Directions:
1. Add pork chops and remaining ingredients into the zip-lock bag, seal bag, and place in the refrigerator overnight.
2. Place marinated pork chops into the baking dish.
3. Select BAKE mode, then set the temperature to 400 F and the time to 15-20 minutes, then press start.
4. When the display shows Add Food then place the baking dish in the vortex plus air fryer oven.
5. Serve and enjoy.

Nutritional Value (Amount per Serving):
Calories 292; Fat 23.5 g; Carbohydrates 1 g; Sugar 0.3 g; Protein 18.2 g; Cholesterol 69 mg

Juicy Pork Tenderloin

Preparation Time: 10 minutes; Cooking Time: 20 minutes; Serve: 6

Ingredients:
- 2 lbs pork tenderloins
- 1 tbsp soy sauce
- 1 tbsp garlic, minced
- 1 tsp dried oregano
- 1 tbsp olive oil
- 1 tsp pepper
- 1 tsp salt

Directions:
1. In a small bowl, mix together soy sauce, garlic, oregano, oil, pepper, and salt.
2. Brush pork tenderloins with soy sauce mixture.
3. Place pork tenderloins onto the cooking tray.
4. Select BAKE mode, then set the temperature to 350 F and the time to 20 minutes, then press start.
5. When the display shows Add Food then place the cooking tray in the vortex plus air fryer oven.
6. Slice and serve.

Nutritional Value (Amount per Serving):
Calories 329; Fat 14.6 g; Carbohydrates 1.1 g; Sugar 0.1 g; Protein 45.5 g; Cholesterol 142 mg

Meatballs

Preparation Time: 10 minutes; Cooking Time: 25 minutes; Serve: 8

Ingredients:
- 1 egg
- 2 lbs ground pork
- 1 tsp pepper
- 3 tbsp sage, chopped
- 1/2 tsp garlic, crushed
- 1 tbsp vinegar
- 2 tbsp Dijon mustard
- 7 oz cheddar cheese, shredded
- 1 tsp salt

Directions:
1. Add all ingredients into the mixing bowl and mix until well combined.
2. Make small balls from mixture and place onto the parchment-lined cooking tray.
3. Select BAKE mode, then set the temperature to 390 F and the time to 20-25 minutes, then press start.
4. When the display shows Add Food then place the cooking tray in the vortex plus air fryer oven.
5. Serve and enjoy.

Nutritional Value (Amount per Serving):
Calories 276; Fat 13 g; Carbohydrates 1.3 g; Sugar 0.2 g; Protein 36.8 g; Cholesterol 129 mg

Flavorful Lamb Chops

Preparation Time: 10 minutes; Cooking Time: 15 minutes; Serve: 4

Ingredients:
- 8 lamb chops
- 2 tsp dried herb de Provence
- 2 garlic cloves, minced
- 2 tbsp olive oil
- 2 tbsp Dijon mustard
- 1/4 tsp salt

Directions:
1. In a small bowl, mix together garlic, oil, Dijon mustard, herb de Provence, and salt and rub all over pork chops.
2. Place pork chops onto the cooking tray.
3. Select BAKE mode, then set the temperature to 400 F and the time to 15 minutes, then press start.

4. When the display shows Add Food then place the cooking tray in the vortex plus air fryer oven.
5. Serve and enjoy.

Nutritional Value (Amount per Serving):
Calories 384; Fat 19.8 g; Carbohydrates 0.9 g; Sugar 0.1 g; Protein 48.2 g; Cholesterol 153 mg

Spicy Jalapeno Sliders

Preparation Time: 10 minutes; Cooking Time: 15 minutes; Serve: 4

Ingredients:
- 1 lb ground beef
- 1/2 tsp garlic powder
- 2 oz cheddar cheese, shredded
- 2 oz shallots, chopped
- 3 pickled jalapenos, chopped
- 1/2 tsp pepper
- 1 tsp salt

Directions:
1. Add all ingredients into the mixing bowl and mix until well combined.
2. Make small patties from meat mixture and place onto the parchment-lined cooking tray.
3. Select BAKE mode, then set the temperature to 400 F and the time to 15 minutes, then press start.
4. When the display shows Add Food then place the cooking tray in the vortex plus air fryer oven.
5. Serve and enjoy.

Nutritional Value (Amount per Serving):
Calories 280; Fat 11.8 g; Carbohydrates 3 g; Sugar 0.2 g; Protein 38.4 g; Cholesterol 116 mg

Flavorful Cheese Casserole

Preparation Time: 10 minutes; Cooking Time: 20 minutes; Serve: 4

Ingredients:
- 1 lb ground beef
- 4 oz cheddar cheese, shredded
- 1 cup heavy whipping cream
- 5 oz blue cheese, crumbled
- 7 oz fresh green beans, chopped
- 1 onion, chopped
- 2 oz butter
- Pepper
- Salt

Directions:
1. Melt butter in a pan over medium heat.
2. Add meat and onion to the pan and cook until meat is browned.
3. Add green beans and crumbled cheese and stir everything well.
4. Add heavy cream and bring to simmer. Season with pepper and salt.
5. Pour meat mixture into the greased baking dish and top with shredded cheddar cheese.
6. Select BAKE mode, then set the temperature to 400 F and the time to 15-20 minutes, then press start.
7. When the display shows Add Food then place the baking dish in the vortex plus air fryer oven.
8. Serve and enjoy.

Nutritional Value (Amount per Serving):
Calories 682; Fat 49.3 g; Carbohydrates 8.2 g; Sugar 2.2 g; Protein 51 g; Cholesterol 229 mg

Simple Herbed Beef Tips

Preparation Time: 10 minutes; Cooking Time: 20 minutes; Serve: 6

Ingredients:

- 2 lbs sirloin steak, cut into 1-inch cubes
- 1/4 tsp red chili flakes
- 1/2 tsp black pepper
- 1/2 tsp dried thyme
- 1 tsp onion powder
- 1 tsp dried oregano
- 2 tbsp lemon juice
- 2 tbsp water
- 1/4 cup olive oil
- 1 cup fresh parsley, chopped
- 2 garlic cloves, minced
- 1/2 tsp salt

Directions:
1. Add meat cubes and remaining ingredients into the zip-lock bag, seal bag, and place in the refrigerator overnight.
2. Place marinated meat cubes onto the parchment-lined cooking tray.
3. Select BAKE mode, then set the temperature to 400 F and the time to 20 minutes, then press start.
4. When the display shows Add Food then place the cooking tray in the vortex plus air fryer oven.
5. Serve and enjoy.

Nutritional Value (Amount per Serving):
Calories 362; Fat 18 g; Carbohydrates 1.7 g; Sugar 0.4 g; Protein 46.4 g; Cholesterol 135 mg

Delicious Blackend Pork Tenderloin

Preparation Time: 10 minutes; Cooking Time: 12 minutes; Serve: 6

Ingredients:
- 1 1/2 lbs pork tenderloin
- 1/2 cup Worcestershire sauce
- 2/3 cup olive oil
- 1/2 tsp black pepper
- 1 tsp ground red pepper
- 1 tbsp dried tarragon
- 1 tbsp paprika
- 1 tbsp dried oregano
- 1 tbsp dried thyme
- 1 tbsp onion powder
- 1 tbsp garlic powder
- 1 tsp salt

Directions:
1. Add pork tenderloin and remaining ingredients into the large zip-lock bag, seal bag, and place in the refrigerator overnight.
2. Remove pork tenderloin from marinade and place onto the parchment-lined cooking tray.
3. Select BAKE mode, then set the temperature to 400 F and the time to 10-12 minutes, then press start.
4. When the display shows Add Food then place the cooking tray in the vortex plus air fryer oven.
5. Slice and serve.

Nutritional Value (Amount per Serving):
Calories 392; Fat 26.7 g; Carbohydrates 7.8 g; Sugar 4.9 g; Protein 30.5 g; Cholesterol 83 mg

Juicy Air Fryer Steak

Preparation Time: 10 minutes; Cooking Time: 12 minutes; Serve: 2

Ingredients:
- 2 ribeye steaks
- 1/2 tsp black pepper
- 1/2 tsp salt

Directions:
1. Season steaks with pepper and salt and place onto the cooking tray.
2. Select AIRFRY mode, then set the temperature to 390 F and the time to 12 minutes, then press start.

3. When the display shows Add Food then place the cooking tray in the vortex plus air fryer oven.
4. Turn steaks halfway through.
5. Serve and enjoy.

Nutritional Value (Amount per Serving):
Calories 181; Fat 12.5 g; Carbohydrates 1.5 g; Sugar 0 g; Protein 15.7 g; Cholesterol 0 mg

Savory Lamb Chops

Preparation Time: 10 minutes; Cooking Time: 10 minutes; Serve: 1

Ingredients:
- 1/3 lb lamb chop
- 1 tbsp fresh thyme, chopped
- 1 tbsp fresh rosemary, chopped
- 1/2 tbsp Dijon mustard
- 1/2 tbsp olive oil
- Pepper
- Salt

Directions:
1. In a small bowl, mix together oil, Dijon mustard, rosemary, thyme, pepper, and salt.
2. Brush lamb chop with oil mixture and place onto the cooking tray.
3. Select AIRFRY mode, then set the temperature to 375 F and the time to 10 minutes, then press start.
4. When the display shows Add Food then place the cooking tray in the vortex plus air fryer oven.
5. Turn lamb chop halfway through.
6. Serve and enjoy.

Nutritional Value (Amount per Serving):
Calories 365; Fat 19.1 g; Carbohydrates 4.3 g; Sugar 0.1 g; Protein 43.2 g; Cholesterol 136 mg

Ribeye Steaks

Preparation Time: 10 minutes; Cooking Time: 10 minutes; Serve: 4

Ingredients:
- 1 lb ribeye steaks, 1-inch thick
- 1 tsp dried oregano
- 1 tbsp garlic, minced
- 1/4 cup fresh lemon juice
- 1/2 cup olive oil
- Pepper
- Salt

Directions:
1. Add steaks and remaining ingredients into the zip-lock bag, seal bag, and place in the refrigerator overnight.
2. Remove steaks from marinade and place onto the cooking tray.
3. Select AIRFRY mode, then set the temperature to 400 F and the time to 10 minutes, then press start.
4. When the display shows Add Food then place the cooking tray in the vortex plus air fryer oven.
5. Serve and enjoy.

Nutritional Value (Amount per Serving):
Calories 383; Fat 36.4 g; Carbohydrates 1.3 g; Sugar 0.4 g; Protein 0.3 g; Cholesterol 0 mg

Mushroom Broccoli Steak Bites

Preparation Time: 10 minutes; Cooking Time: 8 minutes; Serve: 2

Ingredients:
- 1 lb ribeye steak, cut into cubes
- 1 tbsp garlic, minced
- 1 tsp Worcestershire sauce
- 1 cup broccoli florets

- 2 tbsp butter, melted
- 8 oz mushrooms, sliced
- 1 tsp sea salt

Directions:
1. Add steak cubes and remaining ingredients into the mixing bowl and toss well and transfer onto the cooking tray.
2. Select AIRFRY mode, then set the temperature to 400 F and the time to 6-8 minutes, then press start.
3. When the display shows Add Food then place the cooking tray in the vortex plus air fryer oven.
4. Serve and enjoy.

Nutritional Value (Amount per Serving):
Calories 609; Fat 33.8 g; Carbohydrates 8.7 g; Sugar 3.3 g; Protein 66.5 g; Cholesterol 160 mg

Juicy Lime Jalapeno Steak

Preparation Time: 10 minutes; Cooking Time: 10 minutes; Serve: 4

Ingredients:
- 1 lb flank steak
- 1/4 cup olive oil
- 1/2 tsp pepper
- 1/2 tsp paprika
- 1/2 cup fresh cilantro, chopped
- 1 tbsp garlic, minced
- 1 jalapeno pepper, sliced
- 1 lime juice
- 1 lime zest, grated
- Salt

Directions:
1. Add steak and remaining ingredients into the zip-lock bag, seal bag, and place in the refrigerator overnight.
2. Remove marinated steak from marinade and place onto the cooking tray.
3. Select AIRFRY mode, then set the temperature to 400 F and the time to 10 minutes, then press start.
4. When the display shows Add Food then place the cooking tray in the vortex plus air fryer oven.
5. Turn steak halfway through.
6. Serve and enjoy.

Nutritional Value (Amount per Serving):
Calories 337; Fat 22.1 g; Carbohydrates 2.3 g; Sugar 0.4 g; Protein 31.9 g; Cholesterol 62 mg

Steak Tips with Mushrooms

Preparation Time: 10 minutes; Cooking Time: 10 minutes; Serve: 4

Ingredients:
- 1 lb ribeye steaks, cut into bite-size pieces
- 1 1/2 tbsp olive oil
- 2 tbsp Worcestershire sauce
- 8 oz mushrooms, sliced
- Pepper
- Salt

Directions:
1. Add steak pieces, oil, Worcestershire sauce, mushrooms, pepper, and salt into the mixing bowl and toss well.
2. Transfer steak and mushroom mixture onto the parchment-lined cooking tray.
3. Select AIRFRY mode, then set the temperature to 400 F and the time to 10 minutes, then press start.
4. When the display shows Add Food then place the cooking tray in the vortex plus air fryer oven.
5. Stir steak and mushrooms halfway through.

6. Serve and enjoy.

Nutritional Value (Amount per Serving):
Calories 224; Fat 16.4 g; Carbohydrates 3.4 g; Sugar 2.5 g; Protein 1.8 g; Cholesterol 0 mg

Cajun Pork Chops

Preparation Time: 10 minutes; Cooking Time: 10 minutes; Serve: 4

Ingredients:
- 4 pork chops
- 2 tbsp olive oil
- 1 tbsp Cajun seasoning

Directions:
1. Brush pork chops with oil and season with Cajun seasoning.
2. Place pork chops onto the cooking tray.
3. Select AIRFRY mode, then set the temperature to 375 F and the time to 10 minutes, then press start.
4. When the display shows Add Food then place the cooking tray in the vortex plus air fryer oven.
5. Turn pork chops halfway through.
6. Serve and enjoy.

Nutritional Value (Amount per Serving):
Calories 316; Fat 26.9 g; Carbohydrates 0 g; Sugar 0 g; Protein 18 g; Cholesterol 69 mg

Crispy Crusted Pork Chops

Preparation Time: 10 minutes; Cooking Time: 12 minutes; Serve: 2

Ingredients:
- 2 pork chops, boneless
- 1 tsp Cajun seasoning
- 1 tsp Herb de Provence
- 1 tsp paprika
- 3 tbsp parmesan cheese, grated
- 1/3 cup almond flour
- 1 tbsp olive oil

Directions:
1. In a shallow dish, mix together parmesan cheese, almond flour, paprika, Herb de Provence, and Cajun seasoning.
2. Brush pork chops with oil and coat with parmesan cheese mixture.
3. Place coated pork chops onto the parchment-lined cooking tray.
4. Select AIRFRY mode, then set the temperature to 350 F and the time to 8-12 minutes, then press start.
5. When the display shows Add Food then place the cooking tray in the vortex plus air fryer oven.
6. Serve and enjoy.

Nutritional Value (Amount per Serving):
Calories 457; Fat 38.4 g; Carbohydrates 4.9 g; Sugar 0.8 g; Protein 25.5 g; Cholesterol 75 mg

Garlic Herb Pork Chops

Preparation Time: 10 minutes; Cooking Time: 20 minutes; Serve: 4

Ingredients:
- 4 pork chops, bone-in
- 1/2 tsp garlic and herb seasoning
- 2 tbsp olive oil
- Pepper
- Salt

Directions:
1. Brush pork chops with oil and season with garlic herb seasoning, pepper, and salt.
2. Place pork chops onto the cooking tray.

3. Select AIRFRY mode, then set the temperature to 380 F and the time to 20 minutes, then press start.
4. When the display shows Add Food then place the cooking tray in the vortex plus air fryer oven.
5. Flip pork chops after 15 minutes.
6. Serve and enjoy.

Nutritional Value (Amount per Serving):
Calories 316; Fat 26.9 g; Carbohydrates 0 g; Sugar 0 g; Protein 18 g; Cholesterol 69 mg

Pecan Crust Pork Chops

Preparation Time: 10 minutes; Cooking Time: 12 minutes; Serve: 6

Ingredients:
- 1 egg
- 6 pork chops, boneless
- 1 tsp garlic, crushed
- 1 tbsp water
- 1 tsp Dijon mustard
- 1 tsp garlic powder
- 1 tsp onion powder
- 2 tsp Italian seasoning
- 1/3 cup arrowroot
- 1 cup pecan pieces, crushed
- 1/4 tsp sea salt

Directions:
1. In a small bowl, whisk eggs with garlic, water, and Dijon mustard.
2. In a shallow dish, mix together pecans, garlic powder, onion powder, Italian seasoning, arrowroot, and sea salt.
3. Dip pork chop in egg mixture then coats with pecan mixture.
4. Place coated pork chops onto the cooking tray.
5. Select AIRFRY mode, then set the temperature to 400 F and the time to 12 minutes, then press start.
6. When the display shows Add Food then place the cooking tray in the vortex plus air fryer oven.
7. Flip pork chops halfway through.
8. Serve and enjoy.

Nutritional Value (Amount per Serving):
Calories 296; Fat 22.8 g; Carbohydrates 2.3 g; Sugar 0.5 g; Protein 19.6 g; Cholesterol 97 mg

Ranch Pork Chops

Preparation Time: 10 minutes; Cooking Time: 35 minutes; Serve: 6

Ingredients:
- 6 pork chops, boneless
- 2 tbsp ranch seasoning
- 1/4 cup olive oil
- 1 tsp dried parsley
- Pepper
- Salt

Directions:
1. Season pork chops with pepper and salt and place into the baking dish.
2. Mix together olive oil, parsley, and ranch seasoning and pour over pork chops.
3. Select BAKE mode, then set the temperature to 400 F and the time to 35 minutes, then press start.
4. When the display shows Add Food then place the baking dish in the vortex plus air fryer oven.
5. Serve and enjoy.

Nutritional Value (Amount per Serving):
Calories 338; Fat 28.3 g; Carbohydrates 0 g; Sugar 0 g; Protein 18 g; Cholesterol 69 mg

Feta Lamb Patties

Preparation Time: 10 minutes; Cooking Time: 8 minutes; Serve: 4

Ingredients:
- 1 lb ground lamb
- 6 basil leaves, minced
- 8 mint leaves, minced
- 1/4 cup fresh parsley, chopped
- 1 tsp dried oregano
- 1 cup feta cheese, crumbled
- 1 tbsp garlic, minced
- 1 jalapeno pepper, minced
- 1/4 tsp pepper
- 1/2 tsp kosher salt

Directions:
1. Add all ingredients into the large bowl and mix until well combined.
2. Make the equal shape of patties from meat mixture and place onto the parchment-lined cooking tray.
3. Select BAKE mode, then set the temperature to 400 F and the time to 8 minutes, then press start.
4. When the display shows Add Food then place the cooking tray in the vortex plus air fryer oven.
5. Flip patties halfway through.
6. Serve and enjoy.

Nutritional Value (Amount per Serving):
Calories 327; Fat 16.6 g; Carbohydrates 4.9 g; Sugar 1.7 g; Protein 38.3 g; Cholesterol 135 mg

Meatballs

Preparation Time: 10 minutes; Cooking Time: 20 minutes; Serve: 6

Ingredients:
- 2 lbs ground beef
- 1 egg, lightly beaten
- 1 tsp oregano
- 1 tsp cinnamon
- 2 tsp cumin
- 2 tsp coriander
- 1 tsp garlic, minced
- 1 small onion, grated
- 1 tbsp fresh mint, chopped
- 1/4 cup fresh parsley, minced
- 1/2 tsp allspice
- 1 tsp paprika
- 1/4 tsp pepper
- 1/2 tsp salt

Directions:
1. Add all ingredients into the large mixing bowl and mix until well combined.
2. Make small balls from the meat mixture and place them onto the cooking tray.
3. Select BAKE mode, then set the temperature to 400 F and the time to 15-20 minutes, then press start.
4. When the display shows Add Food then place the cooking tray in the vortex plus air fryer oven.
5. Serve and enjoy.

Nutritional Value (Amount per Serving):
Calories 304; Fat 10.4 g; Carbohydrates 2.7 g; Sugar 0.7 g; Protein 47.3 g; Cholesterol 162 mg

Rosemary Thyme Lamb Chops

Preparation Time: 10 minutes; Cooking Time: 12 minutes; Serve: 4

Ingredients:
- 4 lamb loin chops
- 1 tbsp garlic, chopped
- 2 tbsp olive oil
- 1/4 cup lemon juice
- 1/4 tsp cayenne pepper
- 1/2 tsp thyme
- 1 tsp rosemary
- 1 tsp sea salt

Directions:

1. Add lamb chops and remaining ingredients into the zip-lock bag, seal bag, and place in the refrigerator for 1 hour.
2. Place marinated lamb chops onto the cooking tray.
3. Select AIRFRY mode, then set the temperature to 390 F and the time to 12 minutes, then press start.
4. When the display shows Add Food then place the cooking tray in the vortex plus air fryer oven.
5. Flip lamb chops halfway through.
6. Serve and enjoy.

Nutritional Value (Amount per Serving):
Calories 677; Fat 31.2 g; Carbohydrates 1.3 g; Sugar 0.4 g; Protein 92.1 g; Cholesterol 294 mg

Meatballs

Preparation Time: 10 minutes; Cooking Time: 15 minutes; Serve: 4

Ingredients:
- 1 lb ground pork
- 2 tsp curry paste
- 1 tbsp Worcestershire sauce
- 1 tsp garlic paste
- 1 onion, chopped
- 1 tsp coriander
- 1 tsp Chinese spice
- 1 tsp mixed spice
- 1/2 fresh lime juice
- Pepper
- Salt

Directions:
1. Add all ingredients into the bowl and mix until well combined.
2. Make small balls from the meat mixture and place them onto the cooking tray.
3. Select AIRFRY mode, then set the temperature to 350 F and the time to 15 minutes, then press start.
4. When the display shows Add Food then place the cooking tray in the vortex plus air fryer oven.
5. Serve and enjoy.

Nutritional Value (Amount per Serving):
Calories 196; Fat 5.5 g; Carbohydrates 4.7 g; Sugar 2 g; Protein 30.2 g; Cholesterol 83 mg

Air Fryer Pork Ribs

Preparation Time: 10 minutes; Cooking Time: 20 minutes; Serve: 2

Ingredients:
- 1 1/2 lbs pork ribs
- 2 1/2 tbsp olive oil
- 1 1/2 tbsp paprika
- 1 tbsp salt

Directions:
1. Brush pork ribs with oil and season with paprika and salt.
2. Place pork ribs onto the cooking tray.
3. Select AIRFRY mode, then set the temperature to 350 F and the time to 20 minutes, then press start.
4. When the display shows Add Food then place the cooking tray in the vortex plus air fryer oven.
5. Serve and enjoy.

Nutritional Value (Amount per Serving):
Calories 1094; Fat 78.4 g; Carbohydrates 2.9 g; Sugar 0.5 g; Protein 90.9 g; Cholesterol 350 mg

Spicy Pork Chops

Preparation Time: 10 minutes; Cooking Time: 10 minutes; Serve: 4

Ingredients:
- 4 pork chops
- 1/2 tsp black pepper
- 1/2 tsp ground cumin
- 1 tsp paprika
- 1 1/2 tsp olive oil
- 1/2 tsp cayenne pepper
- 1/2 tsp garlic salt

Directions:
1. Add pork chops and remaining ingredients into the zip-lock bag, seal bag and shake well to coat.
2. Place coated pork chops onto the cooking tray.
3. Select AIRFRY mode, then set the temperature to 400 F and the time to 10 minutes, then press start.
4. When the display shows Add Food then place the cooking tray in the vortex plus air fryer oven.
5. Serve and enjoy.

Nutritional Value (Amount per Serving):
Calories 276; Fat 21.8 g; Carbohydrates 1 g; Sugar 0.2 g; Protein 18.2 g; Cholesterol 69 mg

Marinated Pork Chops

Preparation Time: 10 minutes; Cooking Time: 14 minutes; Serve: 2

Ingredients:
- 2 pork chops
- 4 tbsp BBQ sauce, sugar-free
- 1/2 tbsp garlic, minced
- 1/2 tsp olive oil
- Pepper
- Salt

Directions:
1. Add all ingredients into the bowl, mix well, and place in the refrigerator for 1 hour.
2. Place marinated pork chops onto the cooking tray.
3. Select AIRFRY mode, then set the temperature to 390 F and the time to 14 minutes, then press start.
4. When the display shows Add Food then place the cooking tray in the vortex plus air fryer oven.
5. Flip pork chops halfway through.
6. Serve and enjoy.

Nutritional Value (Amount per Serving):
Calories 316; Fat 21.2 g; Carbohydrates 12.1 g; Sugar 8.2 g; Protein 18.5 g; Cholesterol 69 mg

Flavorful Lamb Steak

Preparation Time: 10 minutes; Cooking Time: 15 minutes; Serve: 4

Ingredients:
- 1 lb lamb sirloin steaks, boneless
- 1 tsp ground fennel
- 1 tsp garam masala
- 5 garlic cloves
- 1 tbsp ginger
- 1 tsp cayenne
- 1/2 tsp ground cardamom
- 1 tsp ground cinnamon
- 1/2 onion
- 1 tsp salt

Directions:
1. Add all ingredients except steak into the blender and blend until smooth.
2. Add blended mixture and steak into the bowl and coat well. Cover and place in the refrigerator for 1 hour.
3. Place marinated meat onto the cooking tray.
4. Select AIRFRY mode, then set the temperature to 330 F and the time to 15 minutes, then press start.

5. When the display shows Add Food then place the cooking tray in the vortex plus air fryer oven.
   6. Turn meat half way through.
   7. Serve and enjoy.

Nutritional Value (Amount per Serving):
Calories 252; Fat 10.7 g; Carbohydrates 4.6 g; Sugar 0.7 g; Protein 32.9 g; Cholesterol 104 mg

Asian Pork Shoulder

Preparation Time: 10 minutes; Cooking Time: 15 minutes; Serve: 4

Ingredients:
- 1 lb pork shoulder, boneless and cut into 1/2-inch sliced
- 1 tbsp sesame oil
- 1 tbsp rice wine
- 1 tbsp garlic, minced
- 1 tbsp ginger, minced
- 2 tbsp red pepper paste
- 1 onion, sliced
- 1/4 cup green onions, sliced
- 1 tbsp sesame seeds
- 1 tsp cayenne pepper

Directions:
1. Add all ingredients into the bowl and mix well and place in the refrigerator for 1 hour.
2. Place marinated meat and onion slices onto the cooking tray.
3. Select AIRFRY mode, then set the temperature to 400 F and the time to 15 minutes, then press start.
4. When the display shows Add Food then place the cooking tray in the vortex plus air fryer oven.
5. Turn meat half way through.
6. Serve and enjoy.

Nutritional Value (Amount per Serving):
Calories 403; Fat 29 g; Carbohydrates 7.2 g; Sugar 2.5 g; Protein 27.5 g; Cholesterol 102 mg

Meatloaf

Preparation Time: 10 minutes; Cooking Time: 20 minutes; Serve: 4

Ingredients:
- 1 lb ground pork
- 1 egg, lightly beaten
- 1 tbsp thyme, chopped
- 1/4 tsp garlic powder
- 3 tbsp almond flour
- 1 onion, chopped
- Pepper
- Salt

Directions:
1. Add all ingredients into the bowl and mix until well combined.
2. Pour meat mixture into the greased loaf pan.
3. Select BAKE mode, then set the temperature to 390 F and the time to 20 minutes, then press start.
4. When the display shows Add Food then place the loaf pan in the vortex plus air fryer oven.
5. Serve and enjoy.

Nutritional Value (Amount per Serving):
Calories 221; Fat 7.8 g; Carbohydrates 4.4 g; Sugar 1.5 g; Protein 32.6 g; Cholesterol 124 mg

Meatballs

Preparation Time: 10 minutes; Cooking Time: 12 minutes; Serve: 4

Ingredients:
- 4 oz ground lamb meat
- 1 egg, lightly beaten

- 1 tbsp oregano, chopped
- Pepper
- Salt

Directions:
1. Add all ingredients into the bowl and mix until well combined.
2. Make small balls from meat mixture and place onto the parchment-lined cooking tray.
3. Select BAKE mode, then set the temperature to 400 F and the time to 12 minutes, then press start.
4. When the display shows Add Food then place the cooking tray in the vortex plus air fryer oven.
5. Serve and enjoy.

Nutritional Value (Amount per Serving):
Calories 77; Fat 5 g; Carbohydrates 0.8 g; Sugar 0.1 g; Protein 6.8 g; Cholesterol 61 mg

Baked Beef with Broccoli

Preparation Time: 10 minutes; Cooking Time: 25 minutes; Serve: 2

Ingredients:
- 1/2 lb beef stew meat, cut into pieces
- 1 tbsp vinegar
- 1 garlic clove, minced
- 1 tbsp olive oil
- 1/2 cup broccoli florets
- 1 onion, sliced
- Pepper
- Salt

Directions:
1. Add meat and remaining ingredients into the large bowl and toss well and spread onto the cooking tray.
2. Select BAKE mode, then set the temperature to 390 F and the time to 25 minutes, then press start.
3. When the display shows Add Food then place the cooking tray in the vortex plus air fryer oven.
4. Serve and enjoy.

Nutritional Value (Amount per Serving):
Calories 304; Fat 14.2 g; Carbohydrates 7.3 g; Sugar 2.8 g; Protein 35.8 g; Cholesterol 101 mg

Meatballs

Preparation Time: 10 minutes; Cooking Time: 20 minutes; Serve: 4

Ingredients:
- 1 lb ground beef
- 1/2 small onion, chopped
- 1 egg, lightly beaten
- 2 garlic cloves, minced
- 1 tbsp basil, chopped
- 1/4 cup parmesan cheese, grated
- 1 tbsp parsley, chopped
- 1 tbsp rosemary, chopped
- 2 tbsp coconut milk
- 1/2 cup almond flour
- Pepper
- Salt

Directions:
1. Add all ingredients into the bowl and mix until well combined.
2. Make small balls from meat mixture and place onto the parchment-lined cooking tray.
3. Select BAKE mode, then set the temperature to 375 F and the time to 20 minutes, then press start.
4. When the display shows Add Food then place the cooking tray in the vortex plus air fryer oven.
5. Serve and enjoy.

Nutritional Value (Amount per Serving):
Calories 351; Fat 18.3 g; Carbohydrates 5.7 g; Sugar 1.2 g; Protein 41.1 g; Cholesterol 146 mg

Burger Patties

Preparation Time: 10 minutes; Cooking Time: 15 minutes; Serve: 6

Ingredients:
- 2 lbs ground beef
- 1 tsp garlic powder
- 1 cup mozzarella cheese, grated
- 1 tsp onion powder
- Pepper
- Salt

Directions:
1. Add all ingredients into the large bowl and mix until well combined.
2. Make small patties from meat mixture and place onto the parchment-lined cooking tray.
3. Select BAKE mode, then set the temperature to 400 F and the time to 15 minutes, then press start.
4. When the display shows Add Food then place the cooking tray in the vortex plus air fryer oven.
5. Serve and enjoy.

Nutritional Value (Amount per Serving):
Calories 297; Fat 10.3 g; Carbohydrates 0.8 g; Sugar 0.3 g; Protein 47.3 g; Cholesterol 138 mg

Spicy Lamb Chunks

Preparation Time: 10 minutes; Cooking Time: 10 minutes; Serve: 4

Ingredients:
- 1 lb lamb, cut into 1-inch pieces
- 2 tbsp olive oil
- 1/2 tsp cayenne
- 2 tbsp ground cumin
- 2 chili peppers, chopped
- 1 tbsp garlic, minced
- 1 tsp salt

Directions:
1. Add meat and remaining ingredients into the zip-lock bag, seal bag, and place in the refrigerator for 1 hour.
2. Place marinated meat onto the cooking tray.
3. Select AIRFRY mode, then set the temperature to 360 F and the time to 10 minutes, then press start.
4. When the display shows Add Food then place the cooking tray in the vortex plus air fryer oven.
5. Serve and enjoy.

Nutritional Value (Amount per Serving):
Calories 287; Fat 16 g; Carbohydrates 2.3 g; Sugar 0.2 g; Protein 32.6 g; Cholesterol 102 mg

Thyme Lamb Chops

Preparation Time: 10 minutes; Cooking Time: 12 minutes; Serve: 4

Ingredients:
- 4 lamb chops
- 1 tbsp dried thyme
- 3 tbsp olive oil
- Pepper
- Salt

Directions:
1. Mix together oil, thyme, pepper, and salt.
2. Brush lamb chops with oil mixture and place onto the cooking tray.
3. Select AIRFRY mode, then set the temperature to 390 F and the time to 12 minutes, then press start.
4. When the display shows Add Food then place the cooking tray in the vortex plus air fryer oven.
5. Flip lamb chops halfway through.

6. Serve and enjoy.

Nutritional Value (Amount per Serving):
Calories 700; Fat 34.5 g; Carbohydrates 0.5 g; Sugar 0 g; Protein 91.9 g; Cholesterol 294 mg

Marinated Lamb Chops

Preparation Time: 10 minutes; Cooking Time: 8 minutes; Serve: 4

Ingredients:
- 1 lb lamb chops
- 1 tsp oregano
- 1 tsp thyme
- 1 tsp rosemary
- 2 tbsp lemon juice
- 2 tbsp olive oil
- 1 tsp coriander
- 1 tsp salt

Directions:
1. Add lamb chops and remaining ingredients into the zip-lock bag, seal bag, and place in the refrigerator for 1 hour.
2. Place marinated lamb chops onto the cooking tray.
3. Select AIRFRY mode, then set the temperature to 390 F and the time to 8 minutes, then press start.
4. When the display shows Add Food then place the cooking tray in the vortex plus air fryer oven.
5. Flip lamb chops halfway through.
6. Serve and enjoy.

Nutritional Value (Amount per Serving):
Calories 276; Fat 15.5 g; Carbohydrates 0.8 g; Sugar 0.2 g; Protein 32 g; Cholesterol 102 mg

Dash Pork Chops

Preparation Time: 10 minutes; Cooking Time: 20 minutes; Serve: 4

Ingredients:
- 4 pork chops, boneless
- 1 tbsp olive oil
- 1 tbsp Mr.Dash seasoning
- Pepper
- Salt

Directions:
1. Brush pork chops with oil and season with dash seasoning, pepper, and salt.
2. Place pork chops onto the cooking tray.
3. Select AIRFRY mode, then set the temperature to 360 F and the time to 20 minutes, then press start.
4. When the display shows Add Food then place the cooking tray in the vortex plus air fryer oven.
5. Flip pork chops halfway through.
6. Serve and enjoy.

Nutritional Value (Amount per Serving):
Calories 286; Fat 23.4 g; Carbohydrates 0 g; Sugar 0 g; Protein 18 g; Cholesterol 69 mg

Meatballs

Preparation Time: 10 minutes; Cooking Time: 15 minutes; Serve: 4

Ingredients:
- 10 oz ground pork
- 1/4 cup fresh basil, chopped
- 1 tsp ginger garlic paste
- 1 tsp mustard
- 1 medium onion, peeled and chopped
- Pepper
- Salt

Directions:

1. Add all ingredients into the bowl and mix until well combined.
2. Make small balls from meat mixture and place onto the parchment-lined cooking tray.
3. Select BAKE mode, then set the temperature to 400 F and the time to 15 minutes, then press start.
4. When the display shows Add Food then place the cooking tray in the vortex plus air fryer oven.
5. Serve and enjoy.

Nutritional Value (Amount per Serving):
Calories 123; Fat 3 g; Carbohydrates 3.7 g; Sugar 1.2 g; Protein 19.4 g; Cholesterol 52 mg

Coconut Pork Chops

Preparation Time: 10 minutes; Cooking Time: 16 minutes; Serve: 4
Ingredients:
- 4 pork chops
- 1 tbsp coconut oil
- 1 tbsp coconut butter
- 2 tsp parsley
- 2 tsp garlic, grated
- Pepper
- Salt

Directions:
1. In a small bowl, mix together coconut butter, coconut oil, garlic cloves, parsley, pepper, and salt.
2. Coat pork chops with coconut butter mixture and place in the refrigerator for 1 hour.
3. Place pork chops onto the parchment-lined cooking tray.
4. Select AIRFRY mode, then set the temperature to 350 F and the time to 16 minutes, then press start.
5. When the display shows Add Food then place the cooking tray in the vortex plus air fryer oven.
6. Flip pork chops to halfway through.
7. Serve and enjoy.

Nutritional Value (Amount per Serving):
Calories 301; Fat 23.8 g; Carbohydrates 2.5 g; Sugar 1.4 g; Protein 18.3 g; Cholesterol 69 mg

Meatballs

Preparation Time: 10 minutes; Cooking Time: 15 minutes; Serve: 4
Ingredients:
- 1 lb ground lamb
- 1 tsp onion powder
- 1 tbsp garlic, minced
- 1 tsp ground coriander
- 1 tsp ground cumin
- Pepper
- Salt

Directions:
1. Add all ingredients into the large bowl and mix until well combined.
2. Make small balls from the meat mixture and place them onto the cooking tray.
3. Select BAKE mode, then set the temperature to 400 F and the time to 15 minutes, then press start.
4. When the display shows Add Food then place the cooking tray in the vortex plus air fryer oven.
5. Serve and enjoy.

Nutritional Value (Amount per Serving):
Calories 218; Fat 8.5 g; Carbohydrates 1.4 g; Sugar 0.2 g; Protein 32.1 g; Cholesterol 102 mg

Parmesan Crusted Pork Chops

Preparation Time: 10 minutes; Cooking Time: 30 minutes; Serve: 3
Ingredients:
- 3 pork chops, boneless
- 1 egg, lightly beaten
- 3 tbsp parmesan cheese, grated
- 1/2 cup almond flour
- 2 tbsp coconut milk
- Pepper
- Salt

Directions:
1. In a shallow bowl, whisk the egg with milk.
2. In a shallow dish, mix together parmesan cheese, almond flour, pepper, and salt.
3. Dip pork chops into the egg mixture then coat with parmesan mixture, place coated pork chops onto the cooking tray.
4. Select BAKE mode, then set the temperature to 350 F and the time to 30 minutes, then press start.
5. When the display shows Add Food then place the cooking tray in the vortex plus air fryer oven.
6. Serve and enjoy.

Nutritional Value (Amount per Serving):
Calories 422; Fat 34.1 g; Carbohydrates 4.9 g; Sugar 1.1 g; Protein 25.6 g; Cholesterol 127 mg

Crispy Crusted Pork Chops

Preparation Time: 10 minutes; Cooking Time: 15 minutes; Serve: 2
Ingredients:
- 2 pork chops, bone-in
- 1 tbsp olive oil
- 1 cup pork rinds, crushed
- 1/2 tsp garlic powder
- 1/2 tsp onion powder
- 1/2 tsp paprika
- 1/2 tsp parsley

Directions:
1. In a shallow dish, mix together crushed pork rinds, garlic powder, onion powder, paprika, and parsley.
2. Brush pork chops with oil and coat with crushed pork rinds.
3. Place coated pork chops onto the cooking tray.
4. Select AIRFRY mode, then set the temperature to 400 F and the time to 15 minutes, then press start.
5. When the display shows Add Food then place the cooking tray in the vortex plus air fryer oven.
6. Turn pork chops after 10 minutes.
7. Serve and enjoy.

Nutritional Value (Amount per Serving):
Calories 362; Fat 29.5 g; Carbohydrates 1.3 g; Sugar 0.4 g; Protein 22.8 g; Cholesterol 79 mg

Meatballs

Preparation Time: 10 minutes; Cooking Time: 20 minutes; Serve: 6
Ingredients:
- 1 lb ground beef
- 1 egg, lightly beaten
- 1/2 small onion, minced
- 2 garlic cloves, minced
- 1/4 cup parmesan cheese, grated
- 1/2 cup almond flour
- 1 tbsp fresh basil, chopped
- 1 tbsp fresh parsley, chopped
- 1 tbsp fresh rosemary, chopped
- Pepper
- Salt

Directions:
1. Add all ingredients into the large bowl and mix until well combined.
2. Make small balls from the meat mixture and place them onto the cooking tray.
3. Select AIRFRY mode, then set the temperature to 375 F and the time to 20 minutes, then press start.
4. When the display shows Add Food then place the cooking tray in the vortex plus air fryer oven.
5. Serve and enjoy.

Nutritional Value (Amount per Serving):
Calories 222; Fat 11 g; Carbohydrates 3.5 g; Sugar 0.7 g; Protein 27.2 g; Cholesterol 98 mg

Lemon Pepper Pork Chops

Preparation Time: 10 minutes; Cooking Time: 15 minutes; Serve: 4

Ingredients:
- 4 pork chops, boneless
- 1 tbsp olive oil
- 1 tsp lemon pepper seasoning
- Salt

Directions:
1. Brush pork chops with oil and season with lemon pepper seasoning and salt.
2. Place pork chops onto the cooking tray.
3. Select AIRFRY mode, then set the temperature to 400 F and the time to 15 minutes, then press start.
4. When the display shows Add Food then place the cooking tray in the vortex plus air fryer oven.
5. Serve and enjoy.

Nutritional Value (Amount per Serving):
Calories 287; Fat 23.4 g; Carbohydrates 0.3 g; Sugar 0 g; Protein 18 g; Cholesterol 69 mg

Pork Burger Patties

Preparation Time: 10 minutes; Cooking Time: 35 minutes; Serve: 6

Ingredients:
- 2 lbs ground pork
- 1 egg, lightly beaten
- 1 onion, minced
- 1 carrot, minced
- 1/2 cup almond flour
- 1 tsp garlic powder
- 1 tsp paprika
- Pepper
- Salt

Directions:
1. Add all ingredients into the large bowl and mix until well combined.
2. Make small balls from the meat mixture and place them onto the cooking tray.
3. Select AIRFRY mode, then set the temperature to 375 F and the time to 35 minutes, then press start.
4. When the display shows Add Food then place the cooking tray in the vortex plus air fryer oven.
5. Turn patties after 20 minutes.
6. Serve and enjoy.

Nutritional Value (Amount per Serving):
Calories 294; Fat 10.8 g; Carbohydrates 5.3 g; Sugar 1.8 g; Protein 42.9 g; Cholesterol 138 mg

Stuffed Pork Chops

Preparation Time: 10 minutes; Cooking Time: 35 minutes; Serve: 4

Ingredients:

- 4 pork chops, boneless and thick-cut
- 2 tbsp olives, chopped
- 1 tbsp garlic, minced
- 2 tbsp fresh parsley, chopped
- 2 tbsp sun-dried tomatoes, chopped
- 1/2 cup goat cheese, crumbled

Directions:
1. In a bowl, combine together feta cheese, garlic, parsley, olives, and sun-dried tomatoes.
2. Stuff cheese mixture into each pork chops and place pork chops onto the cooking tray.
3. Select BAKE mode, then set the temperature to 375 F and the time to 35 minutes, then press start.
4. When the display shows Add Food then place the cooking tray in the vortex plus air fryer oven.
5. Serve and enjoy.

Nutritional Value (Amount per Serving):
Calories 317; Fat 24.7 g; Carbohydrates 1.5 g; Sugar 0.4 g; Protein 21.7 g; Cholesterol 81 mg

Meatballs

Preparation Time: 10 minutes; Cooking Time: 20 minutes; Serve: 12

Ingredients:
- 1 lb ground beef
- 2 tbsp fresh parsley, chopped
- 1/2 cup almond flour
- 1/4 cup onion, chopped
- 3 tbsp mushrooms, chopped
- 1/2 tsp pepper
- 1 tsp salt

Directions:
1. In a bowl, mix together ground beef, parsley, onions, and mushrooms.
2. Add remaining ingredients and mix until combined.
3. Make small balls from the mixture and place onto the cooking tray.
4. Select AIRFRY mode, then set the temperature to 350 F and the time to 20 minutes, then press start.
5. When the display shows Add Food then place the cooking tray in the vortex plus air fryer oven.
6. Serve and enjoy.

Nutritional Value (Amount per Serving):
Calories 99; Fat 4.7 g; Carbohydrates 1.4 g; Sugar 0.3 g; Protein 12.6 g; Cholesterol 34 mg

Dill Beef Roast

Preparation Time: 10 minutes; Cooking Time: 45 minutes; Serve: 8

Ingredients:
- 2 1/2 lbs beef roast
- 1 tsp dill
- 1/2 tsp black pepper
- 1/2 tsp garlic powder
- 1 tsp rosemary
- 1/2 tsp onion powder
- 2 tbsp olive oil

Directions:
1. In a small bowl, mix black pepper, garlic powder, onion powder, rosemary, dill, and olive oil and rub all over the beef roast.
2. Place beef roast onto the cooking tray.
3. Select AIRFRY mode, then set the temperature to 360 F and the time to 45 minutes, then press start.
4. When the display shows Add Food then place the cooking tray in the vortex plus air fryer oven.
5. Serve and enjoy.

Nutritional Value (Amount per Serving):

Calories 296; Fat 12.4 g; Carbohydrates 0.5 g; Sugar 0.1 g; Protein 43.1 g; Cholesterol 127 mg

Jamaican Pork Butt

Preparation Time: 10 minutes; Cooking Time: 20 minutes; Serve: 4

Ingredients:
- 1 1/2 lbs pork butt, chopped into pieces
- 1/4 cup jerk paste
- Pepper
- Salt

Directions:
1. Add meat and jerk paste into the bowl and mix well, cover and place in refrigerator overnight.
2. Place marinated meat onto the cooking tray.
3. Select AIRFRY mode, then set the temperature to 390 F and the time to 20 minutes, then press start.
4. When the display shows Add Food then place the cooking tray in the vortex plus air fryer oven.
5. Serve and enjoy.

Nutritional Value (Amount per Serving):
Calories 348; Fat 12.8 g; Carbohydrates 1.4 g; Sugar 1 g; Protein 53.1 g; Cholesterol 156 mg

Meatballs

Preparation Time: 10 minutes; Cooking Time: 20 minutes; Serve: 8

Ingredients:
- 2 lbs ground beef
- 1 cup almond flour
- 1/2 cup coconut flour
- 12 oz jar roasted red peppers
- 2 eggs, lightly beaten
- 1/4 cup fresh parsley, chopped
- 1/2 cup fresh basil, chopped
- 1/3 cup tomato sauce
- 1/4 tsp pepper
- 1/2 tsp salt

Directions:
1. Add all ingredients into the large bowl and mix until well combined.
2. Make small meatballs from mixture and place onto the cooking tray.
3. Select BAKE mode, then set the temperature to 350 F and the time to 20 minutes, then press start.
4. When the display shows Add Food then place the cooking tray in the vortex plus air fryer oven.
5. Serve and enjoy.

Nutritional Value (Amount per Serving):
Calories 367; Fat 15.3 g; Carbohydrates 11.9 g; Sugar 1.1 g; Protein 40.7 g; Cholesterol 142 mg

Sirloin Steak

Preparation Time: 10 minutes; Cooking Time: 10 minutes; Serve: 2

Ingredients:
- 2 sirloin steaks
- 2 tbsp steak seasoning
- 2 tsp olive oil
- Pepper
- Salt

Directions:
1. Brush steak with oil and season with steak seasoning, pepper, and salt.
2. Place steaks onto the cooking tray.
3. Select AIRFRY mode, then set the temperature to 350 F and the time to 10 minutes, then press start.

4. When the display shows Add Food then place the cooking tray in the vortex plus air fryer oven.
5. Slice and serve.

Nutritional Value (Amount per Serving):
Calories 198; Fat 10 g; Carbohydrates 0 g; Sugar 0 g; Protein 25.8 g; Cholesterol 76 mg

Delicious Kebab

Preparation Time: 10 minutes; Cooking Time: 10 minutes; Serve: 4

Ingredients:
- 1/2 lb ground beef
- 1/2 lb ground pork
- 2 tbsp kabab spice mix
- 1 tbsp garlic, minced
- 1/4 cup fresh parsley, chopped
- 1 tbsp olive oil
- 1 tsp salt

Directions:
1. Add all ingredients into the bowl and mix until well combined. Cover and place in the refrigerator for 30 minutes.
2. Divide the mixture evenly in 4 portions and make sausage shape kabab.
3. Place kababs onto the cooking tray.
4. Select AIRFRY mode, then set the temperature to 370 F and the time to 10 minutes, then press start.
5. When the display shows Add Food then place the cooking tray in the vortex plus air fryer oven.
6. Serve and enjoy.

Nutritional Value (Amount per Serving):
Calories 231; Fat 9.3 g; Carbohydrates 2 g; Sugar 0.2 g; Protein 32.8 g; Cholesterol 92 mg

Meatloaf

Preparation Time: 10 minutes; Cooking Time: 20 minutes; Serve: 4

Ingredients:
- 1 lb ground beef
- 3 tbsp almond flour
- 1 egg, lightly beaten
- 2 mushrooms, sliced
- 2 oz sausage, chopped
- 1 tbsp thyme, chopped
- 1 onion, chopped
- Pepper
- Salt

Directions:
1. Add all ingredients into the large bowl and mix until well combined.
2. Transfer meat mixture into the greased loaf pan.
3. Select AIRFRY mode, then set the temperature to 390 F and the time to 20 minutes, then press start.
4. When the display shows Add Food then place the loaf pan in the vortex plus air fryer oven.
5. Serve and enjoy.

Nutritional Value (Amount per Serving):
Calories 319; Fat 14.9 g; Carbohydrates 4.5 g; Sugar 1.6 g; Protein 40.3 g; Cholesterol 154 mg

Montreal Steak

Preparation Time: 10 minutes; Cooking Time: 7 minutes; Serve: 2

Ingredients:
- 12 oz steaks
- 1 tbsp Montreal steak seasoning
- 1 tbsp olive oil
- Pepper

- Salt

Directions:
1. Brush steaks with oil and season with steak seasoning, pepper, and salt and place onto the cooking tray.
2. Select AIRFRY mode, then set the temperature to 375 F and the time to 7 minutes, then press start.
3. When the display shows Add Food then place the cooking tray in the vortex plus air fryer oven.
4. Serve and enjoy.

Nutritional Value (Amount per Serving):
Calories 409; Fat 15.5 g; Carbohydrates 0 g; Sugar 0 g; Protein 61.5 g; Cholesterol 153 mg

Basil Pesto Pork Chops

Preparation Time: 10 minutes; Cooking Time: 18 minutes; Serve: 4

Ingredients:
- 4 pork chops
- 2 tbsp parmesan cheese, grated
- 2 tbsp basil pesto
- Pepper
- Salt

Directions:
1. Season pork chops with pepper and salt and place onto the cooking tray.
2. Spread pesto and cheese on top of pork chops.
3. Select AIRFRY mode, then set the temperature to 350 F and the time to 18 minutes, then press start.
4. When the display shows Add Food then place the cooking tray in the vortex plus air fryer oven.
5. Serve and enjoy.

Nutritional Value (Amount per Serving):
Calories 301; Fat 22.9 g; Carbohydrates 0.6 g; Sugar 0 g; Protein 22.5 g; Cholesterol 79 mg

Creole Cheese Pork Chops

Preparation Time: 10 minutes; Cooking Time: 12 minutes; Serve: 6

Ingredients:
- 1 1/2 lbs pork chops, boneless
- 1 tsp Creole seasoning
- 1/4 cup mozzarella cheese, grated
- 1/3 cup almond flour
- 1 tsp paprika
- 1 tsp garlic powder

Directions:
1. Add pork chops and remaining ingredients into the zip-lock bag, seal bag shakes well.
2. Place coated pork chops onto the parchment-lined cooking tray.
3. Select AIRFRY mode, then set the temperature to 360 F and the time to 12 minutes, then press start.
4. When the display shows Add Food then place the cooking tray in the vortex plus air fryer oven.
5. Serve and enjoy.

Nutritional Value (Amount per Serving):
Calories 404; Fat 31.6 g; Carbohydrates 1.9 g; Sugar 0.4 g; Protein 27.3 g; Cholesterol 98 mg

Garlic & Onion Pork Chops

Preparation Time: 10 minutes; Cooking Time: 12 minutes; Serve: 4

Ingredients:
- 4 pork chops, boneless
- 1/2 tsp granulated onion

- 1/2 tsp granulated garlic
- 2 tsp olive oil
- 1/2 tsp celery seeds
- 1/2 tsp parsley
- 1/2 tsp salt

Directions:
1. In a small bowl, mix together onion, garlic, celery seeds, parsley, and salt.
2. Brush pork chops with oil and rub with garlic mixture.
3. Place pork chops onto the cooking tray.
4. Select AIRFRY mode, then set the temperature to 350 F and the time to 12 minutes, then press start.
5. When the display shows Add Food then place the cooking tray in the vortex plus air fryer oven.
6. Serve and enjoy.

Nutritional Value (Amount per Serving):
Calories 278; Fat 22.3 g; Carbohydrates 0.4 g; Sugar 0.1 g; Protein 18.1 g; Cholesterol 69 mg

Meatballs

Preparation Time: 10 minutes; Cooking Time: 20 minutes; Serve: 4

Ingredients:
- 1/2 lb ground beef
- 1/2 lb Italian sausage
- 1/2 cup mozzarella cheese, shredded
- 1/2 tsp black pepper
- 1/2 tsp garlic powder
- 1/2 tsp onion powder
- Salt

Directions:
1. Add all ingredients into the large mixing bowl and mix until well combined.
2. Make meatballs from mixture and place onto the cooking tray.
3. Select AIRFRY mode, then set the temperature to 370 F and the time to 15-20 minutes, then press start.
4. When the display shows Add Food then place the cooking tray in the vortex plus air fryer oven.
5. Serve and enjoy.

Nutritional Value (Amount per Serving):
Calories 310; Fat 20.3 g; Carbohydrates 0.8 g; Sugar 0.2 g; Protein 29.3 g; Cholesterol 100 mg

Delicious Beef Satay

Preparation Time: 10 minutes; Cooking Time: 8 minutes; Serve: 2

Ingredients:
- 1 lb beef flank steak, sliced into long strips
- 1 tbsp fish sauce
- 2 tbsp olive oil
- 1 tsp hot sauce
- 1 tbsp Swerve
- 1 tbsp garlic, minced
- 1 tbsp ginger, minced
- 1 tbsp soy sauce
- 1/2 cup cilantro, chopped
- 1 tsp ground coriander

Directions:
1. Add all ingredients into the zip-lock bag, seal bag, and shake well. Place into the refrigerator for 1 hour.
2. Place marinated meat onto the cooking tray.
3. Select AIRFRY mode, then set the temperature to 400 F and the time to 8 minutes, then press start.
4. When the display shows Add Food then place the cooking tray in the vortex plus air fryer oven.

5. Serve and enjoy.

Nutritional Value (Amount per Serving):
Calories 568; Fat 28.3 g; Carbohydrates 5.4 g; Sugar 0.7 g; Protein 70.4 g; Cholesterol 203 mg

Easy Steak Fajita

Preparation Time: 10 minutes; Cooking Time: 15 minutes; Serve: 6

Ingredients:
- 1 lb steak, sliced
- 1 tbsp olive oil
- 1 tbsp fajita seasoning, gluten-free
- 1/2 cup onion, sliced
- 3 bell peppers, sliced

Directions:
1. Add all ingredients large bowl and toss until well coated.
2. Transfer fajita mixture into the baking dish.
3. Select AIRFRY mode, then set the temperature to 390 F and the time to 15 minutes, then press start.
4. When the display shows Add Food then place the baking dish in the vortex plus air fryer oven.
5. Serve and enjoy.

Nutritional Value (Amount per Serving):
Calories 199; Fat 6.3 g; Carbohydrates 6.4 g; Sugar 3.4 g; Protein 28 g; Cholesterol 68 mg

Flavorful Beef Fajitas

Preparation Time: 10 minutes; Cooking Time: 8 minutes; Serve: 4

Ingredients:
- 1 lb beef flank steak, sliced
- 1/2 tbsp chili powder
- 3 tbsp olive oil
- 1/2 onion, sliced
- 1 green bell pepper, sliced
- 1 red bell pepper, sliced
- 1 tsp garlic powder
- 1 tsp paprika
- 1 1/2 tsp cumin
- Pepper
- Salt

Directions:
1. Add meat and remaining ingredients into the bowl and toss to coat.
2. Transfer beef mixture into the baking dish.
3. Select AIRFRY mode, then set the temperature to 390 F and the time to 5-8 minutes, then press start.
4. When the display shows Add Food then place the baking dish in the vortex plus air fryer oven.
5. Serve and enjoy.

Nutritional Value (Amount per Serving):
Calories 326; Fat 18.1 g; Carbohydrates 2.4 g; Sugar 2.4 g; Protein 35.3 g; Cholesterol 101 mg

Tasty Stuffed Peppers

Preparation Time: 10 minutes; Cooking Time: 8 minutes; Serve: 12

Ingredients:
- 6 jalapeno peppers, cut in half & remove seeds
- 1 1/2 tbsp taco seasoning
- 1/2 lb ground pork
- 1/4 cup mozzarella cheese, shredded

Directions:
1. Browned the meat in a pan. Remove pan from heat.
2. Add taco seasoning and mix well.

3. Stuff meat into each jalapeno half.
4. Place stuffed jalapeno peppers onto the cooking tray and top with cheese.
5. Select AIRFRY mode, then set the temperature to 320 F and the time to 8 minutes, then press start.
6. When the display shows Add Food then place the cooking tray in the vortex plus air fryer oven.
7. Serve and enjoy.

Nutritional Value (Amount per Serving):
Calories 34; Fat 1 g; Carbohydrates 0.7 g; Sugar 0.2 g; Protein 5.4 g; Cholesterol 15 mg

Delicious Steak Kebab

Preparation Time: 10 minutes; Cooking Time: 10 minutes; Serve: 4

Ingredients:
- 1 lb sirloin steak, cut into 1-inch pieces
- 1 red bell pepper, cut into 1-inch pieces
- 1 onion, cut into 1-inch pieces

For marinade:
- 2 tbsp vinegar
- 2 tbsp olive oil
- 1/4 cup soy sauce
- 1 tsp ginger garlic paste
- 1 tsp pepper

Directions:
1. Add meat and remaining ingredients into the zip-lock bag, seal bag and shake well and place in the refrigerator overnight.
2. Thread marinated steak pieces, bell pepper, and onion onto the skewers.
3. Place skewers onto the cooking tray.
4. Select AIRFRY mode, then set the temperature to 350 F and the time to 10 minutes, then press start.
5. When the display shows Add Food then place the cooking tray in the vortex plus air fryer oven.
6. Serve and enjoy.

Nutritional Value (Amount per Serving):
Calories 309; Fat 14.5 g; Carbohydrates 7.2 g; Sugar 3 g; Protein 36.3 g; Cholesterol 101 mg

Chapter 5: Vegetable Recipes

Perfect Roasted Brussels Sprouts

Preparation Time: 10 minutes; Cooking Time: 25 minutes; Serve: 4
Ingredients:
- 15 oz Brussels sprouts
- 1/4 cup almond flour
- 1/4 cup parmesan cheese, grated
- 1 tbsp garlic, minced
- 1/4 tsp pepper
- 3 tbsp olive oil
- 1/2 tsp kosher salt

Directions:
1. Add Brussels sprouts and remaining ingredients into the mixing bowl and toss well.
2. Transfer brussels sprout mixture onto the parchment-lined cooking tray.
3. Select BAKE mode, then set the temperature to 400 F and the time to 25 minutes, then press start.
4. When the display shows Add Food then place the cooking tray in the vortex plus air fryer oven.
5. Serve and enjoy.

Nutritional Value (Amount per Serving):
Calories 190; Fat 15.8 g; Carbohydrates 10 g; Sugar 2.1 g; Protein 6.2 g; Cholesterol 4 mg

Zucchini Tomato Bake

Preparation Time: 10 minutes; Cooking Time: 25 minutes; Serve: 6
Ingredients:
- 5 tomatoes, sliced
- 2 yellow squash, sliced
- 2 zucchinis, sliced
- 1/2 tsp Italian seasoning
- 1/2 tsp onion powder
- 1/2 tsp garlic powder
- 1/2 tsp pepper
- 1/2 cup parmesan cheese, shredded

Directions:
1. Arrange tomatoes, squash, and zucchini in an alternating pattern in baking dish. Top with spices and cheese.
2. Select BAKE mode, then set the temperature to 375 F and the time to 25-30 minutes, then press start.
3. When the display shows Add Food then place the baking dish in the vortex plus air fryer oven.
4. Serve and enjoy.

Nutritional Value (Amount per Serving):
Calories 67; Fat 2.2 g; Carbohydrates 9.1 g; Sugar 5.1 g; Protein 5 g; Cholesterol 6 mg

Parmesan Yellow Squash

Preparation Time: 10 minutes; Cooking Time: 25 minutes; Serve: 6
Ingredients:
- 6 cups yellow squash, sliced
- 1/8 tsp cayenne pepper
- 1/2 tsp Italian seasoning
- 1/4 tsp pepper
- 1/2 tsp garlic, minced
- 1/2 cup parmesan cheese, grated
- 2 tbsp olive oil
- 1/2 tsp kosher salt

Directions:
1. Add squash and remaining ingredients into the large bowl and toss well.
2. Transfer squash mixture into the baking dish.
3. Select BAKE mode, then set the temperature to 400 F and the time to 20-25 minutes, then press start.

4. When the display shows Add Food then place the baking dish in the vortex plus air fryer oven.
5. Serve and enjoy.

Nutritional Value (Amount per Serving):
Calories 84; Fat 6.6 g; Carbohydrates 4.3 g; Sugar 2 g; Protein 3.8 g; Cholesterol 6 mg

Tasty Baked Cabbage

Preparation Time: 10 minutes; Cooking Time: 25 minutes; Serve: 2

Ingredients:
- 2 lbs medium cabbage, thin shreds
- 3 tbsp butter, melted
- 1 tbsp paprika
- 1 tbsp garlic powder
- 1 tsp salt

Directions:
1. Add cabbage, butter, paprika, garlic powder, and salt into the mixing bowl and toss well.
2. Add cabbage mixture into the baking dish.
3. Select BAKE mode, then set the temperature to 400 F and the time to 25 minutes, then press start.
4. When the display shows Add Food then place the baking dish in the vortex plus air fryer oven.
5. Serve and enjoy.

Nutritional Value (Amount per Serving):
Calories 224; Fat 17.8 g; Carbohydrates 11.8 g; Sugar 1.4 g; Protein 3.7 g; Cholesterol 46 mg

Healthy Cauliflower Roast

Preparation Time: 10 minutes; Cooking Time: 25 minutes; Serve: 4

Ingredients:
- 1 medium cauliflower head, cut into florets
- 1/4 tsp garlic powder
- 1/2 tsp pepper
- 2 tbsp olive oil
- 1 tsp sea salt

Directions:
1. Add cauliflower florets and remaining ingredients into the mixing bowl and toss well.
2. Spread cauliflower florets onto the cooking tray.
3. Select BAKE mode, then set the temperature to 400 F and the time to 25-30 minutes, then press start.
4. When the display shows Add Food then place the cooking tray in the vortex plus air fryer oven.
5. Serve and enjoy.

Nutritional Value (Amount per Serving):
Calories 97; Fat 7.2 g; Carbohydrates 7.9 g; Sugar 3.5 g; Protein 2.9 g; Cholesterol 0 mg

Simple Roasted Beets

Preparation Time: 10 minutes; Cooking Time: 40 minutes; Serve: 4

Ingredients:
- 3 large beets, 1 1/2-inch chunk
- 1 tsp orange zest
- 1/2 tsp pepper
- 1 tsp thyme, minced
- 1 tbsp olive oil
- 1 tsp kosher salt

Directions:
1. In a large bowl, toss beets with remaining ingredients.
2. Spread beets onto the cooking tray.

3. Select BAKE mode, then set the temperature to 400 F and the time to 35-40 minutes, then press start.
4. When the display shows Add Food then place the cooking tray in the vortex plus air fryer oven.
5. Serve and enjoy.

Nutritional Value (Amount per Serving):
Calories 65; Fat 3.7 g; Carbohydrates 7.9 g; Sugar 6 g; Protein 1.3 g; Cholesterol 0 mg

Flavorful Baked Okra

Preparation Time: 10 minutes; Cooking Time: 15 minutes; Serve: 4

Ingredients:
- 1 lb fresh okra, cut into 1/2-inch pieces
- 1 tsp paprika
- 2 tbsp olive oil
- 1/8 tsp cayenne pepper
- Salt

Directions:
1. In a large bowl, add okra and remaining ingredients and toss well.
2. Spread okra onto the cooking tray.
3. Select BAKE mode, then set the temperature to 400 F and the time to 15 minutes, then press start.
4. When the display shows Add Food then place the cooking tray in the vortex plus air fryer oven.
5. Serve and enjoy.

Nutritional Value (Amount per Serving):
Calories 107; Fat 7.3 g; Carbohydrates 8.8 g; Sugar 1.7 g; Protein 2.3 g; Cholesterol 0 mg

Baked Parmesan Fennel

Preparation Time: 10 minutes; Cooking Time: 35 minutes; Serve: 6

Ingredients:
- 3 fennel bulbs, trimmed & split lengthwise
- 4 sprigs thyme
- 1/3 cup parmesan cheese, grated
- 1 tbsp butter, softened
- Pepper
- Salt

Directions:
1. Boil fennel bulbs for 15 minutes or until tender. Drain fennel and pat dry with a paper towel.
2. Place fennel cut side up in the baking dish. Top with butter, cheese, thyme, pepper, and salt.
3. Select BAKE mode, then set the temperature to 400 F and the time to 20 minutes, then press start.
4. When the display shows Add Food then place the baking dish in the vortex plus air fryer oven.
5. Serve and enjoy.

Nutritional Value (Amount per Serving):
Calories 75; Fat 3.4 g; Carbohydrates 10 g; Sugar 0 g; Protein 3.3 g; Cholesterol 9 mg

Air Fryer Mushrooms

Preparation Time: 10 minutes; Cooking Time: 12 minutes; Serve: 2

Ingredients:
- 8 oz mushrooms
- 1 tbsp parsley, chopped
- 1 tsp soy sauce
- 1/2 tsp garlic powder

- 1 tbsp olive oil
- Pepper
- Salt

Directions:
1. In a mixing bowl, toss mushrooms with remaining ingredients.
2. Transfer mushrooms onto the cooking tray.
3. Select AIRFRY mode, then set the temperature to 380 F and the time to 10-12 minutes, then press start.
4. When the display shows Add Food then place the cooking tray in the vortex plus air fryer oven.
5. Serve and enjoy.

Nutritional Value (Amount per Serving):
Calories 89; Fat 7.4 g; Carbohydrates 4.6 g; Sugar 2.2 g; Protein 3.9 g; Cholesterol 0 mg

Air Fryer Asparagus

Preparation Time: 10 minutes; Cooking Time: 9 minutes; Serve: 4

Ingredients:
- 1 lb asparagus, ends trimmed
- 1/8 tsp garlic powder
- 1/8 tsp onion powder
- 1/8 tsp pepper
- 1 tsp olive oil
- 1/8 tsp kosher salt

Directions:
1. Place asparagus onto the parchment-lined cooking tray. Drizzle with oil and season with garlic powder, onion powder, pepper, and salt.
2. Select AIRFRY mode, then set the temperature to 390 F and the time to 8-9 minutes, then press start.
3. When the display shows Add Food then place the cooking tray in the vortex plus air fryer oven.
4. Serve and enjoy.

Nutritional Value (Amount per Serving):
Calories 33; Fat 1.3 g; Carbohydrates 4.6 g; Sugar 2.2 g; Protein 2.5 g; Cholesterol 0 mg

Spicy Garlic Cauliflower

Preparation Time: 10 minutes; Cooking Time: 30 minutes; Serve: 4

Ingredients:
- 1 medium cauliflower head, cut into florets
- 5 garlic cloves, sliced
- 1 medium onion, sliced
- 1 tbsp olive oil
- 1 tbsp sriracha
- 1/2 tsp coconut sugar
- 1 tbsp rice vinegar

Directions:
1. Add cauliflower florets into the baking dish and drizzle with olive oil.
2. Select AIRFRY mode, then set the temperature to 350 F and the time to 10 minutes, then press start.
3. When the display shows Add Food then place the baking dish in the vortex plus air fryer oven.
4. Add onion to the baking dish and mix well and AIRFRY for 10 minutes more.
5. Add garlic and stir well and AIRFRY for 5 minutes.
6. In a small bowl, mix together vinegar, sriracha, coconut sugar, pepper, and salt.
7. Pour vinegar mixture over the cauliflower and stir well and AIRFRY for 5 minutes more.
8. Serve and enjoy.

Nutritional Value (Amount per Serving):
Calories 101; Fat 3.7 g; Carbohydrates 14.6 g; Sugar 4.7 g; Protein 3.5 g; Cholesterol 0 mg

Roasted Carrots Slices

Preparation Time: 10 minutes; Cooking Time: 14 minutes; Serve: 4
Ingredients:
- 6 carrots peel and slice into thick chips
- 1 tbsp fresh parsley, chopped
- 1 tbsp oregano
- 2 tbsp olive oil
- Pepper
- Salt

Directions:
1. Add carrots into the baking dish and drizzle with olive oil.
2. Select AIRFRY mode, then set the temperature to 360 F and the time to 12 minutes, then press start.
3. When the display shows Add Food then place the baking dish in the vortex plus air fryer oven.
4. Add oregano, pepper, and salt in a baking dish and stir well and AIRFRY for 2 minutes more.
5. Garnish with chopped parsley and serve.

Nutritional Value (Amount per Serving):
Calories 81; Fat 7.2 g; Carbohydrates 4.8 g; Sugar 2.1 g; Protein 0.5 g; Cholesterol 0 mg

Air Fry Garlic Broccoli

Preparation Time: 10 minutes; Cooking Time: 8 minutes; Serve: 4
Ingredients:
- 3 cups broccoli florets
- 2 garlic cloves, chopped
- 2 tbsp lemon juice
- 1 tbsp olive oil
- Pepper
- Salt

Directions:
1. Add broccoli florets into the baking dish and drizzle with olive oil.
2. Select AIRFRY mode, then set the temperature to 375 F and the time to 8 minutes, then press start.
3. When the display shows Add Food then place the baking dish in the vortex plus air fryer oven.
4. Transfer cooked broccoli into the bowl. Add garlic, lemon juice, pepper, and salt and toss well.
5. Serve and enjoy.

Nutritional Value (Amount per Serving):
Calories 57; Fat 3.8 g; Carbohydrates 5.2 g; Sugar 1.3 g; Protein 2.1 g; Cholesterol 0 mg

Curried Cauliflower

Preparation Time: 10 minutes; Cooking Time: 10 minutes; Serve: 4
Ingredients:
- 1 medium cauliflower, cut into florets
- 1 tsp curry powder
- 1 tbsp olive oil
- 1/4 tsp pepper
- 1/4 tsp salt

Directions:
1. Add all ingredients into the mixing bowl and toss well.
2. Place cauliflower florets into the baking dish.
3. Select AIRFRY mode, then set the temperature to 390 F and the time to 10 minutes, then press start.
4. When the display shows Add Food then place the baking dish in the vortex plus air fryer oven.
5. Serve and enjoy.

Nutritional Value (Amount per Serving):
Calories 68; Fat 3.7 g; Carbohydrates 8 g; Sugar 3.5 g; Protein 2.9 g; Cholesterol 0 mg

Buffalo Cauliflower

Preparation Time: 10 minutes; Cooking Time: 8 minutes; Serve: 4

Ingredients:
- 12 oz cauliflower florets
- 1/4 tsp pepper
- 3 tbsp hot sauce
- 1/2 tsp salt

Directions:
1. Add all ingredients to the bowl and toss well.
2. Add cauliflower mixture into the baking dish.
3. Select BAKE mode, then set the temperature to 400 F and the time to 8 minutes, then press start.
4. When the display shows Add Food then place the baking dish in the vortex plus air fryer oven.
5. Serve and enjoy.

Nutritional Value (Amount per Serving):
Calories 23; Fat 0.1 g; Carbohydrates 4.8 g; Sugar 2.2 g; Protein 1.8 g; Cholesterol 0 mg

Lemon Garlic Roasted Eggplant

Preparation Time: 10 minutes; Cooking Time: 20 minutes; Serve: 6

Ingredients:
- 2 eggplants remove stems and cut into 1-inch pieces
- 1 tsp garlic powder
- 1 tsp onion powder
- 1 tbsp olive oil
- 1 tbsp lemon juice
- Pepper
- Salt

Directions:
1. Add all ingredients except lemon juice into the bowl and toss well.
2. Place eggplant mixture into the baking dish.
3. Select BAKE mode, then set the temperature to 320 F and the time to 20 minutes, then press start.
4. When the display shows Add Food then place the baking dish in the vortex plus air fryer oven.
5. Stir eggplant mixture after 15 minutes.
6. Serve and enjoy.

Nutritional Value (Amount per Serving):
Calories 24; Fat 3.5 g; Carbohydrates 3.7 g; Sugar 1 g; Protein 0.5 g; Cholesterol 0 mg

Radish Hash Browns

Preparation Time: 10 minutes; Cooking Time: 13 minutes; Serve: 4

Ingredients:
- 16 oz radishes, sliced
- 1 tbsp olive oil
- 1 tsp onion powder
- 1/2 tsp paprika
- 1 onion, sliced
- 1 tsp garlic powder
- 1/4 tsp black pepper
- 3/4 tsp sea salt

Directions:
1. Add onion and radishes into the baking dish. Drizzle with olive oil and toss well.
2. Select AIRFRY mode, then set the temperature to 360 F and the time to 8 minutes, then press start.

3. When the display shows Add Food then place the baking dish in the vortex plus air fryer oven.
4. Transfer radishes and onion in a bowl. Add seasonings and mix well and AIRFRY for 5 minutes more.
5. Serve and enjoy.

Nutritional Value (Amount per Serving):
Calories 65; Fat 3.7 g; Carbohydrates 7.6 g; Sugar 3.7 g; Protein 1.3 g; Cholesterol 0 mg

Air Fry Green Beans

Preparation Time: 10 minutes; Cooking Time: 10 minutes; Serve: 2

Ingredients:
- 2 cups green beans, cut in half
- 1 tbsp shawarma spice
- 2 tbsp olive oil
- 1/2 tsp salt

Directions:
1. Add beans, olive oil, salt, and shawarma into the bowl and toss well.
2. Place beans onto the parchment lined cooking tray.
3. Select AIRFRY mode, then set the temperature to 370 F and the time to 10 minutes, then press start.
4. When the display shows Add Food then place the cooking tray in the vortex plus air fryer oven.
5. Serve and enjoy.

Nutritional Value (Amount per Serving):
Calories 165; Fat 14.5 g; Carbohydrates 9.8 g; Sugar 1.5 g; Protein 2.1 g; Cholesterol 0 mg

Thyme Tomatoes

Preparation Time: 10 minutes; Cooking Time: 15 minutes; Serve: 4

Ingredients:
- 4 tomatoes cut in half
- 1/2 tsp dried thyme
- 1 garlic clove, minced
- 1 tbsp olive oil
- Pepper
- Salt

Directions:
1. Toss tomatoes with olive oil, garlic, pepper, salt, and thyme.
2. Place the tomatoes cut side up in a baking dish.
3. Select BAKE mode, then set the temperature to 390 F and the time to 15 minutes, then press start.
4. When the display shows Add Food then place the baking dish in the vortex plus air fryer oven.
5. Serve and enjoy.

Nutritional Value (Amount per Serving):
Calories 54; Fat 3.8 g; Carbohydrates 5.1 g; Sugar 3.2 g; Protein 1.1 g; Cholesterol 0 mg

Chili Herb Tomatoes

Preparation Time: 10 minutes; Cooking Time: 8 minutes; Serve: 4

Ingredients:
- 2 large tomatoes, cut into 4 slices
- 1 tbsp oregano, dried
- 1/4 tsp black pepper
- 1/4 cup balsamic vinegar
- 1 tsp red pepper flakes
- 1/2 tsp sea salt

Directions:
1. Add vinegar, salt, oregano, red pepper flakes, and pepper into the bowl and stir well.
2. Dip each tomato slice into the vinegar mixture and place it in a baking dish.

3. Select AIRFRY mode, then set the temperature to 360 F and the time to 5-8 minutes, then press start.
4. When the display shows Add Food then place the baking dish in the vortex plus air fryer oven.
5. Serve and enjoy.

Nutritional Value (Amount per Serving):
Calories 25; Fat 0.4 g; Carbohydrates 4.7 g; Sugar 2.6 g; Protein 1 g; Cholesterol 0 mg

Baked Artichoke Hearts

Preparation Time: 10 minutes; Cooking Time: 25 minutes; Serve: 6

Ingredients:
- 18 oz frozen artichoke hearts, defrosted
- 1 tbsp olive oil
- Pepper
- Salt

Directions:
1. Arrange artichoke hearts onto the parchment-lined cooking tray drizzle with olive oil. Season with pepper and salt
2. Select BAKE mode, then set the temperature to 400 F and the time to 25 minutes, then press start.
3. When the display shows Add Food then place the cooking tray in the vortex plus air fryer oven.
4. Serve and enjoy.

Nutritional Value (Amount per Serving):
Calories 60; Fat 2.5 g; Carbohydrates 9 g; Sugar 0.8 g; Protein 2.8 g; Cholesterol 0 mg

Lemon Broccoli & Tomatoes

Preparation Time: 10 minutes; Cooking Time: 10 minutes; Serve: 4

Ingredients:
- 4 cups broccoli florets
- 1/2 tsp lemon zest, grated
- 2 garlic cloves, minced
- 1 tbsp olive oil
- 1 tsp dried oregano
- 10 olives, pitted and sliced
- 1 tbsp fresh lemon juice
- 1 cup cherry tomatoes
- 1/4 tsp salt

Directions:
1. Add broccoli, garlic, oil, tomatoes, and salt in a large bowl and toss well.
2. Spread broccoli mixture onto the cooking tray.
3. Select BAKE mode, then set the temperature to 400 F and the time to 10 minutes, then press start.
4. When the display shows Add Food then place the cooking tray in the vortex plus air fryer oven.
5. Meanwhile, mix together oregano, olives, lemon juice, and lemon zest in a mixing bowl. Add roasted vegetables to the bowl and toss well.
6. Serve and enjoy.

Nutritional Value (Amount per Serving):
Calories 43; Fat 2.6 g; Carbohydrates 4.7 g; Sugar 1.4 g; Protein 1.6 g; Cholesterol 0 mg

Roasted Vegetables

Preparation Time: 10 minutes; Cooking Time: 30 minutes; Serve: 6

Ingredients:
- 1 eggplant, sliced
- 1 onion, sliced

- 1 bell pepper, cut into strips
- 2 zucchinis, sliced
- 2 tomatoes, quartered
- 5 fresh basil leaves, sliced
- 2 tsp Italian seasoning
- 2 tbsp olive oil
- Pepper
- Salt

Directions:
1. Add all ingredients except basil leaves into the mixing bowl and toss well.
2. Transfer veggie mixture on a cooking tray.
3. Select BAKE mode, then set the temperature to 400 F and the time to 30 minutes, then press start.
4. When the display shows Add Food then place the cooking tray in the vortex plus air fryer oven.
5. Garnish with basil and serve.

Nutritional Value (Amount per Serving):
Calories 80; Fat 5.4 g; Carbohydrates 8 g; Sugar 4.6 g; Protein 1.7 g; Cholesterol 0 mg

Parmesan Zucchini

Preparation Time: 10 minutes; Cooking Time: 15 minutes; Serve: 4
Ingredients:
- 1 lb zucchini, sliced
- 1 tsp dried mixed herbs
- 1 garlic clove, minced
- 2 tbsp olive oil
- 1 oz parmesan cheese, grated

Directions:
1. Add all ingredients except parmesan cheese into the large bowl and toss well.
2. Transfer the zucchini mixture to the baking dish and sprinkle with parmesan cheese.
3. Select BAKE mode, then set the temperature to 400 F and the time to 15 minutes, then press start.
4. When the display shows Add Food then place the baking dish in the vortex plus air fryer oven.
5. Serve and enjoy.

Nutritional Value (Amount per Serving):
Calories 103; Fat 8.7 g; Carbohydrates 4.4 g; Sugar 2 g; Protein 3.7 g; Cholesterol 5 mg

Air Fryer Tofu

Preparation Time: 10 minutes; Cooking Time: 15 minutes; Serve: 4
Ingredients:
- 16 oz extra firm tofu, cut into bite-sized pieces
- 1 tbsp olive oil
- 2 tbsp soy sauce
- 1 garlic clove, minced

Directions:
1. Add tofu, garlic, oil, and soy sauce in a bowl and toss well and let sit for 15 minutes.
2. Arrange tofu pieces on a parchment-lined cooking tray.
3. Select AIRFRY mode, then set the temperature to 370 F and the time to 15 minutes, then press start.
4. When the display shows Add Food then place the cooking tray in the vortex plus air fryer oven.
5. Serve and enjoy.

Nutritional Value (Amount per Serving):
Calories 115; Fat 8.2 g; Carbohydrates 2.8 g; Sugar 0.8 g; Protein 9.8 g; Cholesterol 0 mg

Baked Zucchini Patties

Preparation Time: 10 minutes; Cooking Time: 25 minutes; Serve: 6
Ingredients:
- 1 cup zucchini, shredded and squeeze out all liquid
- 1/2 cup almond flour
- 2 tbsp onion, minced
- 1 egg, lightly beaten
- 1/4 tsp red pepper flakes
- 1/4 cup parmesan cheese, grated
- 1/2 tbsp Dijon mustard
- 1/2 tbsp mayonnaise
- Pepper
- Salt

Directions:
1. Add all ingredients into the bowl and mix until well combined.
2. Make small patties from the zucchini mixture and place onto the parchment-lined cooking tray.
3. Select BAKE mode, then set the temperature to 400 F and the time to 25 minutes, then press start.
4. When the display shows Add Food then place the cooking tray in the vortex plus air fryer oven.
5. Turn patties after 15 minutes.
6. Serve and enjoy.

Nutritional Value (Amount per Serving):
Calories 86; Fat 6.7 g; Carbohydrates 3.6 g; Sugar 1 g; Protein 4.5 g; Cholesterol 30 mg

Roasted Asparagus

Preparation Time: 10 minutes; Cooking Time: 15 minutes; Serve: 4
Ingredients:
- 35 asparagus spears, cut the ends
- 1/2 tsp garlic powder
- 1 tbsp olive oil
- Pepper
- Salt

Directions:
1. Add asparagus into the large bowl. Drizzle with oil. Season with garlic powder, pepper, and salt. Toss well.
2. Arrange asparagus onto the parchment-lined cooking tray.
3. Select ROAST mode, then set the temperature to 400 F and the time to 15 minutes, then press start.
4. When the display shows Add Food then place the cooking tray in the vortex plus air fryer oven.
5. Serve and enjoy.

Nutritional Value (Amount per Serving):
Calories 73; Fat 3.8 g; Carbohydrates 8.4 g; Sugar 4 g; Protein 4.7 g; Cholesterol 0 mg

Healthy Broccoli Fritters

Preparation Time: 10 minutes; Cooking Time: 30 minutes; Serve: 4
Ingredients:
- 2 eggs, lightly beaten
- 2 garlic cloves, minced
- 3 cups broccoli florets, steam & chopped
- 2 cups cheddar cheese, shredded
- 1/4 cup almond flour
- Pepper
- Salt

Directions:
1. Add all ingredients into the large bowl and mix until well combined.
2. Make patties from broccoli mixture and place on parchment-lined cooking tray.

3. Select BAKE mode, then set the temperature to 375 F and the time to 30 minutes, then press start.
4. When the display shows Add Food then place the cooking tray in the vortex plus air fryer oven.
5. Turn patties halfway through.
6. Serve and enjoy.

Nutritional Value (Amount per Serving):
Calories 285; Fat 24.7 g; Carbohydrates 7.4 g; Sugar 1.9 g; Protein 20.4 g; Cholesterol 141 mg

Zucchini Casserole

Preparation Time: 10 minutes; Cooking Time: 25 minutes; Serve: 6

Ingredients:
- 2 eggs
- 4 cup zucchini, grated
- 1/2 cup parmesan cheese, grated
- 1 tbsp garlic, minced
- 1/2 cup onion, diced
- 1/2 cup cheddar cheese, shredded
- 1 cup mozzarella cheese, shredded
- 1/2 tsp salt

Directions:
1. Add zucchini and salt into the colander and set aside for 10 minutes. After 10 minutes squeeze out all liquid from zucchini.
2. Combine together zucchini, cheddar cheese, mozzarella cheese, 1/2 parmesan cheese, eggs, garlic, and onion and pour into the greased baking dish.
3. Select BAKE mode, then set the temperature to 375 F and the time to 25 minutes, then press start.
4. When the display shows Add Food then place the baking dish in the vortex plus air fryer oven.
5. Serve and enjoy.

Nutritional Value (Amount per Serving):
Calories 114; Fat 7.2 g; Carbohydrates 4.5 g; Sugar 1.9 g; Protein 9.1 g; Cholesterol 0 mg

Baked Cherry Tomatoes & Zucchini

Preparation Time: 10 minutes; Cooking Time: 35 minutes; Serve: 6

Ingredients:
- 2 1/2 lbs zucchini, cut into quarters
- 6 garlic cloves, crushed
- 10 oz cherry tomatoes cut in half
- 1/3 cup parsley, chopped
- 1 tsp dried basil
- 1/2 cup parmesan cheese, shredded
- 1/2 tsp black pepper
- 3/4 tsp salt

Directions:
1. Add all ingredients except parsley into the large mixing bowl and stir well to combine.
2. Pour egg mixture into the greased baking dish.
3. Select BAKE mode, then set the temperature to 350 F and the time to 35 minutes, then press start.
4. When the display shows Add Food then place the baking dish in the vortex plus air fryer oven.
5. Garnish with parsley and serve.

Nutritional Value (Amount per Serving):
Calories 69; Fat 2.1 g; Carbohydrates 9.8 g; Sugar 4.6 g; Protein 5.4 g; Cholesterol 5 mg

Cauliflower Mac and Cheese

Preparation Time: 10 minutes; Cooking Time: 20 minutes; Serve: 4

Ingredients:

- 1 large cauliflower head, cut into florets
- 2 cups cheddar cheese, shredded
- 1 tsp Dijon mustard
- 2 oz cream cheese
- 1 cup heavy cream
- 1/8 tsp garlic powder
- 1/4 tsp black pepper
- 1/2 tsp kosher salt

Directions:
1. Add water and salt to the pot and bring to boil.
2. Add cauliflower florets into the boiling water and cook about 5 minutes. Drain well and transfer to a baking dish.
3. Add cream into the saucepan and bring to simmer, whisk in mustard and cream cheese until smooth.
4. Stir in 1 1/2 cup cheese, pepper, garlic, and salt. Whisk until cheese melts for 2 minutes. Season with pepper and salt.
5. Remove pan from heat and pour over cauliflower florets and stir well. Top with remaining cheese.
6. Select BAKE mode, then set the temperature to 375 F and the time to 15 minutes, then press start.
7. When the display shows Add Food then place the baking dish in the vortex plus air fryer oven.
8. Serve and enjoy.

Nutritional Value (Amount per Serving):
Calories 531; Fat 43.9 g; Carbohydrates 12.5 g; Sugar 5.4 g; Protein 19.4 g; Cholesterol 155 mg

Baked Cheesy Eggplant Zucchini

Preparation Time: 10 minutes; Cooking Time: 35 minutes; Serve: 6

Ingredients:
- 1 medium eggplant, sliced
- 4 tbsp parsley, chopped
- 4 tbsp basil, chopped
- 3 medium zucchinis, sliced
- 3 oz Parmesan cheese, grated
- 1 tbsp olive oil
- 1 cup cherry tomatoes, halved
- 4 garlic cloves, minced
- 1/4 tsp pepper
- 1/4 tsp salt

Directions:
1. In a mixing bowl, add chopped cherry tomatoes, eggplant, zucchini, olive oil, garlic, cheese, basil, pepper, and salt toss well until combined.
2. Transfer the eggplant mixture into the baking dish.
3. Select BAKE mode, then set the temperature to 350 F and the time to 35 minutes, then press start.
4. When the display shows Add Food then place the baking dish in the vortex plus air fryer oven.
5. Garnish with parsley and serve.

Nutritional Value (Amount per Serving):
Calories 110; Fat 5.8 g; Carbohydrates 10.4 g; Sugar 4.8 g; Protein 7 g; Cholesterol 10 mg

Stuffed Bell Pepper

Preparation Time: 10 minutes; Cooking Time: 25 minutes; Serve: 4

Ingredients:
- 4 eggs
- 2 medium bell peppers, cut in half and deseeded
- 1 tsp dried sage
- 2.5 oz cheddar cheese, grated
- 7 oz almond milk
- 1/4 cup baby broccoli florets
- 1/4 cup cherry tomatoes

- Pepper
- Salt

Directions:
1. In a bowl, whisk together eggs, milk, broccoli, cherry tomatoes, sage, pepper, and salt.
2. Place bell pepper halves in the baking dish.
3. Pour egg mixture into the bell pepper halves.
4. Sprinkle cheese on top of bell pepper.
5. Select BAKE mode, then set the temperature to 390 F and the time to 25 minutes, then press start.
6. When the display shows Add Food then place the baking dish in the vortex plus air fryer oven.
7. Serve and enjoy.

Nutritional Value (Amount per Serving):
Calories 272; Fat 22.3 g; Carbohydrates 8.6 g; Sugar 5.5 g; Protein 11.9 g; Cholesterol 182 mg

Mushrooms & Beans

Preparation Time: 10 minutes; Cooking Time: 25 minutes; Serve: 4

Ingredients:
- 2 cups mushrooms, sliced
- 2 tsp garlic, minced
- 2 cups green beans, clean and cut into pieces
- 1/4 cup olive oil
- 1 tsp black pepper
- 1 tsp sea salt

Directions:
1. Add mushrooms, garlic, green beans, oil, pepper, and salt into the mixing bowl and toss well.
2. Transfer mushrooms and green beans mixture into the baking dish.
3. Select BAKE mode, then set the temperature to 400 F and the time to 25 minutes, then press start.
4. When the display shows Add Food then place the baking dish in the vortex plus air fryer oven.
5. Serve and enjoy.

Nutritional Value (Amount per Serving):
Calories 136; Fat 12.8 g; Carbohydrates 5.9 g; Sugar 1.4 g; Protein 2.3 g; Cholesterol 0 mg

Brussels Sprouts with Garlic

Preparation Time: 10 minutes; Cooking Time: 40 minutes; Serve: 8

Ingredients:
- 2 lbs Brussels sprouts, trimmed and quartered
- 2 tbsp coconut oil, melted
- 6 garlic cloves, sliced
- 1/8 tsp black pepper
- 1 tsp salt

Directions:
1. In a bowl, mix together Brussels sprouts, coconut oil, and garlic.
2. Spread Brussels sprouts onto the cooking tray. Season with pepper and salt.
3. Select BAKE mode, then set the temperature to 400 F and the time to 40 minutes, then press start.
4. When the display shows Add Food then place the cooking tray in the vortex plus air fryer oven.
5. Serve and enjoy.

Nutritional Value (Amount per Serving):
Calories 82; Fat 3.8 g; Carbohydrates 11.1 g; Sugar 2.5 g; Protein 4 g; Cholesterol 0 mg

Lemon Cauliflower

Preparation Time: 10 minutes; Cooking Time: 15 minutes; Serve: 4
Ingredients:
- 1 large cauliflower head, cut into florets
- 1 lemon zest
- 3 tbsp olive oil
- 2 tsp lemon juice
- 1/2 tsp Italian seasoning
- 1/2 tsp garlic powder
- 1/4 tsp pepper
- 1/4 tsp salt

Directions:
1. In a bowl, combine together olive oil, lemon juice, Italian seasoning, garlic powder, lemon zest, pepper, and salt.
2. Add cauliflower florets to the bowl and toss well.
3. Spread cauliflower florets onto the cooking tray.
4. Select BAKE mode, then set the temperature to 400 F and the time to 15 minutes, then press start.
5. When the display shows Add Food then place the cooking tray in the vortex plus air fryer oven.
6. Serve and enjoy.

Nutritional Value (Amount per Serving):
Calories 151; Fat 10.9 g; Carbohydrates 12.9 g; Sugar 5.6 g; Protein 4.4 g; Cholesterol 0 mg

Asparagus Quiche

Preparation Time: 10 minutes; Cooking Time: 45 minutes; Serve: 8
Ingredients:
- 10 eggs
- 2 lbs asparagus, trimmed and cut the ends
- 2 tbsp coconut oil, melted
- 1 tsp salt

Directions:
1. Place asparagus in a greased baking dish.
2. Select ROAST mode, then set the temperature to 400 F and the time to 15 minutes, then press start.
3. When the display shows Add Food then place the baking dish in the vortex plus air fryer oven.
4. Meanwhile, in a bowl, whisk together eggs, coconut oil, and salt until smooth.
5. Pour egg mixture over the asparagus.
6. Select BAKE mode, then set the temperature to 400 F and the time to 30 minutes, then press start.
7. When the display shows Add Food then place the baking dish in the vortex plus air fryer oven.
8. Serve and enjoy.

Nutritional Value (Amount per Serving):
Calories 131; Fat 9 g; Carbohydrates 4.8 g; Sugar 2.6 g; Protein 9.4 g; Cholesterol 205 mg

Baked Parmesan Tomato

Preparation Time: 10 minutes; Cooking Time: 15 minutes; Serve: 6
Ingredients:
- 4 eggs
- 1/2 cup fresh basil, chopped
- 1/3 cup coconut flour
- 1/4 cup water
- 1 cup cherry tomatoes, cut in half
- 1/4 cup parmesan cheese, grated
- 1/4 tsp baking powder
- 1/4 cup butter, melted

- 1/4 tsp black pepper
- 1/4 tsp salt

Directions:
1. In a bowl, whisk together eggs, water, butter, pepper, and salt.
2. Add baking soda and coconut flour and blend until smooth.
3. Add basil, tomatoes, and parmesan cheese and mix well.
4. Pour batter into the greased baking dish.
5. Select BAKE mode, then set the temperature to 400 F and the time to 15 minutes, then press start.
6. When the display shows Add Food then place the baking dish in the vortex plus air fryer oven.
7. Serve and enjoy.

Nutritional Value (Amount per Serving):
Calories 131; Fat 11.6 g; Carbohydrates 2.2 g; Sugar 1.1 g; Protein 5.4 g; Cholesterol 132 mg

Zucchini Gratin

Preparation Time: 10 minutes; Cooking Time: 30 minutes; Serve: 4
Ingredients:
- 1 large egg, lightly beaten
- 1 1/4 cup unsweetened almond milk
- 3 medium zucchinis, sliced
- 1 tbsp Dijon mustard
- 1/2 cup nutritional yeast
- 1 tsp sea salt

Directions:
1. Arrange zucchini slices in the greased baking dish.
2. In a saucepan, heat almond milk over low heat and stir in Dijon mustard, nutritional yeast, and sea salt. Add beaten egg and whisk well.
3. Pour sauce over zucchini slices.
4. Select BAKE mode, then set the temperature to 400 F and the time to 25-30 minutes, then press start.
5. When the display shows Add Food then place the baking dish in the vortex plus air fryer oven.
6. Serve and enjoy.

Nutritional Value (Amount per Serving):
Calories 124; Fat 2.5 g; Carbohydrates 11.2 g; Sugar 1.7 g; Protein 14.1 g; Cholesterol 47 mg

Baked Rutabaga Noodles

Preparation Time: 10 minutes; Cooking Time: 10 minutes; Serve: 4
Ingredients:
- 25 oz rutabaga, peel, cut, and spiralized
- 1/3 cup olive oil
- 1 tsp garlic powder
- 1 tbsp chili powder
- 1 tsp salt

Directions:
1. Add all ingredients into the large bowl and toss until well combined.
2. Spread rutabaga mixture greased baking dish.
3. Select BAKE mode, then set the temperature to 400 F and the time to 10 minutes, then press start.
4. When the display shows Add Food then place the baking dish in the vortex plus air fryer oven.
5. Serve and enjoy.

Nutritional Value (Amount per Serving):
Calories 155; Fat 17.2 g; Carbohydrates 2.2 g; Sugar 0.7 g; Protein 0.4 g; Cholesterol 0 mg

Feta Cheese Stuffed Peppers

Preparation Time: 10 minutes; Cooking Time: 50 minutes; Serve: 4

Ingredients:
- 4 eggs
- 1/4 cup feta cheese, crumbled
- 1/2 cup broccoli, cooked
- 2 bell peppers, cut in half and remove seeds
- 1/2 cup cheddar cheese, grated
- 1/2 tsp garlic powder
- 1 tsp dried thyme
- 1/4 tsp pepper
- 1/2 tsp salt

Directions:
1. Place bell peppers half in a baking dish. Cut side up.
2. Stuff feta and broccoli into the peppers.
3. Beat egg in a bowl with seasoning and pour egg mixture into the pepper over feta and broccoli.
4. Select BAKE mode, then set the temperature to 350 F and the time to 45-50 minutes, then press start.
5. When the display shows Add Food then place the baking dish in the vortex plus air fryer oven.
6. Add grated cheese on top and BAKE for 10 minutes more or until cheese melted.
7. Serve and enjoy.

Nutritional Value (Amount per Serving):
Calories 170; Fat 11.3 g; Carbohydrates 6.7 g; Sugar 4.1 g; Protein 11.4 g; Cholesterol 187 mg

Lemon Parmesan Broccoli

Preparation Time: 10 minutes; Cooking Time: 25 minutes; Serve: 2

Ingredients:
- 4 cups broccoli florets
- 4 garlic cloves, sliced
- 3 tbsp coconut oil
- 1 lemon juice
- 1 cup parmesan cheese, grated
- 1/2 tsp pepper
- 1 1/2 tsp salt

Directions:
1. In a bowl, toss broccoli florets with coconut oil. Add garlic and season with pepper and salt.
2. Spread broccoli in baking dish.
3. Select BAKE mode, then set the temperature to 400 F and the time to 20 minutes, then press start.
4. When the display shows Add Food then place the baking dish in the vortex plus air fryer oven.
5. Sprinkle with half parmesan cheese and BAKE for 5 minutes more.
6. Add remaining parmesan cheese and lemon juice. Stir well and serve.

Nutritional Value (Amount per Serving):
Calories 356; Fat 30.3 g; Carbohydrates 8.4 g; Sugar 1.6 g; Protein 17.1 g; Cholesterol 32 mg

Cauliflower Rice

Preparation Time: 10 minutes; Cooking Time: 15 minutes; Serve: 3

Ingredients:
- 1 cauliflower head, cut into florets
- 2 chilies, chopped
- 2 garlic cloves, chopped
- 1 tomato, chopped
- 1 onion, chopped
- 2 tbsp olive oil
- 1 tsp white pepper
- 1 tsp black pepper
- 1 tbsp dried thyme
- 2 tbsp tomato paste

- 1/2 tsp salt

Directions:
1. Add cauliflower florets into the food processor and process until it looks like rice.
2. Stir in tomato paste, tomatoes, and spices and mix well.
3. Spread cauliflower mixture in a baking dish and drizzle with olive oil.
4. Select BAKE mode, then set the temperature to 400 F and the time to 15 minutes, then press start.
5. When the display shows Add Food then place the baking dish in the vortex plus air fryer oven.
6. Serve and enjoy.

Nutritional Value (Amount per Serving):
Calories 138; Fat 9.7 g; Carbohydrates 12.8 g; Sugar 5.7 g; Protein 3.1 g; Cholesterol 0 mg

Cheesy Squash Noodles

Preparation Time: 10 minutes; Cooking Time: 25 minutes; Serve: 2

Ingredients:
- 1 medium butternut squash, peel and spiralized
- 1/4 cup parmesan cheese
- 1 tsp thyme, chopped
- 1 tbsp sage, chopped
- 1 tsp garlic powder
- 2 tbsp cream cheese
- 3 tbsp cream

Directions:
1. In a bowl, mix together cream cheese, parmesan, thyme, sage, cream, and garlic powder.
2. Add noodles to a baking dish.
3. Select BAKE mode, then set the temperature to 400 F and the time to 25 minutes, then press start.
4. When the display shows Add Food then place the baking dish in the vortex plus air fryer oven.
5. Serve and enjoy.

Nutritional Value (Amount per Serving):
Calories 123; Fat 7.2 g; Carbohydrates 11.4 g; Sugar 2.3 g; Protein 5.6 g; Cholesterol 22 mg

Cauliflower Couscous

Preparation Time: 10 minutes; Cooking Time: 12 minutes; Serve: 4

Ingredients:
- 1 head cauliflower, cut into florets
- 14 oz can artichokes
- 2 tbsp olive oil
- 1/4 cup parsley, chopped
- 1 lemon juice
- 14 black olives
- 1 garlic clove, chopped
- 1/2 tsp pepper
- 1/2 tsp salt

Directions:
1. Add cauliflower florets into the food processor and process until it looks like rice.
2. Spread cauliflower rice in a baking dish and drizzle with olive oil.
3. Select BAKE mode, then set the temperature to 400 F and the time to 12 minutes, then press start.
4. When the display shows Add Food then place the baking dish in the vortex plus air fryer oven.
5. In a bowl, mix together garlic, lemon juice, artichokes, parsley, and olives.
6. Add the cauliflower to the bowl and stir well. Season with pepper and salt.
7. Serve and enjoy.

Nutritional Value (Amount per Serving):

Calories 116; Fat 8.8 g; Carbohydrates 8.4 g; Sugar 3.3 g; Protein 3.3 g; Cholesterol 0 mg

Cheesy Broccoli Casserole

Preparation Time: 10 minutes; Cooking Time: 30 minutes; Serve: 8

Ingredients:
- 2 lbs broccoli florets
- 2 cups cheddar cheese, shredded
- 1/4 cup vegetable stock
- 1/2 cup heavy cream
- 3 tbsp olive oil
- 2 garlic cloves, minced
- 4 oz cream cheese
- 1 cup mozzarella cheese
- Pepper
- Salt

Directions:
1. Arrange broccoli florets in a greased baking dish. Drizzle with olive oil and season with pepper and salt.
2. Select ROAST mode, then set the temperature to 400 F and the time to 15 minutes, then press start.
3. When the display shows Add Food then place the baking dish in the vortex plus air fryer oven.
4. Meanwhile, combine together heavy cream, stock, garlic, cream cheese, mozzarella cheese, and 1 cup cheddar cheese in a medium saucepan over medium-low heat. Stir frequently.
5. Once broccoli is cooked then pour heavy cream mixture over broccoli. Sprinkle remaining cheddar cheese on top.
6. Select BAKE mode, then set the temperature to 400 F and the time to 15 minutes, then press start.
7. When the display shows Add Food then place the baking dish in the vortex plus air fryer oven.
8. Serve and enjoy.

Nutritional Value (Amount per Serving):
Calories 284; Fat 23.3 g; Carbohydrates 8.9 g; Sugar 2.2 g; Protein 12.5 g; Cholesterol 57 mg

Delicious Cheese Cutlet

Preparation Time: 10 minutes; Cooking Time: 10 minutes; Serve: 3

Ingredients:
- 2 cups cottage cheese, grated
- 1/2 tsp garlic powder
- 1 onion, chopped
- 1 cup mozzarella cheese, grated
- 1 tsp butter
- 1/2 tsp oregano
- 1/2 tsp salt

Directions:
1. Add all ingredients into the large mixing bowl and mix well.
2. Make the equal size of cutlets from the mixture and place onto the parchment-lined cooking tray.
3. Select AIRFRY mode, then set the temperature to 350 F and the time to 10 minutes, then press start.
4. When the display shows Add Food then place the cooking tray in the vortex plus air fryer oven.
5. Serve and enjoy.

Nutritional Value (Amount per Serving):
Calories 191; Fat 5.9 g; Carbohydrates 9.7 g; Sugar 2.2 g; Protein 23.9 g; Cholesterol 20 mg

Roasted Squash

Preparation Time: 10 minutes; Cooking Time: 30 minutes; Serve: 4

Ingredients:
- 1 large acorn squash, cut in half lengthwise
- 2 tbsp olive oil
- 1/4 cup parmesan cheese, grated
- 1/4 tsp black pepper
- 8 fresh thyme sprigs

Directions:
1. Remove seed from squash and cut into 3/4-inch slices.
2. Add squash slices, olive oil, thyme, parmesan cheese, pepper, and salt in a bowl and toss to coat.
3. Spread squash onto a cooking tray.
4. Select ROAST mode, then set the temperature to 400 F and the time to 25-30 minutes, then press start.
5. When the display shows Add Food then place the cooking tray in the vortex plus air fryer oven.
6. Serve and enjoy.

Nutritional Value (Amount per Serving):
Calories 100; Fat 8.5 g; Carbohydrates 5.7 g; Sugar 0.1 g; Protein 2.4 g; Cholesterol 4 mg

Baked Broccoli

Preparation Time: 10 minutes; Cooking Time: 15 minutes; Serve: 4

Ingredients:
- 1 lb broccoli, cut into florets
- 1/2 cup mozzarella cheese, shredded
- 1/2 cup heavy cream
- 2 garlic cloves, minced
- 1 tbsp butter
- 1/4 cup parmesan cheese, grated
- 1/2 cup gruyere cheese, shredded

Directions:
1. Melt butter in a pan over medium heat.
2. Add broccoli and season with pepper and salt.
3. Cook broccoli over medium heat for 5 minutes or until tender. Add garlic and stir for a minute.
4. Transfer broccoli into the baking dish. Pour heavy cream over broccoli then top with parmesan cheese, gruyere cheese, and mozzarella cheese.
5. Select BAKE mode, then set the temperature to 375 F and the time to 10 minutes, then press start.
6. When the display shows Add Food then place the baking dish in the vortex plus air fryer oven.
7. Serve and enjoy.

Nutritional Value (Amount per Serving):
Calories 202; Fat 15 g; Carbohydrates 8.8 g; Sugar 2 g; Protein 10.5 g; Cholesterol 49 mg

Roasted Ranch Broccoli

Preparation Time: 10 minutes; Cooking Time: 30 minutes; Serve: 6

Ingredients:
- 4 cups broccoli florets
- 1/4 cup ranch dressing
- 1/4 cup heavy whipping cream
- 1/2 cup cheddar cheese, shredded
- Pepper
- Salt

Directions:
1. Add all ingredients into the bowl and toss until well coated.
2. Spread broccoli in a greased baking dish.
3. Select BAKE mode, then set the temperature to 375 F and the time to 30 minutes, then press start.

4. When the display shows Add Food then place the baking dish in the vortex plus air fryer oven.
5. Serve and enjoy.

Nutritional Value (Amount per Serving):
Calories 79; Fat 5.2 g; Carbohydrates 4.8 g; Sugar 1.4 g; Protein 4.3 g; Cholesterol 17 mg

Spinach Stuffed Peppers

Preparation Time: 10 minutes; Cooking Time: 45 minutes; Serve: 4

Ingredients:
- 4 eggs
- 2 bell peppers, sliced in half and remove seeds
- 1/2 cup parmesan cheese, grated
- 1/2 cup mozzarella cheese, shredded
- 1/2 cup ricotta cheese
- 1/4 cup baby spinach
- 1/4 tsp dried parsley
- 1 tsp garlic powder

Directions:
1. Add three cheeses, parsley, garlic powder, and eggs in food processor and process until combined.
2. Pour egg mixture into each pepper half and top with baby spinach.
3. Place stuffed peppers in a baking dish.
4. Select BAKE mode, then set the temperature to 375 F and the time to 35-45 minutes, then press start.
5. When the display shows Add Food then place the baking dish in the vortex plus air fryer oven.
6. Serve and enjoy.

Nutritional Value (Amount per Serving):
Calories 156; Fat 8.8 g; Carbohydrates 7.4 g; Sugar 3.6 g; Protein 12.7 g; Cholesterol 179 mg

Alfredo Brussels Sprouts

Preparation Time: 10 minutes; Cooking Time: 15 minutes; Serve: 6

Ingredients:
- 2 lbs Brussels sprouts, cleaned and halved
- 4 oz cream cheese
- 2 tbsp water
- 2 tbsp butter
- 1 cup Asiago cheese, shredded
- 1 cup heavy cream

Directions:
1. Melt butter in a large pan over medium-high heat.
2. Add Brussels sprouts and water and cook for 5 minutes.
3. Remove Brussels sprouts from pan and place into a baking dish. Set aside.
4. Add cream cheese to the pan and melt over medium heat.
5. Add Asiago cheese and heavy cream and whisk until smooth.
6. Pour asiago cheese mixture over Brussels sprouts.
7. Select BAKE mode, then set the temperature to 350 F and the time to 10 minutes, then press start.
8. When the display shows Add Food then place the baking dish in the vortex plus air fryer oven.
9. Serve and enjoy.

Nutritional Value (Amount per Serving):
Calories 197; Fat 16.1 g; Carbohydrates 9.9 g; Sugar 2 g; Protein 3.4 g; Cholesterol 51 mg

Cheesy Butternut Squash

Preparation Time: 10 minutes; Cooking Time: 20 minutes; Serve: 6
Ingredients:
- 2 lbs butternut squash, peeled and cut into 1-inch cubes
- 2 tbsp thyme, chopped
- 2 garlic cloves, minced
- 2 tbsp olive oil
- 1/2 cup parmesan cheese, grated
- 1 1/2 cups mozzarella cheese, shredded
- Pepper
- Salt

Directions:
1. Add squash with thyme, garlic, and olive oil in a baking dish and mix well. Season pepper and salt.
2. Select BAKE mode, then set the temperature to 400 F and the time to 15 minutes, then press start.
3. When the display shows Add Food then place the baking dish in the vortex plus air fryer oven.
4. Top with parmesan and mozzarella cheese and BAKE for 5 minutes more.
5. Serve and enjoy.

Nutritional Value (Amount per Serving):
Calories 122; Fat 7.7 g; Carbohydrates 10.3 g; Sugar 1.7 g; Protein 5.3 g; Cholesterol 9 mg

Baked Zucchini Noodles

Preparation Time: 10 minutes; Cooking Time: 35 minutes; Serve: 4
Ingredients:
- 2 medium zucchinis, spiralized
- 2 tbsp butter
- 1 tsp fresh thyme, chopped
- 1 small onion, sliced
- 1 cup Fontina cheese, grated
- 2 tsp Worcestershire sauce
- 1/4 cup vegetable broth
- Pepper
- Salt

Directions:
1. Melt butter in a pan over medium heat.
2. Add the onion in a pan and sauté for a few minutes.
3. Add thyme, Worcestershire sauce, pepper, and salt. Stir for minutes.
4. Add broth in the pan and cook onions for 10 minutes.
5. In a large bowl, combine together zucchini noodles and onion mixture and pour into the greased baking dish. Top with grated cheese.
6. Select BAKE mode, then set the temperature to 400 F and the time to 25 minutes, then press start.
7. When the display shows Add Food then place the baking dish in the vortex plus air fryer oven.
8. Garnish with chopped thyme and serve.

Nutritional Value (Amount per Serving):
Calories 184; Fat 14.5 g; Carbohydrates 6.1 g; Sugar 3.4 g; Protein 8.7 g; Cholesterol 47 mg

Parmesan Green Bean Casserole

Preparation Time: 10 minutes; Cooking Time: 20 minutes; Serve: 4
Ingredients:
- 1 lb green beans, trimmed and cut into pieces
- 1/4 cup olive oil
- 2 oz pecans, crushed
- 1 small onion, chopped
- 2 tbsp lemon zest
- 1/4 cup parmesan cheese, shredded

Directions:
1. Add all ingredients into the mixing bowl and toss well.
2. Spread green bean mixture into the baking dish.
3. Select BAKE mode, then set the temperature to 400 F and the time to 20 minutes, then press start.
4. When the display shows Add Food then place the baking dish in the vortex plus air fryer oven.
5. Serve and enjoy.

Nutritional Value (Amount per Serving):
Calories 269; Fat 24.1 g; Carbohydrates 12.6 g; Sugar 3 g; Protein 5.7 g; Cholesterol 4 mg

Basil Pesto Spaghetti Squash

Preparation Time: 10 minutes; Cooking Time: 10 minutes; Serve: 4
Ingredients:
- 2 cups spaghetti squash, cooked and drained
- 4 oz mozzarella cheese, cubed
- 1/4 cup basil pesto
- 1/2 cup ricotta cheese
- 1 tbsp olive oil
- Pepper
- Salt

Directions:
1. In a bowl, combine together olive oil and squash. Season with pepper and salt.
2. Spread squash mixture in greased baking dish.
3. Spread mozzarella cheese and ricotta cheese on top.
4. Select BAKE mode, then set the temperature to 375 F and the time to 10 minutes, then press start.
5. When the display shows Add Food then place the baking dish in the vortex plus air fryer oven.
6. Drizzle with basil pesto and serve.

Nutritional Value (Amount per Serving):
Calories 169; Fat 11.3 g; Carbohydrates 6.1 g; Sugar 0.1 g; Protein 11.9 g; Cholesterol 25 mg

Healthy Eggplant Salad

Preparation Time: 10 minutes; Cooking Time: 25 minutes; Serve: 6
Ingredients:
- 1 lb eggplant, cut into slices
- 1/4 cup olive oil
- 1 tbsp fresh lemon juice
- 1 tbsp parsley, chopped
- 1 tbsp cilantro, chopped
- 1/2 tsp paprika
- 1 tsp ground cumin
- 1 garlic clove, grated
- 1/2 tsp salt

Directions:
1. Brush eggplant slices with 2 tbsp oil.
2. Place eggplant slices onto a cooking tray.
3. Select BAKE mode, then set the temperature to 400 F and the time to 25 minutes, then press start.
4. When the display shows Add Food then place the cooking tray in the vortex plus air fryer oven.
5. In a bowl, mix together the remaining ingredients and pour over eggplant slices.
6. Mix well and serve.

Nutritional Value (Amount per Serving):
Calories 94; Fat 8.7 g; Carbohydrates 5 g; Sugar 2.4 g; Protein 0.9 g; Cholesterol 0 mg

Eggplant Zucchini Casserole

Preparation Time: 10 minutes; Cooking Time: 35 minutes; Serve: 6
Ingredients:
- 3 zucchinis, sliced
- 1 cup cherry tomatoes, halved
- 1 medium eggplant, sliced
- 1 tbsp olive oil
- 3 garlic cloves, minced
- 4 tbsp basil, chopped
- 3 oz parmesan cheese, grated
- 1/4 cup parsley, chopped
- 1/4 tsp pepper
- 1/4 tsp salt

Directions:
1. Add all ingredients into the large bowl and toss well to combine.
2. Pour eggplant mixture into a greased baking dish.
3. Select BAKE mode, then set the temperature to 350 F and the time to 35 minutes, then press start.
4. When the display shows Add Food then place the baking dish in the vortex plus air fryer oven.
5. Serve and enjoy.

Nutritional Value (Amount per Serving):
Calories 109; Fat 5.8 g; Carbohydrates 10.2 g; Sugar 4.8 g; Protein 7 g; Cholesterol 10 mg

Roasted Radishes

Preparation Time: 10 minutes; Cooking Time: 30 minutes; Serve: 2
Ingredients:
- 3 cups radish, clean and halved
- 8 black peppercorns, crushed
- 3 tbsp olive oil
- 2 tbsp fresh rosemary, chopped
- 2 tsp sea salt

Directions:
1. Add radishes, salt, peppercorns, rosemary, and 2 tablespoons of olive oil in a bowl and toss well.
2. Pour radishes mixture onto the cooking tray.
3. Select BAKE mode, then set the temperature to 400 F and the time to 30 minutes, then press start.
4. When the display shows Add Food then place the cooking tray in the vortex plus air fryer oven.
5. Heat remaining olive oil in a pan over medium heat.
6. Add baked radishes in the pan and sauté for 2 minutes.
7. Serve and enjoy.

Nutritional Value (Amount per Serving):
Calories 220; Fat 21.7 g; Carbohydrates 8.3 g; Sugar 3.2 g; Protein 1.4 g; Cholesterol 0 mg

Broccoli Coconut Loaf

Preparation Time: 10 minutes; Cooking Time: 30 minutes; Serve: 5
Ingredients:
- 5 eggs, lightly beaten
- 3/4 cup broccoli florets, chopped
- 1 cup cheddar cheese, shredded
- 2 tsp baking powder
- 3 1/1 tbsp coconut flour
- 1 tsp salt

Directions:
1. Add all ingredients into the bowl and mix well.
2. Pour egg mixture into the greased loaf pan.
3. Select BAKE mode, then set the temperature to 350 F and the time to 30 minutes, then press start.

4. When the display shows Add Food then place the loaf pan in the vortex plus air fryer oven.
5. Slice and serve.

Nutritional Value (Amount per Serving):
Calories 209; Fat 13.5 g; Carbohydrates 8.9 g; Sugar 1.5 g; Protein 13.2 g; Cholesterol 187 mg

Chapter 6: Snacks & Appetizers

Delicious Broccoli Tots

Preparation Time: 10 minutes; Cooking Time: 16 minutes; Serve: 4
Ingredients:
- 1 egg
- 2 tbsp almond flour
- 2 cups cheddar cheese, shredded
- 2 cups broccoli rice, cooked
- 1 tsp Italian seasoning
- Pepper
- Salt

Directions:
1. Add all ingredients into the mixing bowl and mix until well combined.
2. Make small balls from mixture and place on a cooking tray.
3. Place drip pan into the bottom of the vortex plus air fryer oven cooking chamber.
4. Select BAKE mode, then set the temperature to 400 F and the time to 16 minutes, then press start.
5. When the display shows Add Food then place the cooking tray in the vortex plus air fryer oven.
6. Turn broccoli tots halfway through.
7. Serve and enjoy.

Nutritional Value (Amount per Serving):
Calories 322; Fat 24.4 g; Carbohydrates 8.2 g; Sugar 1.1 g; Protein 17.7 g; Cholesterol 101 mg

Savory Jalapeno Poppers

Preparation Time: 10 minutes; Cooking Time: 10 minutes; Serve: 6
Ingredients:
- 10 jalapenos, cut in half & remove ribs & seeds
- 4 oz cream cheese, softened
- 4 oz cheddar cheese, shredded
- 4 bacon slices, cooked & crumbled
- Pepper
- Salt

Directions:
1. In a bowl, mix together cream cheese, bacon, cheddar cheese, pepper, and salt.
2. Stuff cream cheese mixture into each jalapeno half.
3. Place stuff jalapeno peppers onto the cooking tray.
4. Select BAKE mode, then set the temperature to 350 F and the time to 10 minutes, then press start.
5. When the display shows Add Food then place the cooking tray in the vortex plus air fryer oven.
6. Serve and enjoy.

Nutritional Value (Amount per Serving):
Calories 218; Fat 18.3 g; Carbohydrates 2.3 g; Sugar 1 g; Protein 11.1 g; Cholesterol 55 mg

Cheese Balls

Preparation Time: 10 minutes; Cooking Time: 10 minutes; Serve: 4
Ingredients:
- 2 eggs
- 1/2 tsp baking powder
- 1/2 cup almond flour
- 1/4 cup parmesan cheese, shredded
- 1/4 cup mozzarella cheese, shredded
- 1/2 cup cheddar cheese, shredded
- Pepper
- Salt

Directions:
1. Add eggs into the mixing bowl and whisk until well beaten.

2. Add remaining ingredients into the bowl and mix until well combined.
3. Make 8 balls from cheese mixture and place onto the parchment-lined cooking tray.
4. Select BAKE mode, then set the temperature to 400 F and the time to 10 minutes, then press start.
5. When the display shows Add Food then place the cooking tray in the vortex plus air fryer oven.
6. Serve and enjoy.

Nutritional Value (Amount per Serving):
Calories 192; Fat 15.4 g; Carbohydrates 3.9 g; Sugar 0.7 g; Protein 11.6 g; Cholesterol 102 mg

Crab Stuffed Mushrooms

Preparation Time: 10 minutes; Cooking Time: 18 minutes; Serve: 4

Ingredients:
- 16 oz baby Bella mushrooms, wash & remove stems
- 4 bacon slices, cooked & chopped
- 1 cup mozzarella cheese, shredded
- 6 oz can lump crab meat, drained
- 4 oz cream cheese

Directions:
1. In a bowl, mix together cream cheese, crab meat, shredded cheese, and bacon until well combined.
2. Stuff cream cheese mixture into each mushroom and arrange mushrooms on a cooking tray.
3. Select BAKE mode, then set the temperature to 350 F and the time to 18 minutes, then press start.
4. When the display shows Add Food then place the cooking tray in the vortex plus air fryer oven.
5. Serve and enjoy.

Nutritional Value (Amount per Serving):
Calories 62; Fat 4.3 g; Carbohydrates 1.6 g; Sugar 0.5 g; Protein 4.8 g; Cholesterol 20 mg

Cheesy Pesto Chicken Dip

Preparation Time: 10 minutes; Cooking Time: 30 minutes; Serve: 8

Ingredients:
- 2 cups chicken, cooked & shredded
- 1 bell pepper, chopped
- 1/3 cup basil pesto
- 1/2 cup ricotta cheese
- 1 1/2 cups cheddar cheese, shredded
- 8 oz cream cheese, softened

Directions:
1. Spray an 8*8-inch baking dish with cooking spray and set aside.
2. In a mixing bowl, mix together cream cheese, pesto, 1 cup cheddar cheese, and ricotta cheese until well combined.
3. Stir in the bell pepper and shredded chicken.
4. Pour mixture into the prepared baking dish and spread evenly and top with remaining cheddar cheese.
5. Select BAKE mode, then set the temperature to 350 F and the time to 30 minutes, then press start.
6. When the display shows Add Food then place the baking dish in the vortex plus air fryer oven.
7. Serve and enjoy.

Nutritional Value (Amount per Serving):
Calories 264; Fat 19.3 g; Carbohydrates 3 g; Sugar 1 g; Protein 19.5 g; Cholesterol 85 mg

Crisp Asparagus Fries

Preparation Time: 10 minutes; Cooking Time: 10 minutes; Serve: 6

Ingredients:
- 4 eggs, lightly beaten
- 1 lb asparagus, trimmed & poke using a fork
- 1/4 tsp baking powder
- 1/4 tsp cayenne pepper
- 3/4 cup almond flour
- 1 cup parmesan cheese, grated
- Pepper
- Salt

Directions:
1. Season asparagus spears with pepper and salt and let it sit on a plate for 30 minutes.
2. In a shallow bowl, mix together parmesan cheese, cayenne pepper, and almond flour.
3. In a separate shallow dish, add eggs and whisk well.
4. Dip asparagus spears in eggs then coat with parmesan cheese mixture.
5. Arrange coated asparagus spears onto the cooking tray.
6. Select AIRFRY mode, then set the temperature to 400 F and the time to 10 minutes, then press start.
7. When the display shows Add Food then place the cooking tray in the vortex plus air fryer oven.
8. Turn asparagus spears halfway through.
9. Serve and enjoy.

Nutritional Value (Amount per Serving):
Calories 186; Fat 13.2 g; Carbohydrates 6.9 g; Sugar 2.2 g; Protein 13.2 g; Cholesterol 120 mg

Healthy Zucchini Chips

Preparation Time: 10 minutes; Cooking Time: 15 minutes; Serve: 8

Ingredients:
- 2 medium zucchinis, sliced into rounds
- 3/4 tsp garlic powder
- 2/3 cup Asiago cheese, grated
- 4 tbsp olive oil
- 1/4 tsp smoked paprika
- Pepper
- salt

Directions:
1. In a bowl, toss zucchini with garlic powder, paprika, oil, pepper, and salt until well coated.
2. Arrange zucchini slices onto the cooking tray and sprinkle with grated cheese on top.
3. Select BAKE mode, then set the temperature to 375 F and the time to 15 minutes, then press start.
4. When the display shows Add Food then place the cooking tray in the vortex plus air fryer oven.
5. Serve and enjoy.

Nutritional Value (Amount per Serving):
Calories 93; Fat 8.8 g; Carbohydrates 1.9 g; Sugar 0.9 g; Protein 2.6 g; Cholesterol 1.9 mg

Chicken Stuffed Mushrooms

Preparation Time: 10 minutes; Cooking Time: 30 minutes; Serve: 8

Ingredients:
- 40 mushrooms, clean & remove stems
- 1 tsp garlic, crushed
- 1/4 cup hot sauce
- 1/2 cup mayonnaise
- 4 oz cream cheese, softened
- 1 cup cheddar cheese, shredded
- 2 cups chicken, cooked & chopped
- Pepper
- Salt

Directions:

1. Arrange mushrooms onto the cooking tray.
2. Select BAKE mode, then set the temperature to 400 F and the time to 15 minutes, then press start.
3. When the display shows Add Food then place the cooking tray in the vortex plus air fryer oven.
4. Remove mushrooms from the oven and let it cool completely.
5. In a bowl, mix together chicken, 3/4 cup cheddar cheese, cream cheese, mayonnaise, hot sauce, garlic, pepper, and salt.
6. Stuff chicken mixture into each mushroom and top with remaining cheddar cheese. Arrange mushrooms onto the cooking tray.
7. Select BAKE mode, then set the temperature to 400 F and the time to 15 minutes, then press start.
8. When the display shows Add Food then place the cooking tray in the vortex plus air fryer oven.
9. Serve and enjoy.

Nutritional Value (Amount per Serving):
Calories 237; Fat 15.9 g; Carbohydrates 7.3 g; Sugar 2.7 g; Protein 17.8 g; Cholesterol 61 mg

Cheesy Stuffed Mini Peppers

Preparation Time: 10 minutes; Cooking Time: 12 minutes; Serve: 12
Ingredients:
- 6 mini sweet peppers, sliced in half, remove membranes & seeds
- 1 tsp Worcestershire sauce
- 1/2 cup cheddar cheese, shredded
- 4 bacon slices, cooked and chopped
- 1/2 tsp garlic powder
- 2 tbsp green onions, sliced
- 4 oz cream cheese

Directions:
1. In a small bowl, mix together cream cheese, green onions, garlic powder, bacon slices, cheddar cheese, and Worcestershire sauce until well combined.
2. Stuff cream cheese mixture into each pepper half. Arrange stuff peppers onto the cooking tray.
3. Select BAKE mode, then set the temperature to 400 F and the time to 12 minutes, then press start.
4. When the display shows Add Food then place the cooking tray in the vortex plus air fryer oven.
5. Serve and enjoy.

Nutritional Value (Amount per Serving):
Calories 106; Fat 7.7 g; Carbohydrates 5.1 g; Sugar 3.2 g; Protein 4.9 g; Cholesterol 22 mg

Meatballs

Preparation Time: 10 minutes; Cooking Time: 18 minutes; Serve: 10
Ingredients:
- 1 egg
- 1 lb sausage, casings removed
- 1 tsp garlic, chopped
- 1/2 onion, chopped
- 1 cup spinach, chopped
- 1/2 cup parmesan cheese, grated
- 1/2 cup mozzarella cheese, shredded
- 1 tsp salt

Directions:
1. Add all ingredients into the mixing bowl and mix until well combined.
2. Make small balls from mixture and place onto the parchment-lined cooking tray.
3. Select BAKE mode, then set the temperature to 400 F and the time to 18 minutes, then press start.

4. When the display shows Add Food then place the cooking tray in the vortex plus air fryer oven.
5. Serve and enjoy.

Nutritional Value (Amount per Serving):
Calories 182; Fat 14.5 g; Carbohydrates 1 g; Sugar 0.3 g; Protein 11.4 g; Cholesterol 58 mg

Crispy Baked Broccoli

Preparation Time: 10 minutes; Cooking Time: 15 minutes; Serve: 4

Ingredients:
- 2 large eggs
- 3 1/2 cups broccoli florets
- 1/2 tsp garlic powder
- 1/4 cup cheddar cheese, grated
- 1/2 cup parmesan cheese, grated
- 1/2 cup almond flour
- 1 tbsp unsweetened almond milk
- 1/4 tsp salt

Directions:
1. In a small bowl, whisk together egg and almond milk and set aside.
2. In a separate bowl, mix together almond flour, garlic powder, parmesan cheese, and salt.
3. Dip broccoli floret in the egg mixture then coats with almond flour mixture.
4. Place coated broccoli florets onto the cooking tray and sprinkle with cheddar cheese.
5. Select BAKE mode, then set the temperature to 400 F and the time to 15 minutes, then press start.
6. When the display shows Add Food then place the cooking tray in the vortex plus air fryer oven.
7. Serve and enjoy.

Nutritional Value (Amount per Serving):
Calories 209; Fat 14.6 g; Carbohydrates 9.3 g; Sugar 2.2 g; Protein 13.8 g; Cholesterol 108 mg

Parmesan Artichoke Hearts

Preparation Time: 10 minutes; Cooking Time: 18 minutes; Serve: 5

Ingredients:
- 15 oz can artichoke hearts, drained & quartered
- 1/4 cup almond flour
- 1/4 cup parmesan cheese, grated
- 1/2 tsp garlic powder
- 1/4 cup butter, melted

Directions:
1. Pat dry artichoke hearts with a paper towel.
2. In a small bowl, mix together melted butter and garlic powder.
3. In a separate bowl, mix together parmesan cheese and almond flour.
4. Dip each quartered artichoke heart in melted butter mixture and coat with parmesan cheese mixture.
5. Place coated artichoke hearts onto the parchment-lined cooking tray.
6. Select BAKE mode, then set the temperature to 400 F and the time to 18 minutes, then press start.
7. When the display shows Add Food then place the cooking tray in the vortex plus air fryer oven.
8. Turn artichoke hearts halfway through.
9. Serve and enjoy.

Nutritional Value (Amount per Serving):
Calories 154; Fat 13 g; Carbohydrates 5.8 g; Sugar 1 g; Protein 4.2 g; Cholesterol 28 mg

Perfect Ricotta Cheese Dip

Preparation Time: 10 minutes; Cooking Time: 20 minutes; Serve: 6

Ingredients:
- 2 cups ricotta cheese
- 3 tbsp olive oil
- 2 garlic cloves, minced
- 2 tsp fresh thyme
- 1 lemon zest
- 1/4 cup parmesan cheese, shredded
- 1/2 cup mozzarella cheese, shredded
- Pepper
- Salt

Directions:
1. Grease baking dish with olive oil.
2. Add all ingredients into the mixing bowl and mix until well combined.
3. Pour mixture into the prepared baking dish.
4. Select BAKE mode, then set the temperature to 375 F and the time to 20 minutes, then press start.
5. When the display shows Add Food then place the baking dish in the vortex plus air fryer oven.
6. Serve and enjoy.

Nutritional Value (Amount per Serving):
Calories 198; Fat 14.8 g; Carbohydrates 5.9 g; Sugar 0.5 g; Protein 11.5 g; Cholesterol 30 mg

Tuna Muffins

Preparation Time: 10 minutes; Cooking Time: 25 minutes; Serve: 8

Ingredients:
- 2 large eggs
- 1 can tuna, flaked
- 1 tsp cayenne pepper
- 1 celery stalk, chopped
- 1 1/2 cups cheddar cheese, shredded
- 1/4 cup sour cream
- 1/4 cup mayonnaise
- Pepper
- Salt

Directions:
1. Add eggs and remaining ingredients into the mixing bowl and mix well.
2. Pour mixture into the 8 silicone muffin molds.
3. Select BAKE mode, then set the temperature to 350 F and the time to 25 minutes, then press start.
4. When the display shows Add Food then place silicone muffin molds on the cooking tray and place in the vortex plus air fryer oven.
5. Serve and enjoy.

Nutritional Value (Amount per Serving):
Calories 190; Fat 14.1 g; Carbohydrates 2.6 g; Sugar 0.7 g; Protein 13.1 g; Cholesterol 81 mg

Healthy Zucchini Patties

Preparation Time: 10 minutes; Cooking Time: 30 minutes; Serve: 8

Ingredients:
- 2 eggs
- 2 cups shredded zucchini, squeeze out all liquid
- 1 tsp dried chili flakes
- 1/2 cup parmesan cheese, grated
- 1 tbsp Dijon mustard
- 1 tbsp mayonnaise
- 1 cup almond flour
- 1/4 cup onion, chopped
- Pepper
- Salt

Directions:
1. Add all ingredients into the mixing bowl and mix until well combined.
2. Make patties from mixture and place onto the parchment-lined cooking tray.

3. Select BAKE mode, then set the temperature to 400 F and the time to 30 minutes, then press start.
   4. When the display shows Add Food then place the cooking tray in the vortex plus air fryer oven.
   5. Turn zucchini patties halfway through.
   6. Serve and enjoy.

Nutritional Value (Amount per Serving):
Calories 128; Fat 10 g; Carbohydrates 5.1 g; Sugar 1.4 g; Protein 6.7 g; Cholesterol 45 mg

Garlicky Mushrooms

Preparation Time: 10 minutes; Cooking Time: 12 minutes; Serve: 4

Ingredients:
- 1 lb mushrooms, clean & stems removed
- 1/8 tsp garlic powder
- 2 tbsp chives, sliced
- 1 tsp garlic, minced
- 1 tbsp olive oil
- 1/8 tsp pepper
- 1/8 tsp kosher salt

Directions:
1. Add mushrooms and remaining ingredients into the large bowl and toss until well coated.
2. Spread mushrooms onto the cooking tray.
3. Select BAKE mode, then set the temperature to 400 F and the time to 12 minutes, then press start.
4. When the display shows Add Food then place the cooking tray in the vortex plus air fryer oven.
5. Serve and enjoy.

Nutritional Value (Amount per Serving):
Calories 56; Fat 3.8 g; Carbohydrates 4.2 g; Sugar 2 g; Protein 3.7 g; Cholesterol 0 mg

Sausage Balls

Preparation Time: 10 minutes; Cooking Time: 20 minutes; Serve: 6

Ingredients:
- 1 egg
- 1 lb breakfast sausage, casing removed
- 1 tsp baking powder
- 1 cup almond flour
- 2 tbsp butter, melted
- 1 cup pepper jack cheese, shredded
- 1/4 tsp salt

Directions:
1. Add all ingredients into the large bowl and mix until well combined.
2. Make small balls from mixture and place onto the parchment-lined cooking tray.
3. Select BAKE mode, then set the temperature to 350 F and the time to 20 minutes, then press start.
4. When the display shows Add Food then place the cooking tray in the vortex plus air fryer oven.
5. Serve and enjoy.

Nutritional Value (Amount per Serving):
Calories 467; Fat 40.2 g; Carbohydrates 4.5 g; Sugar 0.7 g; Protein 23.4 g; Cholesterol 117 mg

Spinach Ranch Dip

Preparation Time: 10 minutes; Cooking Time: 25 minutes; Serve: 16

Ingredients:
- 2 cups spinach, washed & chopped
- 1/4 cup parmesan cheese, grated
- 1 1/2 cups mozzarella cheese
- 1 tsp ranch seasoning

- 1/2 cup red pepper, diced
- 1/4 cup green onion, sliced
- 1/2 cup mayonnaise
- 1/2 cup sour cream
- 8 oz cream cheese

Directions:
1. Cook spinach in a pan over medium heat until spinach is wilted. Squeezed out all liquid from spinach.
2. Add spinach, 1 cup mozzarella cheese, and remaining ingredients into the mixing bowl and mix until well combined.
3. Pour mixture into the baking dish and spread evenly. Top with remaining mozzarella cheese.
4. Select BAKE mode, then set the temperature to 350 F and the time to 25 minutes, then press start.
5. When the display shows Add Food then place the baking dish in the vortex plus air fryer oven.
6. Serve and enjoy.

Nutritional Value (Amount per Serving):
Calories 109; Fat 9.7 g; Carbohydrates 3.1 g; Sugar 0.8 g; Protein 2.8 g; Cholesterol 23 mg

Tasty Buffalo Chicken Dip

Preparation Time: 10 minutes; Cooking Time: 20 minutes; Serve: 12
Ingredients:
- 2 cups chicken breast, cooked & diced
- 2 green onions, sliced
- 1 cup mozzarella cheese, shredded
- 1 cup cheddar cheese, shredded
- 1 tsp garlic powder
- 2/3 cup sour cream
- 2/3 cup buffalo sauce
- 8 oz cream cheese, softened

Directions:
1. Add chicken, green onion, 1/2 cup mozzarella cheese, 1/2 cup cheddar cheese, garlic powder, sour cream, buffalo sauce, and cream cheese in a mixing bowl and mix until well combined.
2. Pour mixture into the baking dish and top with remaining cheese.
3. Select BAKE mode, then set the temperature to 350 F and the time to 20 minutes, then press start.
4. When the display shows Add Food then place the baking dish in the vortex plus air fryer oven.
5. Serve and enjoy.

Nutritional Value (Amount per Serving):
Calories 164; Fat 13.2 g; Carbohydrates 2.4 g; Sugar 0.2 g; Protein 8.5 g; Cholesterol 48 mg

Easy Artichoke Dip

Preparation Time: 10 minutes; Cooking Time: 40 minutes; Serve: 8
Ingredients:
- 14 oz can artichoke hearts, drained & chopped
- 1 tbsp garlic, minced
- 1 cup parmesan cheese, shredded
- 1 cup mayonnaise

Directions:
1. Add all ingredients into the baking dish and mix well.
2. Select BAKE mode, then set the temperature to 350 F and the time to 40 minutes, then press start.
3. When the display shows Add Food then place the baking dish in the vortex plus air fryer oven.

4. Serve and enjoy.

Nutritional Value (Amount per Serving):
Calories 167; Fat 12.2 g; Carbohydrates 10.3 g; Sugar 2.3 g; Protein 4.8 g; Cholesterol 16 mg

Creamy Mexican Cheese Dip

Preparation Time: 10 minutes; Cooking Time: 30 minutes; Serve: 10

Ingredients:
- 1/2 cup salsa
- 3 cups cheddar cheese, shredded
- 1 cup sour cream
- 15 oz cream cheese, softened

Directions:
1. Add all ingredients into the mixing bowl and mix until well combined.
2. Pour mixture into the baking dish.
3. Select BAKE mode, then set the temperature to 350 F and the time to 25-30 minutes, then press start.
4. When the display shows Add Food then place the baking dish in the vortex plus air fryer oven.
5. Serve and enjoy.

Nutritional Value (Amount per Serving):
Calories 338; Fat 30.9 g; Carbohydrates 3.4 g; Sugar 0.7 g; Protein 12.6 g; Cholesterol 92 mg

Creamy Spinach Dip

Preparation Time: 10 minutes; Cooking Time: 35 minutes; Serve: 6

Ingredients:
- 10 oz frozen spinach, thawed, drained & chopped
- 8 oz cream cheese, softened
- 1/4 tsp black pepper
- 1 tsp onion powder
- 1/2 cup Asiago cheese, shredded
- 1/2 cup parmesan cheese, grated
- 2 garlic cloves, minced
- 1/2 cup mayonnaise
- 1/4 tsp salt

Directions:
1. In a mixing bowl, add all ingredients except spinach and mix until well combined.
2. Add spinach and mix until well combined.
3. Pour mixture into the baking dish.
4. Select BAKE mode, then set the temperature to 350 F and the time to 35 minutes, then press start.
5. When the display shows Add Food then place the baking dish in the vortex plus air fryer oven.
6. Serve and enjoy.

Nutritional Value (Amount per Serving):
Calories 273; Fat 23.7 g; Carbohydrates 8.4 g; Sugar 1.7 g; Protein 8.8 g; Cholesterol 59 mg

Turkey Meatballs

Preparation Time: 10 minutes; Cooking Time: 25 minutes; Serve: 6

Ingredients:
- 1 lb ground turkey
- 1/4 tsp pepper
- 1/2 tsp ground coriander
- 1 1/2 tsp ginger, grated
- 1 tsp ground cumin
- 2 tbsp red curry paste
- 2 tbsp fresh mint, chopped
- 1/4 cup bell pepper, diced
- 1/2 cup onion, diced
- 1/2 tsp sea salt

Directions:
1. Add all ingredients into the mixing bowl and mix until well combined.

2. Make small balls from meat mixture and place onto the parchment-lined cooking tray.
3. Select BAKE mode, then set the temperature to 350 F and the time to 25 minutes, then press start.
4. When the display shows Add Food then place the cooking tray in the vortex plus air fryer oven.
5. Serve and enjoy.

Nutritional Value (Amount per Serving):
Calories 177; Fat 9.9 g; Carbohydrates 3 g; Sugar 0.7 g; Protein 21 g; Cholesterol 77 mg

Cauliflower Popcorn

Preparation Time: 10 minutes; Cooking Time: 30 minutes; Serve: 6
Ingredients:
- 1 medium cauliflower head, cut into florets
- 2/3 cup water
- 3/4 cup almond flour
- Pepper
- Salt

Directions:
1. Add cauliflower florets into the mixing bowl.
2. Mix together water, almond flour, pepper, and salt and pour over cauliflower florets and toss well.
3. Arrange cauliflower florets onto the parchment-lined cooking tray.
4. Select BAKE mode, then set the temperature to 400 F and the time to 25-30 minutes, then press start.
5. When the display shows Add Food then place the cooking tray in the vortex plus air fryer oven.
6. Serve and enjoy.

Nutritional Value (Amount per Serving):
Calories 104; Fat 7.1 g; Carbohydrates 8.1 g; Sugar 2.8 g; Protein 4.9 g; Cholesterol 0 mg

Tasty Cauliflower Bites

Preparation Time: 10 minutes; Cooking Time: 15 minutes; Serve: 6
Ingredients:
- 1 cup cheddar cheese, shredded
- 1/2 cup cauliflower rice
- 5 eggs whites
- Pepper
- Salt

Directions:
1. Add all ingredients into the mixing bowl and mix until well combined.
2. Pour mixture into mini the silicone muffin pan.
3. Select BAKE mode, then set the temperature to 400 F and the time to 15 minutes, then press start.
4. When the display shows Add Food then place the silicone muffin pan in the vortex plus air fryer oven.
5. Serve and enjoy.

Nutritional Value (Amount per Serving):
Calories 95; Fat 6.4 g; Carbohydrates 1 g; Sugar 0.6 g; Protein 8 g; Cholesterol 20 mg

Air Fryer Herb Mushrooms

Preparation Time: 10 minutes; Cooking Time: 14 minutes; Serve: 4
Ingredients:
- 1 lb mushrooms
- 1 tbsp basil, minced
- 1 tsp rosemary, chopped
- 1 tsp thyme, chopped

- 1 garlic clove, minced
- 1/2 tbsp vinegar
- Pepper
- Salt

Directions:
1. Add all ingredients into the large bowl and toss well.
2. Spread mushrooms onto the cooking tray.
3. Select AIRFRY mode, then set the temperature to 350 F and the time to 14 minutes, then press start.
4. When the display shows Add Food then place the cooking tray in the vortex plus air fryer oven.
5. Serve and enjoy.

Nutritional Value (Amount per Serving):
Calories 28; Fat 0.4 g; Carbohydrates 4.4 g; Sugar 2 g; Protein 3.7 g; Cholesterol 0 mg

Tasty Brussels Sprouts

Preparation Time: 10 minutes; Cooking Time: 35 minutes; Serve: 6

Ingredients:
- 2 cups Brussels sprouts, halved
- 1/4 tsp chili pepper
- 1/4 tsp garlic powder
- 1/4 tsp onion powder
- 1/4 cup olive oil
- 1/4 tsp salt

Directions:
1. Add all ingredients into the large bowl and toss well.
2. Transfer Brussels sprouts onto the cooking tray.
3. Select BAKE mode, then set the temperature to 400 F and the time to 35 minutes, then press start.
4. When the display shows Add Food then place the cooking tray in the vortex plus air fryer oven.
5. Serve and enjoy.

Nutritional Value (Amount per Serving):
Calories 86; Fat 8.5 g; Carbohydrates 2.9 g; Sugar 0.7 g; Protein 1 g; Cholesterol 0 mg

Cheesy Spinach Dip

Preparation Time: 10 minutes; Cooking Time: 20 minutes; Serve: 12

Ingredients:
- 3 oz frozen spinach, defrosted & chopped
- 8 oz cream cheese
- 1 cup sour cream
- 2 cups mozzarella cheese, shredded
- Salt

Directions:
1. Add all ingredients into the bowl and mix until well combined.
2. Transfer mixture into the greased baking dish.
3. Select BAKE mode, then set the temperature to 350 F and the time to 20 minutes, then press start.
4. When the display shows Add Food then place the baking dish in the vortex plus air fryer oven.
5. Serve and enjoy.

Nutritional Value (Amount per Serving):
Calories 122; Fat 11.5 g; Carbohydrates 1.8 g; Sugar 0.1 g; Protein 3.6 g; Cholesterol 32 mg

Cheese Dip

Preparation Time: 10 minutes; Cooking Time: 20 minutes; Serve: 12
Ingredients:

- 8 oz cream cheese, softened
- 4.5 oz Asiago cheese, shredded
- 1 cup sour cream
- 1 tbsp garlic, minced
- 1 cup mozzarella cheese, shredded
- 1/4 tsp onion powder

Directions:
1. Add all ingredients into the bowl and mix until well combined.
2. Pour mixture into the greased baking dish.
3. Select BAKE mode, then set the temperature to 350 F and the time to 20 minutes, then press start.
4. When the display shows Add Food then place the baking dish in the vortex plus air fryer oven.
5. Serve and enjoy.

Nutritional Value (Amount per Serving):
Calories 153; Fat 14.1 g; Carbohydrates 1.7 g; Sugar 0.1 g; Protein 5.4 g; Cholesterol 40 mg

Ricotta Dip

Preparation Time: 10 minutes; Cooking Time: 15 minutes; Serve: 6
Ingredients:
- 1 cup ricotta cheese, shredded
- 1 tbsp lemon juice
- 1/4 cup parmesan cheese, grated
- 1/2 cup mozzarella cheese, shredded
- 2 tbsp olive oil
- 1 tsp garlic, minced
- Pepper
- Salt

Directions:
1. Add all ingredients into the mixing bowl and mix until well combined.
2. Pour mixture into the greased baking dish.
3. Select BAKE mode, then set the temperature to 400 F and the time to 15 minutes, then press start.
4. When the display shows Add Food then baking dish in the vortex plus air fryer oven.
5. Serve and enjoy.

Nutritional Value (Amount per Serving):
Calories 117; Fat 9.2 g; Carbohydrates 2.6 g; Sugar 0.2 g; Protein 6.6 g; Cholesterol 17 mg

Cheesy Onion Dip

Preparation Time: 10 minutes; Cooking Time: 40 minutes; Serve: 8
Ingredients:
- 1 cup mozzarella cheese, shredded
- 1 cup cheddar cheese, shredded
- 1 1/2 cup mayonnaise
- 2 onions, chopped
- 1 1/2 cup Swiss cheese, shredded
- Pepper
- Salt

Directions:
1. Add all ingredients into the bowl and mix until well combined.
2. Pour mixture into the greased baking dish.
3. Select BAKE mode, then set the temperature to 350 F and the time to 40 minutes, then press start.
4. When the display shows Add Food then place the baking dish in the vortex plus air fryer oven.
5. Serve and enjoy.

Nutritional Value (Amount per Serving):
Calories 249; Fat 21.4 g; Carbohydrates 3.9 g; Sugar 1.2 g; Protein 9.5 g; Cholesterol 33 mg

Air Fryer Walnuts

Preparation Time: 10 minutes; Cooking Time: 5 minutes; Serve: 6
Ingredients:
- 2 cups walnuts
- 1 tsp olive oil
- 1/4 tsp garlic powder
- Pepper
- Salt

Directions:
1. Add walnuts, oil, garlic powder, pepper, and salt into the bowl and toss well.
2. Spread walnuts onto the cooking tray.
3. Select AIRFRY mode, then set the temperature to 350 F and the time to 4 minutes, then press start.
4. When the display shows Add Food then place the cooking tray in the vortex plus air fryer oven.
5. Serve and enjoy.

Nutritional Value (Amount per Serving):
Calories 265; Fat 25.4 g; Carbohydrates 4.2 g; Sugar 0.5 g; Protein 10.1 g; Cholesterol 0 mg

Spicy Almonds

Preparation Time: 10 minutes; Cooking Time: 20 minutes; Serve: 6
Ingredients:
- 1 1/2 cups almonds
- 1/2 tsp cayenne
- 1/4 tsp onion powder
- 1/4 tsp dried basil
- 1/2 tsp garlic powder
- 1/2 tsp cumin
- 1 1/2 tsp chili powder
- 2 tsp Worcestershire sauce
- 2 tbsp butter, melted
- 1/2 tsp sea salt

Directions:
1. Add almonds and remaining ingredients into the mixing bowl and mix well.
2. Spread almonds onto the parchment-lined cooking tray.
3. Select BAKE mode, then set the temperature to 350 F and the time to 18-20 minutes, then press start.
4. When the display shows Add Food then place the cooking tray in the vortex plus air fryer oven.
5. Serve and enjoy.

Nutritional Value (Amount per Serving):
Calories 177; Fat 15.9 g; Carbohydrates 6.2 g; Sugar 1.5 g; Protein 5.2 g; Cholesterol 10 mg

Easy Brussels Sprouts Chips

Preparation Time: 10 minutes; Cooking Time: 10 minutes; Serve: 4
Ingredients:
- 20 Brussels sprouts split leaves
- 2 tbsp olive oil
- 1/4 tsp garlic powder
- 1/4 tsp pepper
- 1/2 tsp salt

Directions:
1. Add brussels sprouts, oil, garlic, pepper, and salt into the mixing bowl and toss well.
2. Spread Brussels sprouts onto the cooking tray.
3. Select BAKE mode, then set the temperature to 350 F and the time to 10 minutes, then press start.
4. When the display shows Add Food then place the cooking tray in the vortex plus air fryer oven.
5. Serve and enjoy.

Nutritional Value (Amount per Serving):
Calories 102; Fat 7.3 g; Carbohydrates 8.9 g; Sugar 2.1 g; Protein 3.3 g; Cholesterol 0 mg

Crispy Onion Rings

Preparation Time: 10 minutes; Cooking Time: 25 minutes; Serve: 4

Ingredients:
- 2 eggs
- 2 large sweet onion, cut into rings
- 1/2 tsp garlic powder
- 1/2 tsp pepper
- 1/2 tsp salt
- 1 1/2 cups almond flour

Directions:
1. In a bowl, mix together almond flour, garlic powder, thyme, garlic powder, and salt.
2. In a separate bowl, whisk eggs.
3. Dip onion ring in egg mixture then coats with almond flour mixture.
4. Place coated onion ring onto the cooking tray.
5. Select BAKE mode, then set the temperature to 400 F and the time to 25 minutes, then press start.
6. When the display shows Add Food then place the cooking tray in the vortex plus air fryer oven.
7. Serve and enjoy.

Nutritional Value (Amount per Serving):
Calories 123; Fat 7.5 g; Carbohydrates 9.9 g; Sugar 3.8 g; Protein 5.9 g; Cholesterol 82 mg

Cinnamon Cashews

Preparation Time: 10 minutes; Cooking Time: 15 minutes; Serve: 4

Ingredients:
- 1 cup cashews, soak in water for overnight
- 2 tbsp cinnamon

Directions:
1. Drain cashews well and pat dry with a paper towel.
2. Place cashews onto the cooking tray and sprinkle with cinnamon.
3. Select BAKE mode, then set the temperature to 350 F and the time to 15-20 minutes, then press start.
4. When the display shows Add Food then place the cooking tray in the vortex plus air fryer oven.
5. Store in an air-tight container.

Nutritional Value (Amount per Serving):
Calories 198; Fat 14 g; Carbohydrates 11.7 g; Sugar 2.1 g; Protein 5.1 g; Cholesterol 0 mg

Broccoli Nuggets

Preparation Time: 10 minutes; Cooking Time: 20 minutes; Serve: 4

Ingredients:
- 2 egg whites
- 2 cups broccoli florets, chopped
- 1 cup cheddar cheese, shredded
- 1/4 cup almond flour
- 1/4 tsp garlic powder
- 1/8 tsp salt

Directions:
1. Add all ingredients into the mixing bowl and mix until well combined.
2. Drop 20 scoops onto cooking tray and press lightly into a nugget shape.
3. Select BAKE mode, then set the temperature to 350 F and the time to 20 minutes, then press start.

4. When the display shows Add Food then place the cooking tray in the vortex plus air fryer oven.
5. Serve and enjoy.

Nutritional Value (Amount per Serving):
Calories 179; Fat 13 g; Carbohydrates 5.1 g; Sugar 1.3 g; Protein 11.6 g; Cholesterol 30 mg

Healthy Carrot Fries

Preparation Time: 10 minutes; Cooking Time: 15 minutes; Serve: 2

Ingredients:
- 1/2 lb carrots, peeled and cut into 4 inch long pieces
- 1/4 tsp paprika
- 1/4 tsp cumin
- 1/2 tbsp olive oil
- 1/4 tsp salt

Directions:
1. In a large bowl, add all ingredients and toss until well coated.
2. Spread carrots fries onto the cooking tray.
3. Select BAKE mode, then set the temperature to 400 F and the time to 15 minutes, then press start.
4. When the display shows Add Food then place the cooking tray in the vortex plus air fryer oven.
5. Stir carrot fries halfway through.
6. Serve and enjoy.

Nutritional Value (Amount per Serving):
Calories 78; Fat 3.6 g; Carbohydrates 11.4 g; Sugar 5.6 g; Protein 1 g; Cholesterol 0 mg

Crispy Bacon

Preparation Time: 5 minutes; Cooking Time: 10 minutes; Serve: 10

Ingredients:
- 10 bacon slices

Directions:
1. Arrange bacon slices onto the cooking tray.
2. Select BAKE mode, then set the temperature to 400 F and the time to 10 minutes, then press start.
3. When the display shows Add Food then place the cooking tray in the vortex plus air fryer oven.
4. Serve and enjoy.

Nutritional Value (Amount per Serving):
Calories 103; Fat 7.9 g; Carbohydrates 0.3 g; Sugar 0 g; Protein 7 g; Cholesterol 21 mg

Salsa Jalapeno Poppers

Preparation Time: 10 minutes; Cooking Time: 13 minutes; Serve: 4

Ingredients:
- 4 jalapeno peppers, slice in half and deseeded
- 1/4 tsp chili powder
- 1/2 tsp garlic, minced
- 2 tbsp salsa
- 4 oz feta cheese, crumbled
- Pepper
- Salt

Directions:
1. In a small bowl, mix together cheese, salsa, chili powder, garlic, pepper, and salt.
2. Spoon cheese mixture into each jalapeno halves and place onto the cooking tray.
3. Select BAKE mode, then set the temperature to 350 F and the time to 13 minutes, then press start.

4. When the display shows Add Food then place the cooking tray in the vortex plus air fryer oven.
   5. Serve and enjoy.

Nutritional Value (Amount per Serving):
Calories 84; Fat 6.3 g; Carbohydrates 2.9 g; Sugar 1.9 g; Protein 4.4 g; Cholesterol 25 mg

Chestnuts Spinach Dip

Preparation Time: 10 minutes; Cooking Time: 40 minutes; Serve: 8

Ingredients:
- 8 oz cream cheese, softened
- 1 cup mayonnaise
- 1 cup cheddar cheese, grated
- 1 cup frozen spinach, thawed and squeeze out all liquid
- 1/4 tsp garlic powder
- 1/2 cup onion, minced
- 1/3 cup water chestnuts, drained and chopped

Directions:
1. Add all ingredients into the bowl and mix until well combined.
2. Transfer bowl mixture into the greased baking dish.
3. Select BAKE mode, then set the temperature to 300 F and the time to 35-40 minutes, then press start.
4. When the display shows Add Food then place the baking dish in the vortex plus air fryer oven.
5. Serve and enjoy.

Nutritional Value (Amount per Serving):
Calories 282; Fat 24.4 g; Carbohydrates 10.6 g; Sugar 2.4 g; Protein 6.3 g; Cholesterol 54 mg

Zucchini Fries

Preparation Time: 10 minutes; Cooking Time: 10 minutes; Serve: 4

Ingredients:
- 1 egg, lightly beaten
- 2 medium zucchinis, cut into fries shape
- 1 tsp Italian seasoning
- 1/2 cup parmesan cheese, grated
- 1/2 cup almond flour
- Pepper
- Salt

Directions:
1. Add egg in a bowl and whisk well.
2. In a shallow dish, mix together almond flour, parmesan cheese, Italian seasoning, pepper, and salt.
3. Dip zucchini fries in egg then coat with almond flour mixture and place onto the cooking tray.
4. Select BAKE mode, then set the temperature to 400 F and the time to 10 minutes, then press start.
5. When the display shows Add Food then place the cooking tray in the vortex plus air fryer oven.
6. Serve and enjoy.

Nutritional Value (Amount per Serving):
Calories 151; Fat 11 g; Carbohydrates 6.9 g; Sugar 2.4 g; Protein 9.2 g; Cholesterol 50 mg

Chicken Dip

Preparation Time: 10 minutes; Cooking Time: 20 minutes; Serve: 6

Ingredients:
- 2 cups chicken, cooked and shredded
- 3/4 cup sour cream

- 6 oz cream cheese, softened
- 4 tbsp hot sauce

Directions:
1. Add all ingredients in a mixing bowl and mix until well combined.
2. Pour mixture into the greased baking dish.
3. Select BAKE mode, then set the temperature to 325 F and the time to 20 minutes, then press start.
4. When the display shows Add Food then place the cooking tray in the vortex plus air fryer oven.
5. Serve and enjoy.

Nutritional Value (Amount per Serving):
Calories 232; Fat 17.4 g; Carbohydrates 2.2 g; Sugar 0.2 g; Protein 16.6 g; Cholesterol 80 mg

Delicious Jalapeno Poppers

Preparation Time: 10 minutes; Cooking Time: 5 minutes; Serve: 5

Ingredients:
- 10 fresh jalapeno peppers, cut in half and remove seeds
- 1/4 cup mozzarella cheese, shredded
- 6 oz cream cheese, softened
- 4 bacon slices, cooked and crumbled
- Pepper
- Salt

Directions:
1. In a bowl, mix together bacon, cream cheese, mozzarella cheese, pepper, and salt.
2. Stuff each jalapeno half with cheese mixture.
3. Place stuffed jalapeno peppers onto the cooking tray.
4. Select BAKE mode, then set the temperature to 370 F and the time to 5 minutes, then press start.
5. When the display shows Add Food then place the cooking tray in the vortex plus air fryer oven.
6. Serve and enjoy.

Nutritional Value (Amount per Serving):
Calories 217; Fat 18.9 g; Carbohydrates 3.3 g; Sugar 1 g; Protein 9 g; Cholesterol 55 mg

Baked Eggplant Chips

Preparation Time: 5 minutes; Cooking Time: 20 minutes; Serve: 4

Ingredients:
- 1 eggplant, cut into 1-inch slices
- 1/2 tsp Italian seasoning
- 1 tsp paprika
- 2 tbsp olive oil
- 1/8 tsp cayenne
- 1/2 tsp red pepper
- 1 tsp garlic powder

Directions:
1. Add all ingredients into the mixing bowl and toss well.
2. Arrange eggplant slices onto the cooking tray.
3. Select AIRFRY mode, then set the temperature to 375 F and the time to 20 minutes, then press start.
4. When the display shows Add Food then place the cooking tray in the vortex plus air fryer oven.
5. Turn eggplant slices halfway through.
6. Serve and enjoy.

Nutritional Value (Amount per Serving):
Calories 99; Fat 7.5 g; Carbohydrates 8.8 g; Sugar 4.5 g; Protein 1.5 g; Cholesterol 0 mg

Salmon Bites

Preparation Time: 10 minutes; Cooking Time: 12 minutes; Serve: 4

Ingredients:
- 1 lb salmon fillets, boneless and cubes
- 1/2 tsp chili powder
- 2 tsp olive oil
- Pepper
- Salt

Directions:
1. Add all ingredients into the bowl and toss well.
2. Arrange salmon cubes onto the cooking tray.
3. Select AIRFRY mode, then set the temperature to 350 F and the time to 12 minutes, then press start.
4. When the display shows Add Food then place the cooking tray in the vortex plus air fryer oven.
5. Turn halfway through.
6. Serve and enjoy.

Nutritional Value (Amount per Serving):
Calories 171; Fat 9.4 g; Carbohydrates 0.2 g; Sugar 0 g; Protein 22 g; Cholesterol 50 mg

Flavors Turkey Dip

Preparation Time: 10 minutes; Cooking Time: 25 minutes; Serve: 6

Ingredients:
- 1 lb turkey breast, skinless, boneless, and minced
- 2 shallots, chopped
- 1 tbsp olive oil
- 1/4 cup heavy cream
- 1 cup tomatoes, chopped
- 1 tbsp garlic, minced
- Pepper
- Salt

Directions:
1. Add all ingredients into the large bowl and mix until well combined.
2. Pour mixture into the greased baking dish.
3. Select BAKE mode, then set the temperature to 380 F and the time to 25 minutes, then press start.
4. When the display shows Add Food then place the baking dish in the vortex plus air fryer oven.
5. Serve and enjoy.

Nutritional Value (Amount per Serving):
Calories 134; Fat 5.5 g; Carbohydrates 7.3 g; Sugar 3.5 g; Protein 13.7 g; Cholesterol 39 mg

Air Fryer Mushrooms

Preparation Time: 10 minutes; Cooking Time: 14 minutes; Serve: 4

Ingredients:
- 1 lb mushroom caps
- 1 garlic clove, minced
- 1/2 tbsp vinegar
- 1/2 tsp ground coriander
- 1/4 tsp garlic powder
- 1/4 tsp onion powder
- 1/4 tsp cayenne
- Pepper
- Salt

Directions:
1. Add all ingredients into the large bowl and toss well.
2. Spread mushrooms onto the cooking tray.
3. Select AIRFRY mode, then set the temperature to 350 F and the time to 14 minutes, then press start.

4. When the display shows Add Food then place the cooking tray in the vortex plus air fryer oven.
  5. Serve and enjoy.

Nutritional Value (Amount per Serving):
Calories 27; Fat 0.3 g; Carbohydrates 4.3 g; Sugar 2.1 g; Protein 3.7 g; Cholesterol 0 mg

Creamy Shrimp Dip

Preparation Time: 10 minutes; Cooking Time: 8 minutes; Serve: 6

Ingredients:
- 1 lb shrimp, peeled, deveined, and chopped
- 1 tsp chili powder
- 1 cup heavy cream
- 2 tbsp olive oil

Directions:
1. Add all ingredients into the mixing bowl and mix until well combined.
2. Pour mixture into the greased baking dish.
3. Select BAKE mode, then set the temperature to 380 F and the time to 8 minutes, then press start.
4. When the display shows Add Food then place the baking dish in the vortex plus air fryer oven.
5. Serve and enjoy.

Nutritional Value (Amount per Serving):
Calories 200; Fat 13.4 g; Carbohydrates 2 g; Sugar 0.1 g; Protein 17.7 g; Cholesterol 187 mg

Roasted Pecans

Preparation Time: 10 minutes; Cooking Time: 6 minutes; Serve: 6

Ingredients:
- 2 cups pecan halves
- 1 tbsp olive oil
- Pepper
- Salt

Directions:
1. Add pecans, oil, and salt in a bowl and toss well.
2. Transfer pecans onto the cooking tray.
3. Select AIRFRY mode, then set the temperature to 200 F and the time to 6 minutes, then press start.
4. When the display shows Add Food then place the cooking tray in the vortex plus air fryer oven.
5. Stir after every 2 minutes.
6. Serve and enjoy.

Nutritional Value (Amount per Serving):
Calories 159; Fat 16.6 g; Carbohydrates 2.9 g; Sugar 0.7 g; Protein 2.1 g; Cholesterol 0 mg

Cajun Zucchini Slices

Preparation Time: 10 minutes; Cooking Time: 16 minutes; Serve: 2

Ingredients:
- 1 1/4 cup zucchini slices
- 1 tsp Cajun seasoning
- 1 tbsp olive oil
- Pepper
- Salt

Directions:
1. Toss zucchini slices with oil, cajun seasoning, pepper, and salt.
2. Arrange zucchini slices onto the cooking tray.

3. Select AIRFRY mode, then set the temperature to 370 F and the time to 16 minutes, then press start.
4. When the display shows Add Food then place the cooking tray in the vortex plus air fryer oven.
5. Turn Zucchini slices halfway through.
6. Serve and enjoy.

Nutritional Value (Amount per Serving):
Calories 179; Fat 13.9 g; Carbohydrates 11.9 g; Sugar 1.3 g; Protein 1.3 g; Cholesterol 0 mg

Ranch Chicken Wings

Preparation Time: 10 minutes; Cooking Time: 20 minutes; Serve: 4

Ingredients:
- 1 lb chicken wings
- 2 tbsp olive oil
- 1 1/2 tbsp ranch seasoning
- 3 garlic cloves, minced

Directions:
1. Toss chicken wings with garlic, oil, and ranch seasoning.
2. Arrange chicken wings onto the cooking tray.
3. Select AIRFRY mode, then set the temperature to 360 F and the time to 20 minutes, then press start.
4. When the display shows Add Food then place the cooking tray in the vortex plus air fryer oven.
5. Turn chicken wings halfway through.
6. Serve and enjoy.

Nutritional Value (Amount per Serving):
Calories 290; Fat 15.4 g; Carbohydrates 0.7 g; Sugar 0 g; Protein 0 g; Cholesterol 101 mg

Meatballs

Preparation Time: 10 minutes; Cooking Time: 14 minutes; Serve: 4

Ingredients:
- 1 lb ground beef
- 1 cup olives, pitted and chopped
- 1 tbsp oregano, chopped
- 1 tbsp almond flour
- 1 tbsp chives, chopped
- Pepper
- Salt

Directions:
1. Add all ingredients into the mixing bowl and mix until well combined.
2. Make small balls from the meat mixture and place them onto the cooking tray.
3. Select AIRFRY mode, then set the temperature to 400 F and the time to 14 minutes, then press start.
4. When the display shows Add Food then place the cooking tray in the vortex plus air fryer oven.
5. Turn meatballs halfway through.
6. Serve and enjoy.

Nutritional Value (Amount per Serving):
Calories 263; Fat 11.7 g; Carbohydrates 3.3 g; Sugar 0.1 g; Protein 35.2 g; Cholesterol 101 mg

Tasty Parmesan Carrot Fries

Preparation Time: 10 minutes; Cooking Time: 15 minutes; Serve: 4

Ingredients:
- 4 carrots, peeled and cut into fries
- 2 tbsp parmesan cheese, grated
- 2 tbsp olive oil
- Pepper

- Salt

Directions:
1. Add carrots and remaining ingredients into the bowl and toss well.
2. Arrange carrots fries onto the cooking tray.
3. Select AIRFRY mode, then set the temperature to 350 F and the time to 15 minutes, then press start.
4. When the display shows Add Food then place the cooking tray in the vortex plus air fryer oven.
5. Stir halfway through.
6. Serve and enjoy.

Nutritional Value (Amount per Serving):
Calories 98; Fat 7.9 g; Carbohydrates 6.2 g; Sugar 3 g; Protein 1.8 g; Cholesterol 3 mg

Broccoli Cheese Balls

Preparation Time: 10 minutes; Cooking Time: 30 minutes; Serve: 4

Ingredients:
- 2 cups broccoli florets
- 1/4 cup onion, minced
- 1 cup cheddar cheese, shredded
- 1/2 cup almond flour
- 2 eggs, lightly beaten
- 1 tsp Cajun seasoning
- 1 garlic clove, minced
- 2 tbsp fresh cilantro, chopped
- Pepper
- Salt

Directions:
1. Add broccoli into the boiling water and cook until tender.
2. Drain broccoli well and transfer in food processor and process until minced. Transfer to the bowl.
3. Add remaining ingredients and mix until just combined.
4. Make small balls and place them onto the cooking tray.
5. Select BAKE mode, then set the temperature to 400 F and the time to 25-30 minutes, then press start.
6. When the display shows Add Food then place the cooking tray in the vortex plus air fryer oven.
7. Serve and enjoy.

Nutritional Value (Amount per Serving):
Calories 251; Fat 18.8 g; Carbohydrates 8.9 g; Sugar 2.6 g; Protein 14.5 g; Cholesterol 112 mg

Basil Pesto Poppers

Preparation Time: 10 minutes; Cooking Time: 15 minutes; Serve: 6

Ingredients:
- 3 jalapeno peppers, halved and remove seeds
- 1/2 cup cheddar cheese, shredded
- 1/4 cup cream cheese
- 3 tbsp basil pesto

Directions:
1. In a bowl, mix together pesto, shredded cheese, and cream cheese.
2. Stuff pesto cheese mixture into each jalapeno half and place onto the cooking tray.
3. Select BAKE mode, then set the temperature to 400 F and the time to 12-15 minutes, then press start.
4. When the display shows Add Food then place the cooking tray in the vortex plus air fryer oven.
5. Serve and enjoy.

Nutritional Value (Amount per Serving):

Calories 75; Fat 6.6 g; Carbohydrates 0.9 g; Sugar 0.3 g; Protein 3.2 g; Cholesterol 21 mg

Meatballs

Preparation Time: 10 minutes; Cooking Time: 25 minutes; Serve: 6
Ingredients:
- 1 egg, lightly beaten
- 1 lb ground turkey
- 1 tsp garlic powder
- 1 1/2 tbsp olive oil
- 3/4 cup parmesan cheese, grated
- 1/4 cup fresh parsley, chopped
- 1/2 tsp cayenne
- 1 tsp paprika
- 1 tsp onion powder
- 1/2 tsp salt

Directions:
1. Add all ingredients into the mixing bowl and mix until well combined.
2. Make small balls from the meat mixture and place them onto the cooking tray.
3. Select BAKE mode, then set the temperature to 400 F and the time to 25 minutes, then press start.
4. When the display shows Add Food then place the cooking tray in the vortex plus air fryer oven.
5. Serve and enjoy.

Nutritional Value (Amount per Serving):
Calories 229; Fat 15 g; Carbohydrates 1.6 g; Sugar 0.4 g; Protein 25.5 g; Cholesterol 112 mg

Meatballs

Preparation Time: 10 minutes; Cooking Time: 15 minutes; Serve: 8
Ingredients:
- 2 lbs ground turkey
- 1/2 cup coconut flour
- 1 tbsp fresh ginger, grated
- 1 tsp garlic, minced
- 2 tbsp fresh cilantro, chopped
- 2 tbsp green onion, sliced
- 2 eggs, lightly beaten
- 1 tbsp sesame oil
- 1 tsp sea salt

Directions:
1. Add all ingredients into the large bowl and mix until well combined.
2. Make small balls from the meat mixture and place them onto the cooking tray.
3. Select BAKE mode, then set the temperature to 400 F and the time to 15 minutes, then press start.
4. When the display shows Add Food then place the cooking tray in the vortex plus air fryer oven.
5. Serve and enjoy.

Nutritional Value (Amount per Serving):
Calories 259; Fat 15.4 g; Carbohydrates 1.3 g; Sugar 0.2 g; Protein 32.7 g; Cholesterol 157 mg

Tasty Cauliflower Hummus

Preparation Time: 10 minutes; Cooking Time: 35 minutes; Serve: 8
Ingredients:
- 1 cauliflower head, cut into florets
- 1/3 cup tahini
- 3 tbsp olive oil
- 1/2 tsp ground cumin
- 1 tsp garlic, chopped
- 2 tbsp fresh lemon juice
- Pepper
- Salt

Directions:
1. Spread cauliflower onto the cooking tray.

2. Select BAKE mode, then set the temperature to 400 F and the time to 30-35 minutes, then press start.
3. When the display shows Add Food then place the cooking tray in the vortex plus air fryer oven.
4. Transfer roasted cauliflower and remaining ingredients into the food processor and process until smooth.
5. Serve and enjoy.

Nutritional Value (Amount per Serving):
Calories 115; Fat 10.7 g; Carbohydrates 4.2 g; Sugar 0.9 g; Protein 2.4 g; Cholesterol 0 mg

Tasty Cauliflower Tots

Preparation Time: 10 minutes; Cooking Time: 18 minutes; Serve: 16

Ingredients:
- 1 large egg
- 1 tbsp butter
- 2 cups cauliflower, steamed and shredded
- 1/4 tsp onion powder
- 1/4 tsp garlic powder
- 1/2 cup parmesan cheese, shredded
- Pepper
- Salt

Directions:
1. Add all ingredients into the bowl and mix until well combined.
2. Make small tots from mixture and place onto the cooking tray.
3. Select BAKE mode, then set the temperature to 400 F and the time to 18 minutes, then press start.
4. When the display shows Add Food then place the cooking tray in the vortex plus air fryer oven.
5. Serve and enjoy.

Nutritional Value (Amount per Serving):
Calories 23; Fat 1.6 g; Carbohydrates 0.9 g; Sugar 0.3 g; Protein 1.6 g; Cholesterol 16 mg

Chapter 7: Seafood Recipes

Delicious Baked Tilapia

Preparation Time: 10 minutes; Cooking Time: 15 minutes; Serve: 6

Ingredients:
- 6 tilapia fillets, pat dry with a paper towel
- 1/2 cup Asiago cheese, grated
- 1/4 tsp dried basil
- 1/4 tsp dried thyme
- 1/4 tsp onion powder
- 1/4 tsp garlic powder
- 1/2 cup mayonnaise
- 1/8 tsp black pepper
- 1/4 tsp salt

Directions:
1. Arrange tilapia fillets onto the parchment-lined cooking tray.
2. In a small bowl, mix together mayonnaise, garlic powder, onion powder, thyme, basil, cheese, pepper, and salt.
3. Spread mayonnaise mixture on top of each tilapia fillet.
4. Select BAKE mode, then set the temperature to 350 F and the time to 15 minutes, then press start.
5. When the display shows Add Food then place the cooking tray in the vortex plus air fryer oven.
6. Serve and enjoy.

Nutritional Value (Amount per Serving):
Calories 125; Fat 8.9 g; Carbohydrates 4.9 g; Sugar 1.3 g; Protein 6.7 g; Cholesterol 24 mg

Lemon Butter Tilapia

Preparation Time: 10 minutes; Cooking Time: 15 minutes; Serve: 4

Ingredients:
- 4 tilapia fillets
- 1 lemon, sliced
- 1 tsp pepper
- 1 tsp parsley, chopped
- 1 tsp old bay seasoning
- 2 tbsp butter, melted

Directions:
1. Arrange fish fillets onto the cooking tray.
2. In a small bowl, mix together butter, old bay seasoning, parsley, and pepper. Brush fish fillets with butter mixture.
3. Arrange lemon slices on top of fish fillets.
4. Select BAKE mode, then set the temperature to 400 F and the time to 10-15 minutes, then press start.
5. When the display shows Add Food then place the cooking tray in the vortex plus air fryer oven.
6. Serve and enjoy.

Nutritional Value (Amount per Serving):
Calories 131; Fat 6.6 g; Carbohydrates 1.7 g; Sugar 0.4 g; Protein 17 g; Cholesterol 59 mg

Baked Catfish

Preparation Time: 10 minutes; Cooking Time: 20 minutes; Serve: 4

Ingredients:
- 4 catfish fillets
- 1/4 tsp garlic powder
- 2 tbsp butter, melted
- 1 lemon juice
- 1/2 tsp pepper
- 1/2 tsp dried basil
- 1/2 tsp dried oregano
- 1/2 tsp dried thyme
- 3/4 tsp paprika
- 2 tbsp parsley, chopped

- 1 tsp salt

Directions:
1. Place fish fillets into the baking dish.
2. Mix together the remaining ingredients and pour over fish fillets.
3. Select BAKE mode, then set the temperature to 350 F and the time to 15-20 minutes, then press start.
4. When the display shows Add Food then place the baking dish in the vortex plus air fryer oven.
5. Serve and enjoy.

Nutritional Value (Amount per Serving):
Calories 274; Fat 18.1 g; Carbohydrates 1.1 g; Sugar 0.4 g; Protein 25.2 g; Cholesterol 90 mg

Easy Parmesan Tilapia

Preparation Time: 10 minutes; Cooking Time: 12 minutes; Serve: 4

Ingredients:
- 1 lb tilapia fillets
- 1/2 tsp pepper
- 1 tbsp olive oil
- 1 tbsp dried parsley
- 1 tbsp paprika
- 1 cup parmesan cheese, grated
- 1/2 tsp salt

Directions:
1. In a shallow dish, mix together parmesan cheese, paprika, dried parsley, pepper, and salt.
2. Brush fish fillets with oil and coat with parmesan mixture.
3. Place coated fish fillets onto the cooking tray.
4. Select BAKE mode, then set the temperature to 400 F and the time to 12 minutes, then press start.
5. When the display shows Add Food then place the cooking tray in the vortex plus air fryer oven.
6. Serve and enjoy.

Nutritional Value (Amount per Serving):
Calories 202; Fat 9.6 g; Carbohydrates 2 g; Sugar 0.2 g; Protein 28.6 g; Cholesterol 71 mg

Garlic Butter Cod

Preparation Time: 10 minutes; Cooking Time: 20 minutes; Serve: 2

Ingredients:
- 8 oz cod fillets
- 1 tbsp parsley, chopped
- 1/8 tsp paprika
- 2 garlic cloves, minced
- 1 tbsp olive oil
- 2 tbsp butter
- 1/8 tsp salt

Directions:
1. Arrange fish fillets onto the cooking tray.
2. In a small bowl, mix together butter, oil, garlic, paprika, parsley, and salt.
3. Brush fish fillets with butter mixture.
4. Select BAKE mode, then set the temperature to 400 F and the time to 20 minutes, then press start.
5. When the display shows Add Food then place the cooking tray in the vortex plus air fryer oven.
6. Serve and enjoy.

Nutritional Value (Amount per Serving):
Calories 258; Fat 19.6 g; Carbohydrates 1.2 g; Sugar 0.1 g; Protein 20.6 g; Cholesterol 86 mg

Easy Baked Tilapia

Preparation Time: 10 minutes; Cooking Time: 20 minutes; Serve: 4
Ingredients:
- 4 tilapia fillets
- 2 tbsp butter, melted
- 2 tsp paprika
- 1/2 tsp salt

Directions:
1. Arrange fish fillets onto the cooking tray.
2. In a small bowl, mix together butter, paprika, and salt.
3. Brush fish fillets with butter mixture.
4. Select BAKE mode, then set the temperature to 400 F and the time to 15-20 minutes, then press start.
5. When the display shows Add Food then place the cooking tray in the vortex plus air fryer oven.
6. Serve and enjoy.

Nutritional Value (Amount per Serving):
Calories 128; Fat 6.7 g; Carbohydrates 0.6 g; Sugar 0.1 g; Protein 17 g; Cholesterol 59 mg

Baked Parmesan Cod

Preparation Time: 10 minutes; Cooking Time: 15 minutes; Serve: 2
Ingredients:
- 2 cod fillets
- 1/4 tbsp olive oil
- 1/2 tsp parsley
- 1/2 tsp paprika
- 1/4 cup parmesan cheese, grated
- Pepper
- Salt

Directions:
1. In a shallow dish, mix together parmesan cheese, paprika, and parsley.
2. Brush fish fillets with oil and season with pepper and salt.
3. Coat fish fillets with parmesan cheese mixture and place onto the cooking tray.
4. Select BAKE mode, then set the temperature to 400 F and the time to 15 minutes, then press start.
5. When the display shows Add Food then place the cooking tray in the vortex plus air fryer oven.
6. Serve and enjoy.

Nutritional Value (Amount per Serving):
Calories 143; Fat 5.2 g; Carbohydrates 0.8 g; Sugar 0.1 g; Protein 23.7 g; Cholesterol 63 mg

Delicious Baked Cod

Preparation Time: 10 minutes; Cooking Time: 25 minutes; Serve: 4
Ingredients:
- 1 lb cod fillets
- 1 1/2 tsp lemon juice
- 1 tsp olive oil
- 1 garlic clove, chopped
- 1/2 tsp pepper
- 1/2 tsp ground cumin
- 1/8 tsp ground turmeric
- 1/2 tsp salt

Directions:
1. Add fish fillets and remaining ingredients into the zip-lock bag, seal bag, and place in the refrigerator overnight.
2. Place marinated fish fillets onto the cooking tray.
3. Select BAKE mode, then set the temperature to 400 F and the time to 20-25 minutes, then press start.

4. When the display shows Add Food then place the cooking tray in the vortex plus air fryer oven.
5. Serve and enjoy.

Nutritional Value (Amount per Serving):
Calories 105; Fat 2.3 g; Carbohydrates 0.6 g; Sugar 0.1 g; Protein 20.4 g; Cholesterol 56 mg

Lemon Parmesan Cod

Preparation Time: 10 minutes; Cooking Time: 15 minutes; Serve: 4

Ingredients:
- 1 1/2 lbs cod fillets, boneless
- 1 tsp paprika
- 3/4 cup parmesan cheese, grated
- 2 garlic cloves, minced
- 1/4 cup butter, melted

Directions:
1. In a small dish, mix together butter and garlic.
2. In a shallow dish, mix together parmesan cheese and paprika.
3. Dip fish fillet in butter mixture then coats with parmesan mixture and place onto the cooking tray.
4. Select BAKE mode, then set the temperature to 400 F and the time to 15 minutes, then press start.
5. When the display shows Add Food then place the cooking tray in the vortex plus air fryer oven.
6. Serve and enjoy.

Nutritional Value (Amount per Serving):
Calories 296; Fat 16.7 g; Carbohydrates 1.4 g; Sugar 0.1 g; Protein 36.1 g; Cholesterol 103 mg

Garlic Herb Cod

Preparation Time: 10 minutes; Cooking Time: 12 minutes; Serve: 4

Ingredients:
- 2 lbs cod fillets
- 1 garlic clove, grated
- 2 tbsp parsley, chopped
- 2 tbsp basil, chopped
- 1/3 cup parmesan cheese, grated
- 1/3 cup mayonnaise
- Pepper
- Salt

Directions:
1. Arrange fish fillets onto the cooking tray.
2. In a small bowl, mix together mayonnaise, cheese, basil, parsley, garlic, pepper, and salt.
3. Spread mayonnaise mixture on top of fish fillets.
4. Select BAKE mode, then set the temperature to 400 F and the time to 10-12 minutes, then press start.
5. When the display shows Add Food then place the cooking tray in the vortex plus air fryer oven.
6. Serve and enjoy.

Nutritional Value (Amount per Serving):
Calories 285; Fat 10.2 g; Carbohydrates 5.4 g; Sugar 1.3 g; Protein 43.2 g; Cholesterol 122 mg

Lemon Pepper Sea Bass

Preparation Time: 10 minutes; Cooking Time: 20 minutes; Serve: 1

Ingredients:
- 3.5 oz sea bass fillet
- 1/2 tsp paprika
- 1/2 tsp lemon pepper
- 1/2 lemon juice
- 2 garlic cloves, minced
- 1/2 tsp pink salt

Directions:
1. Place the fish fillet in a baking dish.
2. Mix together lemon juice, garlic, lemon pepper, paprika, and salt and pour over the fish fillet.
3. Select BAKE mode, then set the temperature to 400 F and the time to 15-20 minutes, then press start.
4. When the display shows Add Food then place the baking dish in the vortex plus air fryer oven.
5. Serve and enjoy.

Nutritional Value (Amount per Serving):
Calories 143; Fat 2.9 g; Carbohydrates 3.7 g; Sugar 0.7 g; Protein 24.3 g; Cholesterol 53 mg

Lemon Butter Shrimp

Preparation Time: 10 minutes; Cooking Time: 12 minutes; Serve: 4

Ingredients:
- 1 1/2 lbs shrimp, peeled & deveined
- 2 tbsp parsley, chopped
- 1/8 tsp chili flakes
- 2 tbsp lemon juice
- 1 tbsp garlic, minced
- 1/4 cup butter, melted
- Pepper
- Salt

Directions:
1. Add shrimp and remaining ingredients into the baking dish and mix well.
2. Select BAKE mode, then set the temperature to 350 F and the time to 10-12 minutes, then press start.
3. When the display shows Add Food then place the baking dish in the vortex plus air fryer oven.
4. Serve and enjoy.

Nutritional Value (Amount per Serving):
Calories 310; Fat 14.5 g; Carbohydrates 3.6 g; Sugar 0.2 g; Protein 39.1 g; Cholesterol 389 mg

Shrimp with Cherry Tomatoes

Preparation Time: 10 minutes; Cooking Time: 25 minutes; Serve: 4

Ingredients:
- 1 lb shrimp, peeled and deveined
- 1 tbsp olive oil
- 4 garlic cloves, sliced
- 2 cups grape tomatoes
- 1/2 tsp salt

Directions:
1. Add shrimp and remaining ingredients into the baking dish and mix well.
2. Select BAKE mode, then set the temperature to 400 F and the time to 25 minutes, then press start.
3. When the display shows Add Food then place the baking dish in the vortex plus air fryer oven.
4. Serve and enjoy.

Nutritional Value (Amount per Serving):
Calories 185; Fat 5.6 g; Carbohydrates 6.2 g; Sugar 2.4 g; Protein 26.8 g; Cholesterol 239 mg

Greek Shrimp

Preparation Time: 10 minutes; Cooking Time: 20 minutes; Serve: 4

Ingredients:
- 1 lb shrimp, peeled and deveined
- 3/4 cup feta cheese, crumbled
- 1/8 tsp red chili flakes
- 1/2 tsp oregano

- 2 garlic cloves, minced
- 1 tbsp olive oil
- 14.5 oz can tomato, diced
- 1/4 tsp salt

Directions:
1. Add shrimp into the baking dish. Mix together remaining ingredients and pour over shrimp.
2. Select BAKE mode, then set the temperature to 375 F and the time to 20 minutes, then press start.
3. When the display shows Add Food then place the baking dish in the vortex plus air fryer oven.
4. Serve and enjoy.

Nutritional Value (Amount per Serving):
Calories 164; Fat 11.4 g; Carbohydrates 8.7 g; Sugar 4.7 g; Protein 30.9 g; Cholesterol 264 mg

Flavorful Baked Shrimp

Preparation Time: 10 minutes; Cooking Time: 10 minutes; Serve: 4

Ingredients:
- 1 lb shrimp, peeled & deveined
- 1/8 tsp ground pepper
- 1/4 tsp onion powder
- 1/4 tsp cumin
- 1/2 tsp garlic powder
- 1/2 tsp chili powder
- 2 tbsp olive oil
- 1/4 tsp sea salt

Directions:
1. In a large bowl, toss shrimp with remaining ingredients.
2. Transfer shrimp into the baking dish.
3. Select BAKE mode, then set the temperature to 400 F and the time to 10 minutes, then press start.
4. When the display shows Add Food then place the baking dish in the vortex plus air fryer oven.
5. Serve and enjoy.

Nutritional Value (Amount per Serving):
Calories 198; Fat 9 g; Carbohydrates 2.4 g; Sugar 0.2 g; Protein 26 g; Cholesterol 239 mg

Italian Shrimp

Preparation Time: 10 minutes; Cooking Time: 10 minutes; Serve: 4

Ingredients:
- 1 lb shrimp, peeled & deveined
- 3/4 cup fresh Italian parsley
- 1/2 cup olive oil
- 3 tbsp lemon juice
- 1/4 tsp pepper
- 1/4 tsp salt

Directions:
1. Add shrimp into the baking dish.
2. Add parsley, oil, lemon juice, pepper, and salt into the blender and blend until smooth.
3. Pour blended mixture over shrimp and mix well.
4. Select BAKE mode, then set the temperature to 400 F and the time to 10 minutes, then press start.
5. When the display shows Add Food then place the baking dish in the vortex plus air fryer oven.
6. Serve and enjoy.

Nutritional Value (Amount per Serving):
Calories 358; Fat 27.3 g; Carbohydrates 2.8 g; Sugar 0.3 g; Protein 26.3 g; Cholesterol 239 mg

Lemon Dill White Fish Fillets

Preparation Time: 10 minutes; Cooking Time: 25 minutes; Serve: 2
Ingredients:
- 2 white fish fillets
- 2 tbsp butter, melted
- 1 tsp dried dill

Directions:
1. Place fish fillets in the baking dish.
2. Mix together melted butter and dill and pour over fish fillets.
3. Select BAKE mode, then set the temperature to 400 F and the time to 15-25 minutes, then press start.
4. When the display shows Add Food then place the baking dish in the vortex plus air fryer oven.
5. Serve and enjoy.

Nutritional Value (Amount per Serving):
Calories 368; Fat 23.1 g; Carbohydrates 0.3 g; Sugar 0 g; Protein 37.9 g; Cholesterol 149 mg

Herb Salmon

Preparation Time: 10 minutes; Cooking Time: 8 minutes; Serve: 2
Ingredients:
- 8 oz salmon fillets
- 1 tbsp butter, melted
- 2 tbsp olive oil
- 1/4 tsp pepper
- 1 tsp herb de province
- 1/4 tsp sea salt

Directions:
1. In a small bowl, mix together oil, pepper, herb de Provence, and salt.
2. Brush salmon fillets with oil and place them onto the cooking tray.
3. Select AIRFRY mode, then set the temperature to 390 F and the time to 5-8 minutes, then press start.
4. When the display shows Add Food then place the cooking tray in the vortex plus air fryer oven.
5. Pour melted butter over salmon and serve.

Nutritional Value (Amount per Serving):
Calories 353; Fat 27.8 g; Carbohydrates 0.2 g; Sugar 0 g; Protein 27.4 g; Cholesterol 39 mg

Flavorful Crab Cakes

Preparation Time: 10 minutes; Cooking Time: 10 minutes; Serve: 4
Ingredients:
- 8 oz lump crab meat
- 1 tsp old bay seasoning
- 1 tbsp Dijon mustard
- 2 tbsp almond flour
- 2 tbsp mayonnaise
- 2 green onion, chopped
- 1/4 cup bell pepper, chopped

Directions:
1. Add all ingredients into the mixing bowl and mix until well combined.
2. Make small patties from mixture and place onto the parchment-lined cooking tray.
3. Select AIRFRY mode, then set the temperature to 370 F and the time to 10 minutes, then press start.
4. When the display shows Add Food then place the cooking tray in the vortex plus air fryer oven.
5. Serve and enjoy.

Nutritional Value (Amount per Serving):
Calories 97; Fat 9 g; Carbohydrates 4.7 g; Sugar 1.2 g; Protein 9.4 g; Cholesterol 34 mg

Lemon Garlic Scallops

Preparation Time: 10 minutes; Cooking Time: 10 minutes; Serve: 2
Ingredients:
- 8 scallops, cleaned and pat dry
- 1/2 tsp garlic, chopped
- 1 tsp lemon zest, grated
- 2 tsp capers, chopped
- 2 tbsp parsley, chopped
- 1/4 cup olive oil
- 1/4 tsp pepper
- 1/8 tsp salt

Directions:
1. Add scallops and remaining ingredients into the baking dish and mix well.
2. Select AIRFRY mode, then set the temperature to 400 F and the time to 12 minutes, then press start.
3. When the display shows Add Food then place the baking dish in the vortex plus air fryer oven.
4. Flip scallops halfway through.
5. Serve and enjoy.

Nutritional Value (Amount per Serving):
Calories 326; Fat 26.2 g; Carbohydrates 3.8 g; Sugar 0.1 g; Protein 20.4 g; Cholesterol 40 mg

Broiled Tilapia

Preparation Time: 10 minutes; Cooking Time: 5 minutes; Serve: 6
Ingredients:
- 24 oz tilapia fish fillets
- 1/4 tsp cinnamon
- 1/2 tsp paprika
- 1 tsp dry mustard powder
- 1/2 tsp basil
- 1 tbsp olive oil
- 2 lemons, sliced
- 1/8 tsp cayenne pepper
- 1/2 tsp salt

Directions:
1. In a small bowl, mix together all dry spices.
2. Place fish fillets onto the parchment-lined cooking tray. Brush fish fillets with oil and sprinkle with spice mixture.
3. Arrange lemon slices on top of fish fillets and place the cooking tray in vortex plus air fryer oven.
4. Select BROIL mode, then set the temperature to 400 F and the time to 5 minutes, then press start.
5. Serve and enjoy.

Nutritional Value (Amount per Serving):
Calories 33; Fat 2.6 g; Carbohydrates 2.2 g; Sugar 0.5 g; Protein 1.3 g; Cholesterol 2 mg

Salmon with Tomato Salsa

Preparation Time: 10 minutes; Cooking Time: 15 minutes; Serve: 4
Ingredients:
- 4 salmon fillets
- 2 tbsp olive oil
- 1/4 tsp pepper
- 1/2 tsp salt

For salsa:
- 2 tsp olive oil
- 2 tsp fresh lemon juice
- 1 tbsp fresh parsley, chopped
- 1 tbsp fresh basil, chopped
- 2 tbsp onion, chopped
- 1 cup zucchini, chopped
- 1 1/2 cups tomato, chopped
- 1 garlic clove, minced
- 1 1/2 tsp capers
- 1/2 bell pepper, chopped
- 1/8 tsp pepper
- 1/4 tsp salt

Directions:
1. Place salmon in a greased baking dish and drizzle with oil and season with pepper and salt.
2. Select BAKE mode, then set the temperature to 400 F and the time to 12-15 minutes, then press start.
3. When the display shows Add Food then place the baking dish in the vortex plus air fryer oven.
4. In a bowl, mix together all salsa ingredients.
5. Top fish fillets with salsa and serve.

Nutritional Value (Amount per Serving):
Calories 342; Fat 20.6 g; Carbohydrates 5.7 g; Sugar 3.3 g; Protein 35.8 g; Cholesterol 78 mg

Delicious Tuna Patties

Preparation Time: 10 minutes; Cooking Time: 20 minutes; Serve: 4
Ingredients:
- 14.5 oz can tuna, drained
- 1 tbsp garlic, minced
- 2 eggs, lightly beaten
- 1/4 cup almond flour
- 1/2 cup parsley, chopped
- 1 tbsp Dijon mustard
- Pepper
- Salt

Directions:
1. In a mixing bowl, mix together tuna, parsley, mustard, garlic, eggs, almond flour, pepper, and salt.
2. Make small patties from mixture and place onto the parchment-lined cooking tray.
3. Select BAKE mode, then set the temperature to 400 F and the time to 20 minutes, then press start.
4. When the display shows Add Food then place the cooking tray in the vortex plus air fryer oven.
5. Turn patties halfway through.
6. Serve and enjoy.

Nutritional Value (Amount per Serving):
Calories 199; Fat 6.8 g; Carbohydrates 3.1 g; Sugar 0.5 g; Protein 31 g; Cholesterol 113 mg

Feta Tuna Patties

Preparation Time: 10 minutes; Cooking Time: 15 minutes; Serve: 6
Ingredients:
- 10 oz can tuna, drained
- 1 tbsp lemon juice
- 2 tbsp green onion, minced
- 3 tbsp flax meal
- 1/2 cup feta cheese, crumbled
- 1 egg, lightly beaten
- 1 garlic clove, minced
- 1/2 tsp lemon zest
- 1 tsp dried oregano
- 2 tbsp fresh mint, chopped

Directions:
1. Add all ingredients into the bowl and mix until well combined.
2. Make small patties from tuna mixture and place onto the parchment-lined cooking tray.
3. Select BAKE mode, then set the temperature to 400 F and the time to 12-15 minutes, then press start.
4. When the display shows Add Food then place the cooking tray in the vortex plus air fryer oven.
5. Turn patties halfway through.
6. Serve and enjoy.

Nutritional Value (Amount per Serving):

Calories 117; Fat 5.1 g; Carbohydrates 2.3 g; Sugar 0.7 g; Protein 15.7 g; Cholesterol 53 mg

Salmon with Spread

Preparation Time: 10 minutes; Cooking Time: 35 minutes; Serve: 6

Ingredients:
- 6 salmon fillets
- 2 garlic cloves, minced
- 1/2 lemon juice

For spread:
- 1/2 cup olives, chopped
- 4 tomatoes, diced
- 3 tbsp fresh basil, chopped
- 1/2 cup feta cheese, crumbled
- Pepper
- Salt

Directions:
1. Place salmon fillets into the baking dish.
2. Pour lemon juice over fish fillets and sprinkle with garlic.
3. Select BAKE mode, then set the temperature to 375 F and the time to 25-30 minutes, then press start.
4. When the display shows Add Food then place the baking dish in the vortex plus air fryer oven.
5. In a bowl, mix together all spread ingredients.
6. Top cooked salmon with spread and serve.

Nutritional Value (Amount per Serving):
Calories 299; Fat 15.1 g; Carbohydrates 4.9 g; Sugar 2.8 g; Protein 37.3 g; Cholesterol 90 mg

Rosemary Salmon

Preparation Time: 10 minutes; Cooking Time: 20 minutes; Serve: 2

Ingredients:
- 2 salmon fillets
- 4 fresh rosemary sprigs
- 1 lemon, sliced
- 1 tbsp olive oil
- Salt

Directions:
1. Place half lemon slices and 2 rosemary sprigs into the baking dish and top with salmon fillets.
2. Arrange remaining lemon slices and rosemary sprigs on top of salmon fillets.
3. Drizzle fish fillet with oil and season with salt.
4. Select BAKE mode, then set the temperature to 400 F and the time to 20 minutes, then press start.
5. When the display shows Add Food then place the baking dish in the vortex plus air fryer oven.
6. Serve and enjoy.

Nutritional Value (Amount per Serving):
Calories 312; Fat 18.5 g; Carbohydrates 4.2 g; Sugar 0.7 g; Protein 35 g; Cholesterol 78 mg

Basil Tomato Salmon

Preparation Time: 10 minutes; Cooking Time: 20 minutes; Serve: 2

Ingredients:
- 2 salmon fillets
- 1 tomato, sliced
- 1 tbsp dried basil
- 2 tbsp parmesan cheese, grated
- 1 tbsp olive oil
- Pepper
- Salt

Directions:

1. Place fish fillets int a baking dish. Season with basil.
2. Arrange tomato slices on top of salmon fillets. Drizzle with oil and sprinkle cheese on top.
3. Select BAKE mode, then set the temperature to 375 F and the time to 20 minutes, then press start.
4. When the display shows Add Food then place the baking dish in the vortex plus air fryer oven.
5. Serve and enjoy.

Nutritional Value (Amount per Serving):
Calories 319; Fat 19.2 g; Carbohydrates 1.5 g; Sugar 0.8 g; Protein 36.6 g; Cholesterol 82 mg

Lemon Herb Tilapia

Preparation Time: 10 minutes; Cooking Time: 18 minutes; Serve: 4
Ingredients:
- 1 lb tilapia fillets
- 1 tsp fresh lemon juice
- 2 tsp olive oil
- 1/2 tsp garlic powder
- 1/2 tsp dried thyme
- 1/2 tsp dried oregano
- 1/4 tsp pepper
- 1 tsp salt

Directions:
1. Brush fish fillets with oil and lemon juice and place onto the parchment-lined cooking tray.
2. In a small bowl, mix oregano, garlic powder, thyme, pepper, and salt and sprinkle over fish fillets.
3. Select BAKE mode, then set the temperature to 400 F and the time to 15-18 minutes, then press start.
4. When the display shows Add Food then place the cooking tray in the vortex plus air fryer oven.
5. Serve and enjoy.

Nutritional Value (Amount per Serving):
Calories 116; Fat 3.4 g; Carbohydrates 0.6 g; Sugar 0.1 g; Protein 21.2 g; Cholesterol 55 mg

Italian Baked Cod

Preparation Time: 10 minutes; Cooking Time: 20 minutes; Serve: 4
Ingredients:
- 1 1/2 lbs cod fillet
- 1 tbsp olive oil
- 1 lb cherry tomatoes, halved
- 2 garlic cloves, crushed
- 1 small onion, chopped
- 1/4 cup of water
- 1 tsp Italian seasoning
- 1/4 cup olives, sliced
- Pepper
- Salt

Directions:
1. Place fish fillets, olives, tomatoes, garlic, and onion in a greased baking dish.
2. Drizzle with oil and sprinkle with Italian seasoning, pepper, and salt. Pour water into the dish.
3. Select BAKE mode, then set the temperature to 400 F and the time to 15-20 minutes, then press start.
4. When the display shows Add Food then place the baking dish in the vortex plus air fryer oven.
5. Serve and enjoy.

Nutritional Value (Amount per Serving):
Calories 210; Fat 6.5 g; Carbohydrates 7.2 g; Sugar 3.8 g; Protein 31.7 g; Cholesterol 84 mg

Air Fryer Catfish

Preparation Time: 10 minutes; Cooking Time: 20 minutes; Serve: 4
Ingredients:
- 4 catfish fillets
- 1 tbsp olive oil
- 1 tbsp parsley, chopped
- Pepper
- Salt

Directions:
1. Brush fish fillets with oil and season with pepper and salt.
2. Place fish fillets onto the parchment-lined cooking tray. Sprinkle parsley on top of fish fillets.
3. Select AIRFRY mode, then set the temperature to 400 F and the time to 20 minutes, then press start.
4. When the display shows Add Food then place the cooking tray in the vortex plus air fryer oven.
5. Turn fish fillets halfway through.
6. Serve and enjoy.

Nutritional Value (Amount per Serving):
Calories 246; Fat 15.7 g; Carbohydrates 0.1 g; Sugar 0 g; Protein 24.9 g; Cholesterol 75 mg

Shrimp & Vegetables

Preparation Time: 10 minutes; Cooking Time: 20 minutes; Serve: 4
Ingredients:
- 2 lbs shrimp, peeled and deveined
- 1 bag of frozen mixed vegetables
- 1 tbsp Cajun seasoning
- Pepper
- Salt

Directions:
1. Arrange shrimp and vegetables onto the cooking tray and season with cajun seasoning, pepper, and salt.
2. Select AIRFRY mode, then set the temperature to 350 F and the time to 20 minutes, then press start.
3. When the display shows Add Food then place the cooking tray in the vortex plus air fryer oven.
4. Stir shrimp and vegetables halfway through.
5. Serve and enjoy.

Nutritional Value (Amount per Serving):
Calories 314; Fat 3.9 g; Carbohydrates 12.5 g; Sugar 2.2 g; Protein 53.7 g; Cholesterol 478 mg

Garlic Lemon Shrimp

Preparation Time: 10 minutes; Cooking Time: 8 minutes; Serve: 4
Ingredients:
- 1 lb shrimp, peeled
- 1 lemon juice
- 1 lemon zest
- 4 garlic cloves, minced
- 1 tbsp olive oil
- 1/4 cup parsley, chopped
- 1/4 tsp red pepper flakes
- 1/4 tsp sea salt

Directions:
1. Add all ingredients into the bowl and toss well and transfer into the baking dish.
2. Select AIRFRY mode, then set the temperature to 400 F and the time to 5-8 minutes, then press start.
3. When the display shows Add Food then place the baking dish in the vortex plus air fryer oven.

4. Serve and enjoy.

Nutritional Value (Amount per Serving):
   Calories 178; Fat 5.6 g; Carbohydrates 4.6 g; Sugar 0.7 g; Protein 26.4 g; Cholesterol 239 mg

Air Fryer Shrimp Scampi

Preparation Time: 10 minutes; Cooking Time: 6 minutes; Serve: 4

Ingredients:
- 1 lb shrimp
- 2 tsp red pepper flakes
- 1 tbsp garlic, minced
- 1 tbsp fresh lemon juice
- 4 tbsp butter
- 2 tbsp white wine
- 1 tsp dried basil
- 1 tsp dried chives

Directions:
1. Add all ingredients into the baking dish and mix well.
2. Select AIRFRY mode, then set the temperature to 350 and the time to 5-6 minutes, then press start.
3. When the display shows Add Food then place the cooking tray in the vortex plus air fryer oven.
4. Serve and enjoy.

Nutritional Value (Amount per Serving):
   Calories 250; Fat 13.6 g; Carbohydrates 3.2 g; Sugar 0.3 g; Protein 26.3 g; Cholesterol 269 mg

Spicy Shrimp

Preparation Time: 10 minutes; Cooking Time: 10 minutes; Serve: 2

Ingredients:
- 1/2 lb shrimp, peeled and deveined
- 1/4 tsp cayenne pepper
- 1/4 tsp paprika
- 1/2 tsp old bay seasoning
- Pinch of salt

Directions:
1. Add all ingredients into the mixing bowl and mix well.
2. Transfer shrimp onto the parchment-lined cooking tray.
3. Select AIRFRY mode, then set the temperature to 390 F and the time to 8-10 minutes, then press start.
4. When the display shows Add Food then place the cooking tray in the vortex plus air fryer oven.
5. Serve and enjoy.

Nutritional Value (Amount per Serving):
   Calories 136; Fat 2 g; Carbohydrates 2 g; Sugar 0.1 g; Protein 25.9 g; Cholesterol 239 mg

Air Fryer Mackerel

Preparation Time: 10 minutes; Cooking Time: 20 minutes; Serve: 2

Ingredients:
- 1 1/2 lbs mackerel fish fillets
- 1/2 tsp olive oil
- Pepper
- Salt

Directions:
1. Place the fish fillet in a baking dish and drizzle with oil and season with pepper and salt.
2. Select AIRFRY mode, then set the temperature to 390 F and the time to 20 minutes, then press start.
3. When the display shows Add Food then place the baking dish in the vortex plus air fryer oven.
4. Serve and enjoy.

Nutritional Value (Amount per Serving):
Calories 185; Fat 13.9 g; Carbohydrates 0 g; Sugar 0 g; Protein 15 g; Cholesterol 0 mg

Air Fryer Hot Shrimp

Preparation Time: 10 minutes; Cooking Time: 8 minutes; Serve: 4
Ingredients:
- 12 shrimp
- 1 tsp chili flakes
- 1/2 tsp pepper
- 1 tsp chili powder
- 1/2 tsp salt

Directions:
1. Add all ingredients to the bowl and toss well.
2. Add marinated shrimp onto the parchment-lined cooking tray.
3. Select AIRFRY mode, then set the temperature to 350 F and the time to 8 minutes, then press start.
4. When the display shows Add Food then place the cooking tray in the vortex plus air fryer oven.
5. Serve and enjoy.

Nutritional Value (Amount per Serving):
Calories 81; Fat 1.2 g; Carbohydrates 1.6 g; Sugar 0.1 g; Protein 15.2 g; Cholesterol 139 mg

Creole Seasoned Shrimp

Preparation Time: 10 minutes; Cooking Time: 7 minutes; Serve: 2
Ingredients:
- 1/2 lb shrimp, deveined and shelled
- 1 tsp Creole seasoning
- 1 tsp vinegar
- 1/8 tsp cayenne pepper
- 1/4 tsp paprika
- 1 tbsp olive oil

Directions:
1. Add all ingredients into the bowl and mix well.
2. Add marinated shrimp into the baking dish.
3. Select AIRFRY mode, then set the temperature to 400 F and the time to 5-7 minutes, then press start.
4. When the display shows Add Food then place the baking dish in the vortex plus air fryer oven.
5. Serve and enjoy.

Nutritional Value (Amount per Serving):
Calories 196; Fat 9 g; Carbohydrates 1.9 g; Sugar 0.1 g; Protein 25.9 g; Cholesterol 239 mg

Shrimp with Cherry Tomatoes

Preparation Time: 10 minutes; Cooking Time: 25 minutes; Serve: 4
Ingredients:
- 2 cups cherry tomatoes
- 1 tbsp olive oil
- 1 lb shrimp, peeled
- 1 tbsp garlic, sliced
- Pepper
- Salt

Directions:
1. Add shrimp, oil, garlic, tomatoes, pepper, and salt into the bowl and toss well.
2. Transfer shrimp mixture into the baking dish.
3. Select AIRFRY mode, then set the temperature to 400 F and the time to 25 minutes, then press start.
4. When the display shows Add Food then place the baking dish in the vortex plus air fryer oven.

5. Serve and enjoy.

Nutritional Value (Amount per Serving):
Calories 184; Fat 5.6 g; Carbohydrates 5.9 g; Sugar 2.4 g; Protein 26.8 g; Cholesterol 239 mg

Spicy Lemon Garlic Shrimp

Preparation Time: 10 minutes; Cooking Time: 6 minutes; Serve: 4

Ingredients:
- 1 lb shrimp
- 1 tsp steak seasoning
- 1/4 tsp red pepper flakes
- 2 garlic cloves, minced
- 1 tbsp parsley, chopped
- 2 tsp fresh lemon juice
- 1 tsp lemon zest, grated
- 2 tsp olive oil
- Pepper
- Salt

Directions:
1. Add shrimp and remaining ingredients into the bowl and toss well.
2. Transfer shrimp onto the cooking tray.
3. Select AIRFRY mode, then set the temperature to 400 F and the time to 6 minutes, then press start.
4. When the display shows Add Food then place the cooking tray in the vortex plus air fryer oven.
5. Serve and enjoy.

Nutritional Value (Amount per Serving):
Calories 159; Fat 4.3 g; Carbohydrates 2.5 g; Sugar 0.1 g; Protein 26 g; Cholesterol 239 mg

Flavorful Crab Cakes

Preparation Time: 10 minutes; Cooking Time: 10 minutes; Serve: 5

Ingredients:
- 18 oz can crab meat, drained
- 1 tsp Old bay seasoning
- 1 1/2 tbsp Dijon mustard
- 2 1/2 tbsp mayonnaise
- 2 eggs, lightly beaten
- 1/4 cup almond flour
- 1 1/2 tsp dried parsley
- 1 tbsp dried celery
- Pepper
- Salt

Directions:
1. Add all ingredients into the bowl and mix until well combined.
2. Make small patties from mixture and place onto the parchment-lined cooking tray.
3. Select AIRFRY mode, then set the temperature to 320 F and the time to 10 minutes, then press start.
4. When the display shows Add Food then place the cooking tray in the vortex plus air fryer oven.
5. Serve and enjoy.

Nutritional Value (Amount per Serving):
Calories 151; Fat 7.1 g; Carbohydrates 5.1 g; Sugar 2.4 g; Protein 17.3 g; Cholesterol 127 mg

Lemon Pepper Tilapia

Preparation Time: 10 minutes; Cooking Time: 10 minutes; Serve: 2

Ingredients:
- 2 tilapia fillets
- 1/2 tsp lemon pepper seasoning
- 1/2 tsp garlic powder
- 1/2 tsp onion powder
- Salt

Directions:

1. Spray tilapia with cooking spray and season with lemon pepper seasoning, garlic powder, onion powder, and salt.
2. Place tilapia onto the parchment-lined cooking tray.
3. Select AIRFRY mode, then set the temperature to 360 F and the time to 10 minutes, then press start.
4. When the display shows Add Food then place the cooking tray in the vortex plus air fryer oven.
5. Serve and enjoy.

Nutritional Value (Amount per Serving):
Calories 99; Fat 1.1 g; Carbohydrates 1.3 g; Sugar 0.4 g; Protein 21.3 g; Cholesterol 55 mg

Easy Salmon Patties

Preparation Time: 10 minutes; Cooking Time: 7 minutes; Serve: 2
Ingredients:
- 1 egg, lightly beaten
- 8 oz salmon fillet, minced
- 1/4 tsp garlic powder
- Pepper
- Salt

Directions:
1. Add all ingredients into the bowl and mix until well combined.
2. Make small patties from salmon mixture and place onto the parchment-lined cooking tray.
3. Select AIRFRY mode, then set the temperature to 390 F and the time to 7 minutes, then press start.
4. When the display shows Add Food then place the cooking tray in the vortex plus air fryer oven.
5. Serve and enjoy.

Nutritional Value (Amount per Serving):
Calories 183; Fat 9.2 g; Carbohydrates 0.5 g; Sugar 0.3 g; Protein 24.8 g; Cholesterol 132 mg

Herb Butter Salmon

Preparation Time: 10 minutes; Cooking Time: 5 minutes; Serve: 2
Ingredients:
- 2 salmon fillets
- 1/4 tsp paprika
- 1 tsp herb de Provence
- 1 tbsp butter, melted
- 2 tbsp olive oil
- Pepper
- Salt

Directions:
1. Brush salmon fillets with oil and sprinkle with paprika, herb de Provence, pepper, and salt.
2. Place salmon fillets onto the parchment-lined cooking tray.
3. Select AIRFRY mode, then set the temperature to 390 F and the time to 5 minutes, then press start.
4. When the display shows Add Food then place the cooking tray in the vortex plus air fryer oven.
5. Drizzle melted butter over salmon and serve.

Nutritional Value (Amount per Serving):
Calories 411; Fat 31 g; Carbohydrates 0.2 g; Sugar 0 g; Protein 35.1 g; Cholesterol 94 mg

Lemon Herb Tilapia

Preparation Time: 10 minutes; Cooking Time: 15 minutes; Serve: 4
Ingredients:

- 1 lb tilapia
- 1 lemon, sliced
- 1 tsp fresh lemon juice
- 2 tsp olive oil
- 1 tsp garlic powder
- 1/2 tsp dried thyme
- 1/2 tsp dried oregano
- 1/2 tsp pepper
- 1 tsp salt

Directions:
1. Place a fish fillets in a baking dish and brush with lemon juice and olive oil.
2. Mix together garlic powder, thyme, oregano, pepper, and salt and sprinkle over fish fillets.
3. Arrange lemon slices on top of fish fillet.
4. Select BAKE mode, then set the temperature to 400 F and the time to 15-18 minutes, then press start.
5. When the display shows Add Food then place the baking dish in the vortex plus air fryer oven.
6. Serve and enjoy.

Nutritional Value (Amount per Serving):
Calories 122; Fat 3.5 g; Carbohydrates 2.3 g; Sugar 0.6 g; Protein 21.4 g; Cholesterol 55 mg

Greek Salmon

Preparation Time: 10 minutes; Cooking Time: 15 minutes; Serve: 2
Ingredients:
- 2 salmon filets
- 1/2 cup olives, chopped
- 1 tbsp balsamic vinegar
- 1 tbsp olive oil
- 1 tbsp parsley, chopped
- 1/3 cup feta cheese, crumbled
- 1/2 cup tomato, diced
- Pepper
- Salt

Directions:
1. Season salmon with pepper and salt.
2. Place salmon on the cooking tray.
3. Select BAKE mode, then set the temperature to 350 F and the time to 15 minutes, then press start.
4. When the display shows Add Food then place the cooking tray in the vortex plus air fryer oven.
5. Meanwhile, mix together tomato, olive oil, vinegar, olives, feta cheese, and parsley.
6. Remove salmon from oven and top with tomato mixture.
7. Serve and enjoy.

Nutritional Value (Amount per Serving):
Calories 275; Fat 17 g; Carbohydrates 5.1 g; Sugar 2.3 g; Protein 28.3 g; Cholesterol 67 mg

Orange Chili Salmon

Preparation Time: 10 minutes; Cooking Time: 20 minutes; Serve: 4
Ingredients:
- 2 lbs salmon fillet, skinless and boneless
- 2 lemon juice
- 1 orange juice
- 1 tbsp olive oil
- 1 bunch fresh dill
- 1 chili, sliced
- Pepper
- Salt

Directions:
1. Place salmon fillets in a baking dish and drizzle with olive oil, lemon juice, and orange juice.
2. Sprinkle chili slices over the salmon and season with pepper and salt.

3. Select BAKE mode, then set the temperature to 350 F and the time to 20 minutes, then press start.
4. When the display shows Add Food then place the baking dish in the vortex plus air fryer oven.
5. Garnish with dill and serve.

Nutritional Value (Amount per Serving):
Calories 351; Fat 18 g; Carbohydrates 3.4 g; Sugar 2.3 g; Protein 44.6 g; Cholesterol 101 mg

Parmesan Walnut Salmon

Preparation Time: 10 minutes; Cooking Time: 15 minutes; Serve: 4

Ingredients:
- 4 salmon fillets
- 1/4 cup parmesan cheese, grated
- 1/2 cup walnuts
- 1 tsp olive oil
- 1 tbsp lemon rind

Directions:
1. Add walnuts into the food processor and process until finely ground.
2. Mix together ground walnuts, cheese, oil, and lemon rind.
3. Place salmon fillets into the baking dish and spread the walnut mixture on top of fish fillets.
4. Select BAKE mode, then set the temperature to 400 F and the time to 15 minutes, then press start.
5. When the display shows Add Food then place the baking dish in the vortex plus air fryer oven.
6. Serve and enjoy.

Nutritional Value (Amount per Serving):
Calories 361; Fat 22.6 g; Carbohydrates 2.1 g; Sugar 0.3 g; Protein 40.1 g; Cholesterol 83 mg

Taco Shrimp Fajitas

Preparation Time: 10 minutes; Cooking Time: 22 minutes; Serve: 6

Ingredients:
- 1 lb shrimp, tail-off
- 1 green bell pepper, diced
- 1 red bell pepper, diced
- 2 tbsp taco seasoning
- 1/2 cup onion, diced
- Pepper
- Salt

Directions:
1. Add shrimp, taco seasoning, onion, and bell peppers into the bowl and toss well.
2. Place shrimp mixture onto the cooking tray.
3. Select AIRFRY mode, then set the temperature to 390 F and the time to 22 minutes, then press start.
4. When the display shows Add Food then place the cooking tray in the vortex plus air fryer oven.
5. Stir shrimp halfway through.
6. Serve and enjoy.

Nutritional Value (Amount per Serving):
Calories 108; Fat 1.5 g; Carbohydrates 5.2 g; Sugar 2.4 g; Protein 17.8 g; Cholesterol 159 mg

Chipotle Shrimp

Preparation Time: 10 minutes; Cooking Time: 8 minutes; Serve: 4

Ingredients:
- 1 1/2 lbs shrimp, peeled and deveined
- 2 tsp chipotle in adobo

- 2 tbsp olive oil
- 4 tbsp lime juice
- 1/4 tsp ground cumin

Directions:
1. Add shrimp, oil, lime juice, cumin, and chipotle in a zip-lock bag, seal bag, and place in the fridge for 30 minutes.
2. Thread marinated shrimp onto skewers and place skewers onto the cooking tray.
3. Select AIRFRY mode, then set the temperature to 350 F and the time to 8 minutes, then press start.
4. When the display shows Add Food then place the cooking tray in the vortex plus air fryer oven.
5. Serve and enjoy.

Nutritional Value (Amount per Serving):
Calories 275; Fat 10 g; Carbohydrates 6.4 g; Sugar 0.7 g; Protein 39 g; Cholesterol 359 mg

Lime Shrimp Kababs

Preparation Time: 10 minutes; Cooking Time: 8 minutes; Serve: 2

Ingredients:
- 1 cup raw shrimp
- 1 garlic clove, minced
- 1 lime juice
- Pepper
- Salt

Directions:
1. In a bowl, mix shrimp, lime juice, garlic, pepper, and salt.
2. Thread shrimp onto the skewers and place them onto the cooking tray.
3. Select AIRFRY mode, then set the temperature to 350 F and the time to 8 minutes, then press start.
4. When the display shows Add Food then place the cooking tray in the vortex plus air fryer oven.
5. Serve and enjoy.

Nutritional Value (Amount per Serving):
Calories 21; Fat 0.2 g; Carbohydrates 2.6 g; Sugar 0.4 g; Protein 2.7 g; Cholesterol 23 mg

Curried Cod Fillets

Preparation Time: 10 minutes; Cooking Time: 10 minutes; Serve: 2

Ingredients:
- 2 cod fillets
- 1/4 tsp curry powder
- 1 tbsp butter, melted
- 1 tbsp basil, sliced
- 1/8 tsp garlic powder
- 1/8 tsp paprika
- 1/8 tsp sea salt

Directions:
1. In a small bowl, mix together curry powder, garlic powder, paprika, and salt and set aside.
2. Place cod fillets onto the cooking tray and brush with butter and sprinkle with dry spice mixture.
3. Select BAKE mode, then set the temperature to 360 F and the time to 10 minutes, then press start.
4. When the display shows Add Food then place the cooking tray in the vortex plus air fryer oven.
5. Garnish with basil and serve.

Nutritional Value (Amount per Serving):
Calories 143; Fat 6.8 g; Carbohydrates 0.4 g; Sugar 0.1 g; Protein 20.2 g; Cholesterol 70 mg

Air Fryer Cajun Scallops

Preparation Time: 10 minutes; Cooking Time: 6 minutes; Serve: 2

Ingredients:
- 12 scallops, clean and pat dry
- 1 tsp Cajun seasoning
- Salt

Directions:
1. Season scallops with Cajun seasoning and salt and place onto the cooking tray.
2. Select AIRFRY mode, then set the temperature to 400 F and the time to 6 minutes, then press start.
3. When the display shows Add Food then place the cooking tray in the vortex plus air fryer oven.
4. Serve and enjoy.

Nutritional Value (Amount per Serving):
Calories 158; Fat 1.4 g; Carbohydrates 4.3 g; Sugar 0 g; Protein 30.2 g; Cholesterol 59 mg

Tender Cod Fillets

Preparation Time: 10 minutes; Cooking Time: 12 minutes; Serve: 2

Ingredients:
- 1 lb cod fillets
- 1 lemon, sliced
- 1/4 cup butter, melted
- 1 tsp salt

Directions:
1. Brush cod fillets with melted butter and season with salt.
2. Place cod fillets into a baking dish and top with sliced lemon.
3. Select BAKE mode, then set the temperature to 400 F and the time to 10-12 minutes, then press start.
4. When the display shows Add Food then place the baking dish in the vortex plus air fryer oven.
5. Serve and enjoy.

Nutritional Value (Amount per Serving):
Calories 394; Fat 25.1 g; Carbohydrates 2.7 g; Sugar 0.8 g; Protein 41.1 g; Cholesterol 172 mg

Dill Salmon Patties

Preparation Time: 10 minutes; Cooking Time: 10 minutes; Serve: 2

Ingredients:
- 1 egg
- 14 oz salmon
- 1/4 cup onion, diced
- 1 tsp dill weed
- 1/2 cup almond flour

Directions:
1. Add all ingredients into the bowl and mix well.
2. Make patties from mixture and place onto the parchment-lined cooking tray.
3. Select AIRFRY mode, then set the temperature to 375 F and the time to 10 minutes, then press start.
4. When the display shows Add Food then place the cooking tray in the vortex plus air fryer oven.
5. Serve and enjoy.

Nutritional Value (Amount per Serving):
Calories 461; Fat 28.5 g; Carbohydrates 7.8 g; Sugar 1.8 g; Protein 47.5 g; Cholesterol 169 mg

Lemon Garlic Cod

Preparation Time: 10 minutes; Cooking Time: 20 minutes; Serve: 4

Ingredients:
- 1 1/2 lb cod fillet
- 1 lemon, sliced
- 1/4 cup butter, diced
- 4 garlic cloves, minced
- 2 lemon juice
- 2 tbsp olive oil
- Pepper
- Salt

Directions:
1. Place fish fillets in the baking dish and season with pepper and salt.
2. Whisk together garlic, lemon juice, and oil and pour over fish fillets.
3. Arrange butter pieces and lemon slices on top of fish fillets.
4. Select BAKE mode, then set the temperature to 400 F and the time to 20 minutes, then press start.
5. When the display shows Add Food then place the cooking tray in the vortex plus air fryer oven.
6. Serve and enjoy.

Nutritional Value (Amount per Serving):
Calories 313; Fat 20.3 g; Carbohydrates 2.9 g; Sugar 0.9 g; Protein 31 g; Cholesterol 114 mg

Salmon with Creamy Sauce

Preparation Time: 10 minutes; Cooking Time: 30 minutes; Serve: 4

Ingredients:
- 1 lb salmon
- 1 tbsp dill, chopped
- 1 tbsp mayonnaise
- 1/3 cup sour cream
- 1/2 lemon juice
- 1 tbsp garlic, minced
- 1 tbsp dijon mustard
- Pepper
- Salt

Directions:
1. In a bowl, mix together sour cream, lemon juice, dill, dijon, and mayonnaise.
2. Place salmon in a baking dish and top with garlic, pepper, and salt. Pour half sour cream mixture over salmon.
3. Cover baking dish with foil.
4. Select BAKE mode, then set the temperature to 400 F and the time to 30 minutes, then press start.
5. When the display shows Add Food then place the baking dish in the vortex plus air fryer oven.
6. Serve with sauce.

Nutritional Value (Amount per Serving):
Calories 215; Fat 12.5 g; Carbohydrates 3.2 g; Sugar 0.4 g; Protein 23.2 g; Cholesterol 59 mg

BBQ Parmesan Salmon

Preparation Time: 10 minutes; Cooking Time: 15 minutes; Serve: 5

Ingredients:
- 1 1/2 lbs salmon fillets
- 4 tbsp parsley, chopped
- 3 garlic cloves, minced
- 1/2 cup parmesan cheese, shredded
- 1 tsp BBQ seasoning
- 1 tsp paprika
- 1 tbsp olive oil
- Pepper
- Salt

Directions:
1. Place salmon in a baking dish.
2. Brush salmon with oil and sprinkle with seasoning.
3. In a small bowl, mix together parsley, cheese, and garlic and sprinkle on top of salmon.

4. Select BAKE mode, then set the temperature to 400 F and the time to 15 minutes, then press start.
5. When the display shows Add Food then place the baking dish in the vortex plus air fryer oven.
6. Serve and enjoy.

Nutritional Value (Amount per Serving):
Calories 239; Fat 13.2 g; Carbohydrates 1.4 g; Sugar 0.1 g; Protein 29.6 g; Cholesterol 66 mg

Delicious Parmesan Halibut

Preparation Time: 10 minutes; Cooking Time: 15 minutes; Serve: 6

Ingredients:
- 1 lb halibut fillets
- 1 tbsp almond flour
- 3 tbsp parmesan cheese, grated
- 1 tbsp dried parsley
- 2 tsp garlic powder
- 1 stick butter
- Pepper
- Salt

Directions:
1. In a bowl, mix together all ingredients except fish fillets.
2. Place fish fillets in a baking dish and spread bowl mixture on top of fish fillets.
3. Select BAKE mode, then set the temperature to 400 F and the time to 10-12 minutes, then press start.
4. When the display shows Add Food then place the baking dish in the vortex plus air fryer oven.
5. Serve and enjoy.

Nutritional Value (Amount per Serving):
Calories 260; Fat 18.2 g; Carbohydrates 1.1 g; Sugar 0.3 g; Protein 21.9 g; Cholesterol 78 mg

Ginger Garlic Fish Fillet

Preparation Time: 10 minutes; Cooking Time: 20 minutes; Serve: 2

Ingredients:
- 12 oz white fish fillets
- 2 garlic cloves, minced
- 2 tsp ginger, grated
- 1 lime zest
- 2 tbsp butter, cut into pieces
- 1/4 tsp onion powder
- Pepper
- Salt

Directions:
1. Place fish fillets in a baking dish. Top with ginger, garlic, and lime zest.
2. Season with onion powder, pepper, and salt.
3. Spread butter pieces on top of fish fillets.
4. Select BAKE mode, then set the temperature to 350 F and the time to 20 minutes, then press start.
5. When the display shows Add Food then place the baking dish in the vortex plus air fryer oven.
6. Serve and enjoy.

Nutritional Value (Amount per Serving):
Calories 408; Fat 24.4 g; Carbohydrates 3 g; Sugar 0.3 g; Protein 42.2 g; Cholesterol 162 mg

Chili Prawns

Preparation Time: 10 minutes; Cooking Time: 8 minutes; Serve: 2

Ingredients:
- 6 prawns
- 1 tsp chili flakes
- 1/4 tsp pepper
- 1 tsp chili powder

- 1/4 tsp salt

Directions:
1. In a bowl, add all ingredients and toss well.
2. Transfer prawns onto the cooking tray.
3. Select AIRFRY mode, then set the temperature to 350 F and the time to 6-8 minutes, then press start.
4. When the display shows Add Food then place the cooking tray in the vortex plus air fryer oven.
5. Serve and enjoy.

Nutritional Value (Amount per Serving):
Calories 83; Fat 1.4 g; Carbohydrates 1.9 g; Sugar 0.1 g; Protein 15.2 g; Cholesterol 139 mg

Chapter 8: Desserts Recipes

Zesty Lemon Muffins

Preparation Time: 10 minutes; Cooking Time: 15 minutes; Serve: 6
Ingredients:
- 2 eggs, separated
- 1 tsp baking powder
- 1 1/2 cups almond flour
- 1 lemon juice
- 1 lemon zest, grated
- 3 tbsp Swerve
- 1/4 cup heavy cream

Directions:
1. In a mixing bowl, mix together egg yolks, heavy cream, Sweetener, lemon zest, lemon juice, almond flour, and baking powder until well combined.
2. In a separate bowl, beat egg whites until soft peaks form.
3. Slowly add egg whites into the egg yolk mixture and fold well.
4. Divide mixture into the 6 silicone muffin molds.
5. Select BAKE mode, then set the temperature to 350 F and the time to 15 minutes, then press start.
6. When the display shows Add Food then place silicone muffin molds on the cooking tray and place in the vortex plus air fryer oven.
7. Serve and enjoy.

Nutritional Value (Amount per Serving):
Calories 204; Fat 17.4 g; Carbohydrates 7.9 g; Sugar 1.3 g; Protein 8 g; Cholesterol 61 mg

Chocolate Chip Muffins

Preparation Time: 10 minutes; Cooking Time: 12 minutes; Serve: 6
Ingredients:
- 3 eggs
- 1/2 cup unsweetened chocolate chips
- 1 tbsp Swerve
- 1 tsp baking powder
- 1 cup almond flour
- 1 1/2 cups mozzarella cheese, shredded

Directions:
1. In a bowl, whisk eggs with shredded cheese until well combined.
2. Add Swerve, baking powder, and almond flour and mix until well combined.
3. Add chocolate chips and fold well.
4. Divide mixture into the 6 silicone muffin molds.
5. Select BAKE mode, then set the temperature to 400 F and the time to 12 minutes, then press start.
6. When the display shows Add Food then place silicone muffin molds on the cooking tray and place in the vortex plus air fryer oven.
7. Serve and enjoy.

Nutritional Value (Amount per Serving):
Calories 293; Fat 23.5 g; Carbohydrates 10.5 g; Sugar 0.8 g; Protein 11.4 g; Cholesterol 86 mg

Fudgey Flourless Chocolate Cake

Preparation Time: 10 minutes; Cooking Time: 30 minutes; Serve: 12
Ingredients:
- 3 large eggs
- 1 tbsp vanilla
- 1/2 cup unsweetened cocoa powder
- 3/4 cup coconut sugar
- 1/2 cup butter
- 1 cup unsweetened chocolate chips
- 1/2 tsp sea salt

Directions:
1. Line 8-inch cake pan with parchment paper and set aside.
2. Melt butter in a small saucepan over medium heat then add chocolate chips and remove the pan from heat. Stir until chocolate chips in melted.
3. Add remaining ingredients and whisk until smooth.
4. Pour batter into the prepared cake pan.
5. Select BAKE mode, then set the temperature to 375 F and the time to 30 minutes, then press start.
6. When the display shows Add Food then place the cake pan in the vortex plus air fryer oven.
7. Slice and serve.

Nutritional Value (Amount per Serving):
Calories 236; Fat 20.1 g; Carbohydrates 8.7 g; Sugar 0.3 g; Protein 5.1 g; Cholesterol 67 mg

Chocolate Cookies

Preparation Time: 10 minutes; Cooking Time: 10 minutes; Serve: 20
Ingredients:
- 3 tbsp ground chia
- 1 cup almond flour
- 2 tbsp chocolate protein powder
- 1 cup sunflower seed butter

Directions:
1. In a large bowl, add all ingredients and mix until combined.
2. Make small balls from mixture and place onto the parchment-lined cooking sheet. Press down lightly.
3. Select BAKE mode, then set the temperature to 350 F and the time to 10 minutes, then press start.
4. When the display shows Add Food then place the cooking tray in the vortex plus air fryer oven.
5. Serve and enjoy.

Nutritional Value (Amount per Serving):
Calories 115; Fat 9 g; Carbohydrates 5 g; Sugar 1.4 g; Protein 5.3 g; Cholesterol 4 mg

Pumpkin Blondies

Preparation Time: 10 minutes; Cooking Time: 40 minutes; Serve: 12
Ingredients:
- 1 cup can pumpkin puree
- 1 tbsp pumpkin pie spice
- 1/4 cup Erythritol
- 1/4 cup coconut flour
- 1/2 cup tahini
- 1 tsp baking powder
- 1 tsp vanilla extract
- 1 tbsp vinegar

Directions:
1. Mix together in a bowl pumpkin, vinegar, vanilla, sweetener, and tahini.
2. In a separate dish mix together coconut flour, baking powder, and spices.
3. Add dry ingredients to the wet ingredients and stir until well combined.
4. Pour batter into the greased 8-inch baking pan.
5. Select BAKE mode, then set the temperature to 350 F and the time to 40 minutes, then press start.
6. When the display shows Add Food then place the baking pan in the vortex plus air fryer oven.
7. Slice and serve.

Nutritional Value (Amount per Serving):
Calories 68; Fat 5.5 g; Carbohydrates 3.7 g; Sugar 0.5 g; Protein 1.9 g; Cholesterol 0 mg

Almond Butter Blondie's

Preparation Time: 10 minutes; Cooking Time: 20 minutes; Serve: 16
Ingredients:
- 1 cup almond butter
- 3 tbsp water
- 1 tbsp ground chia seeds
- 1/4 cup dark chocolate chips
- 1/2 tsp baking soda
- 1 tsp vanilla
- 1/2 cup coconut sugar
- 1/4 tsp salt

Directions:
1. In a large bowl, mix together ground chia seeds and water. Stir well and let sit for 5 minutes.
2. Add almond butter, baking soda, vanilla, coconut sugar, and salt. Stir well. Add chocolate chips and fold well.
3. Pour batter into greased baking dish.
4. Select BAKE mode, then set the temperature to 350 F and the time to 20 minutes, then press start.
5. When the display shows Add Food then place the baking pan in the vortex plus air fryer oven.
6. Slice and serve.

Nutritional Value (Amount per Serving):
Calories 20; Fat 1.1 g; Carbohydrates 2.2 g; Sugar 1.1 g; Protein 0.4 g; Cholesterol 0 mg

Healthy Chia Muffins

Preparation Time: 10 minutes; Cooking Time: 35 minutes; Serve: 6
Ingredients:
- 2 tbsp coconut flour
- 20 drops liquid stevia
- 1/4 cup almond flour
- 1/2 cup ground flax
- 2 tbsp ground chia
- 1/4 cup water
- 1/4 tsp vanilla
- 1/4 tsp baking soda
- 1/2 tsp baking powder
- 1 tsp cinnamon

Directions:
1. In a small bowl, add 6 tablespoons of water and ground chia. Mix well and set aside.
2. In a large bowl, mix together ground flax, baking soda, baking powder, cinnamon, coconut flour, and almond flour.
3. Add chia seed mixture, vanilla, water, and stevia and stir to combine.
4. Pour mixture into the 6 silicone muffin molds.
5. Select BAKE mode, then set the temperature to 350 F and the time to 35 minutes, then press start.
6. When the display shows Add Food then place silicone muffin molds on the cooking tray and place in the vortex plus air fryer oven.
7. Serve and enjoy.

Nutritional Value (Amount per Serving):
Calories 84; Fat 6 g; Carbohydrates 6.4 g; Sugar 0.2 g; Protein 3.6 g; Cholesterol 0 mg

Easy Choco Brownies

Preparation Time: 10 minutes; Cooking Time: 15 minutes; Serve: 4
Ingredients:
- 1/2 cup almond butter, melted
- 1 scoop vanilla protein powder
- 2 tbsp unsweetened cocoa powder
- 1 cup bananas, overripe

Directions:
1. Add all ingredients into the blender and blend until smooth.

2. Pour blended mixture into the greased baking dish.
3. Select BAKE mode, then set the temperature to 350 F and the time to 15 minutes, then press start.
4. When the display shows Add Food then place the baking dish in the vortex plus air fryer oven.
5. Slice and serve.

Nutritional Value (Amount per Serving):
Calories 80; Fat 1.6 g; Carbohydrates 10.6 g; Sugar 4.8 g; Protein 8.1 g; Cholesterol 0 mg

Moist Cinnamon Muffins

Preparation Time: 10 minutes; Cooking Time: 15 minutes; Serve: 20
Ingredients:
- 2 scoops vanilla protein powder
- 1/2 cup almond flour
- 1/2 cup coconut oil
- 1/2 cup pumpkin puree
- 1/2 cup almond butter
- 1 tbsp cinnamon
- 1 tsp baking powder

Directions:
1. In a large bowl, combine together all dry ingredients and mix well.
2. Add wet ingredients into the dry ingredients and mix until well combined.
3. Divide mixture into the 20 silicone muffin molds.
4. Select BAKE mode, then set the temperature to 350 F and the time to 15 minutes, then press start.
5. When the display shows Add Food then place silicone muffin molds on the cooking tray and place in the vortex plus air fryer oven.
6. Serve and enjoy.

Nutritional Value (Amount per Serving):
Calories 80; Fat 7.1 g; Carbohydrates 1.6 g; Sugar 0.4 g; Protein 3.5 g; Cholesterol 0 mg

Cinnamon Strawberry Muffins

Preparation Time: 10 minutes; Cooking Time: 20 minutes; Serve: 12
Ingredients:
- 3 eggs
- 2/3 cup strawberries, diced
- 1 tsp vanilla
- 1/2 cup Swerve
- 5 tbsp butter, melted
- 1 tsp cinnamon
- 2 tsp baking powder
- 2 1/2 cups almond flour
- 1/3 cup heavy cream
- 1/4 tsp Himalayan salt

Directions:
1. In a bowl, beat together butter and swerve. Add eggs, cream, and vanilla and beat until frothy.
2. Sift together almond flour, cinnamon, baking powder, and salt.
3. Add almond flour mixture to the wet ingredients and mix until well combined. Add strawberries and fold well.
4. Pour mixture into the 12 silicone muffin molds.
5. Select BAKE mode, then set the temperature to 350 F and the time to 20 minutes, then press start.
6. When the display shows Add Food then place silicone muffin molds on the cooking tray and place in the vortex plus air fryer oven.
7. Serve and enjoy.

Nutritional Value (Amount per Serving):
Calories 208; Fat 18.8 g; Carbohydrates 6.4 g; Sugar 1.3 g; Protein 6.6 g; Cholesterol 58 mg

Vanilla Pecan Muffins

Preparation Time: 10 minutes; Cooking Time: 20 minutes; Serve: 12

Ingredients:
- 4 eggs
- 1/4 cup almond milk
- 2 tbsp butter, melted
- 1/2 cup swerve
- 1 tsp psyllium husk
- 1 tbsp baking powder
- 1 1/2 cups almond flour
- 1/2 cup pecans, chopped
- 1/2 tsp ground cinnamon
- 2 tsp allspice
- 1 tsp vanilla

Directions:
1. Beat eggs, almond milk, vanilla, sweetener, and butter in a bowl using a hand blender until smooth.
2. Add remaining ingredients and mix until well combined.
3. Divide mixture into the 12 silicone muffin molds.
4. Select BAKE mode, then set the temperature to 400 F and the time to 15-20 minutes, then press start.
5. When the display shows Add Food then place silicone muffin molds on the cooking tray and place in the vortex plus air fryer oven.
6. Serve and enjoy.

Nutritional Value (Amount per Serving):
Calories 159; Fat 14 g; Carbohydrates 5.8 g; Sugar 0.9 g; Protein 5.4 g; Cholesterol 60 mg

Almond Blueberry Muffins

Preparation Time: 10 minutes; Cooking Time: 20 minutes; Serve: 12

Ingredients:
- 3 large eggs
- 3/4 cup blueberries
- 1 1/2 tsp baking powder
- 1/2 cup Swerve
- 2 1/2 cups almond flour
- 1/2 tsp vanilla
- 1/3 cup unsweetened almond milk
- 1/3 cup coconut oil, melted

Directions:
1. In a large bowl, stir together almond flour, baking powder, erythritol.
2. Mix in the coconut oil, vanilla, eggs, and almond milk. Fold in blueberries.
3. Divide mixture into the 12 silicone muffin molds.
4. Select BAKE mode, then set the temperature to 350 F and the time to 20 minutes, then press start.
5. When the display shows Add Food then place silicone muffin molds on the cooking tray and place in the vortex plus air fryer oven.
6. Serve and enjoy.

Nutritional Value (Amount per Serving):
Calories 211; Fat 19.1 g; Carbohydrates 6.9 g; Sugar 1.9 g; Protein 6.7 g; Cholesterol 47 mg

Coconut Pumpkin Muffins

Preparation Time: 10 minutes; Cooking Time: 25 minutes; Serve: 10

Ingredients:
- 4 large eggs
- 1 tbsp baking powder
- 2/3 cup erythritol
- 1/2 cup almond flour
- 1/2 cup coconut flour
- 1 tsp vanilla
- 1/3 cup coconut oil, melted
- 1/2 cup pumpkin puree
- 1 tbsp pumpkin pie spice
- 1/2 tsp sea salt

Directions:

1. Preheat the oven to 350 F/ 180 C.
2. Spray a muffin tray with cooking spray and set aside.
3. In a large bowl, stir together coconut flour, pumpkin pie spice, baking powder, erythritol, almond flour, and sea salt.
4. Stir in eggs, vanilla, coconut oil, and pumpkin puree until well combined.
5. Pour batter into the 10 silicone muffin molds.
6. Select BAKE mode, then set the temperature to 350 F and the time to 25 minutes, then press start.
7. When the display shows Add Food then place silicone muffin molds on the cooking tray and place in the vortex plus air fryer oven.
8. Serve and enjoy.

Nutritional Value (Amount per Serving):
Calories 135; Fat 12.3 g; Carbohydrates 3.9 g; Sugar 1.3 g; Protein 4 g; Cholesterol 74 mg

Lemon Blueberry Muffins

Preparation Time: 10 minutes; Cooking Time: 25 minutes; Serve: 12
Ingredients:
- 2 large eggs
- 1/2 cup fresh blueberries
- 1 tsp baking powder
- 5 drops stevia
- 1/4 cup butter, melted
- 1 cup heavy whipping cream
- 2 cups almond flour
- 1/4 tsp lemon zest
- 1/2 tsp lemon extract

Directions:
1. Add eggs to the mixing bowl and whisk until good mix.
2. Add remaining ingredients to the eggs and mix well to combine.
3. Pour batter into the 12 silicone muffin molds.
4. Select BAKE mode, then set the temperature to 350 F and the time to 25 minutes, then press start.
5. When the display shows Add Food then place silicone muffin molds on the cooking tray and place in the vortex plus air fryer oven.
6. Serve and enjoy.

Nutritional Value (Amount per Serving):
Calories 191; Fat 17.7 g; Carbohydrates 5.4 g; Sugar 1.4 g; Protein 5.4 g; Cholesterol 55 mg

Moist Chocolate Muffins

Preparation Time: 10 minutes; Cooking Time: 30 minutes; Serve: 10
Ingredients:
- 2 eggs, lightly beaten
- 1 cup almond flour
- 1 tbsp baking powder
- 4 tbsp Erythritol
- 1/2 cup cocoa powder
- 1/2 cup heavy cream
- 1/2 tsp vanilla
- Pinch of salt

Directions:
1. In a bowl, mix together almond flour, baking powder, Erythritol, cocoa powder, and salt.
2. In a separate bowl, beat eggs with cream, and vanilla.
3. Pour egg mixture into the almond flour mixture and mix well.
4. Divide mixture into the 10 silicone muffin molds.
5. Select BAKE mode, then set the temperature to 375 F and the time to 30 minutes, then press start.
6. When the display shows Add Food then place silicone muffin molds on the cooking tray and place in the vortex plus air fryer oven.

7. Serve and enjoy.

Nutritional Value (Amount per Serving):
Calories 109; Fat 9.3 g; Carbohydrates 5.7 g; Sugar 0.6 g; Protein 4.4 g; Cholesterol 41 mg

Cranberry Bread Loaf

Preparation Time: 10 minutes; Cooking Time: 30 minutes; Serve: 10

Ingredients:
- 1 large egg
- 2 egg whites
- 1/3 cup cassava flour
- 1 tsp vanilla
- 1/2 tbsp vinegar
- 1 tsp stevia
- 3 tbsp cranberries, chopped
- 1/2 tsp baking soda
- 1/2 tbsp cinnamon
- 3 tbsp butter, melted
- 1/4 tsp salt

Directions:
1. In a bowl, whisk egg whites and egg.
2. Add vanilla, vinegar, and butter. Mix well.
3. Add cranberries, salt, stevia, baking soda, cinnamon, and cassava flour. Mix well.
4. Pour batter into the greased loaf pan.
5. Select BAKE mode, then set the temperature to 350 F and the time to 30 minutes, then press start.
6. When the display shows Add Food then place the loaf pan in the vortex plus air fryer oven.
7. Slice and serve.

Nutritional Value (Amount per Serving):
Calories 48; Fat 4 g; Carbohydrates 1.5 g; Sugar 0.2 g; Protein 1.4 g; Cholesterol 28 mg

Banana Almond Butter Bread

Preparation Time: 10 minutes; Cooking Time: 40 minutes; Serve: 12

Ingredients:
- 3 large eggs
- 3 bananas, mashed
- 1/2 tsp baking powder
- 1/4 cup coconut flour
- 1 1/2 tsp vanilla extract
- 1/4 cup coconut oil, melted
- 1/2 cup almond butter
- 1/8 cup chocolate chips
- 1/4 tsp sea salt
- 1/2 tsp cinnamon
- 1/2 tsp baking soda

Directions:
1. In a large bowl, combine together bananas, vanilla, coconut oil, almond butter, and eggs.
2. Add all dry ingredients and mix well to combine.
3. Pour batter into the greased loaf pan.
4. Select BAKE mode, then set the temperature to 350 F and the time to 40 minutes, then press start.
5. When the display shows Add Food then place the loaf pan in the vortex plus air fryer oven.
6. Slice and serve.

Nutritional Value (Amount per Serving):
Calories 100; Fat 6.8 g; Carbohydrates 8.4 g; Sugar 4.7 g; Protein 2.2 g; Cholesterol 47 mg

Zucchini Chocolate Bread

Preparation Time: 10 minutes; Cooking Time: 30 minutes; Serve: 6

Ingredients:

- 2 large eggs
- 1 cup zucchini, shredded
- 1 tbsp cocoa powder
- 1 cup almond butter
- 2 tbsp chocolate chips
- 1/2 tsp baking soda
- 1 tsp apple cider vinegar
- 1 tsp stevia
- 1 tbsp vanilla extract
- 1/4 tsp sea salt

Directions:
1. In a bowl, blend together almond butter, sea salt, cocoa powder, vanilla, stevia, and eggs until 2 minutes.
2. Add vinegar and soda and fold into the batter. Stir in shredded zucchini.
3. Pour batter into the greased loaf pan and then top with chocolate chips.
4. Select BAKE mode, then set the temperature to 350 F and the time to 30 minutes, then press start.
5. When the display shows Add Food then place the loaf pan in the vortex plus air fryer oven.
6. Slice and serve.

Nutritional Value (Amount per Serving):
Calories 70; Fat 4.4 g; Carbohydrates 4.1 g; Sugar 2.7 g; Protein 3.3 g; Cholesterol 63 mg

Delicious Mug Brownie

Preparation Time: 10 minutes; Cooking Time: 10 minutes; Serve: 1
Ingredients:
- 1 scoop chocolate protein powder
- 1 tbsp cocoa powder
- 1/2 tsp baking powder
- 1/4 cup almond milk

Directions:
1. Add baking powder, protein powder, and cocoa powder in a ramekin. Add milk and stir well.
2. Select BAKE mode, then set the temperature to 390 F and the time to 10 minutes, then press start.
3. When the display shows Add Food then place the ramekin on the cooking tray and place it in the vortex plus air fryer oven.
4. Serve and enjoy.

Nutritional Value (Amount per Serving):
Calories 207; Fat 15.8 g; Carbohydrates 9.5 g; Sugar 3.1 g; Protein 12.4 g; Cholesterol 20 mg

Chocolate Cookies

Preparation Time: 10 minutes; Cooking Time: 10 minutes; Serve: 20
Ingredients:
- 2 tbsp chocolate protein powder
- 1 cup sunflower seed butter
- 3 tbsp ground chia
- 1 cup almond flour

Directions:
1. In a large bowl, add all ingredients and mix until well combined.
2. Make small balls from the mixture and place onto the parchment-lined cooking tray.
3. Select BAKE mode, then set the temperature to 350 F and the time to 10 minutes, then press start.
4. When the display shows Add Food then place the cooking tray in the vortex plus air fryer oven.
5. Serve and enjoy.

Nutritional Value (Amount per Serving):
Calories 111; Fat 9.3 g; Carbohydrates 5.2 g; Sugar 0.2 g; Protein 4 g; Cholesterol 0 mg

Vanilla Cinnamon Mug Cake

Preparation Time: 10 minutes; Cooking Time: 10 minutes; Serve: 1
Ingredients:
- 1 tbsp almond flour
- 1/2 tsp baking powder
- 1/4 tsp vanilla
- 1/4 cup almond milk, unsweetened
- 1 scoop vanilla protein powder
- 1/2 tsp cinnamon
- 1 tsp Swerve

Directions:
1. Add protein powder, sweetener, cinnamon, almond flour, and baking powder into the ramekin and mix well.
2. Add vanilla extract and almond milk and stir well.
3. Select BAKE mode, then set the temperature to 390 F and the time to 10 minutes, then press start.
4. When the display shows Add Food then place the ramekin on the cooking tray and place it in the vortex plus air fryer oven.
5. Serve and enjoy.

Nutritional Value (Amount per Serving):
Calories 296; Fat 20.8 g; Carbohydrates 12 g; Sugar 2 g; Protein 17 g; Cholesterol 0 mg

Tasty Chocolate Brownies

Preparation Time: 10 minutes; Cooking Time: 30 minutes; Serve: 8
Ingredients:
- 3 eggs
- 1/2 cup unsweetened chocolate chips
- 1 tsp vanilla
- 1/4 cup Truvia
- 1/2 cup butter

Directions:
1. Add chocolate chips and butter into the microwave-safe bowl and microwave for 1 minute. Remove from microwave and stir well.
2. In a bowl, add eggs, vanilla, and sweetener and blend until frothy.
3. Pour melted chocolate and butter into the bowl and beat until well combined.
4. Pour batter into the greased baking pan.
5. Select BAKE mode, then set the temperature to 350 F and the time to 30 minutes, then press start.
6. When the display shows Add Food then place the baking pan in the vortex plus air fryer oven.
7. Slice and serve.

Nutritional Value (Amount per Serving):
Calories 227; Fat 21.2 g; Carbohydrates 4.2 g; Sugar 0.2 g; Protein 4.2 g; Cholesterol 92 mg

Coconut Muffins

Preparation Time: 10 minutes; Cooking Time: 12 minutes; Serve: 1
Ingredients:
- 1 egg
- 2 tsp coconut flour
- Pinch of salt
- Pinch of baking soda

Directions:
1. In a small bowl, mix together all ingredients and pour into the greased ramekin.
2. Select AIRFRY mode, then set the temperature to 400 F and the time to 12 minutes, then press start.
3. When the display shows Add Food then place the ramekin on the cooking tray and place it in the vortex plus air fryer oven.

4. Serve and enjoy.

Nutritional Value (Amount per Serving):
Calories 183; Fat 8 g; Carbohydrates 16 g; Sugar 2 g; Protein 9 g; Cholesterol 164 mg

Vanilla Coconut Pie

Preparation Time: 10 minutes; Cooking Time: 12 minutes; Serve: 6

Ingredients:
- 2 eggs
- 1 cup shredded coconut
- 1 tsp vanilla
- 4 tbsp butter
- 1 1/2 cups coconut milk
- 1/2 cup coconut flour
- 1/2 cup monk fruit

Directions:
1. In a large bowl, add all ingredients and mix until well blended.
2. Pour batter into the greased 6-inch pie dish.
3. Select AIRFRY mode, then set the temperature to 350 F and the time to 10-12 minutes, then press start.
4. When the display shows Add Food then place the pie dish on the cooking tray and place it in the vortex plus air fryer oven.
5. Serve and enjoy.

Nutritional Value (Amount per Serving):
Calories 281; Fat 28 g; Carbohydrates 6 g; Sugar 3 g; Protein 3 g; Cholesterol 75 mg

Tasty Brownie Muffins

Preparation Time: 10 minutes; Cooking Time: 15 minutes; Serve: 6

Ingredients:
- 3 eggs
- 1/3 cup butter, melted
- 1/3 cup cocoa powder
- 1/2 cup Erythritol
- 1 cup almond flour
- 1 tbsp gelatin

Directions:
1. Add all ingredients into the bowl and stir until just combined.
2. Divide mixture into the 6 silicone muffin molds.
3. Select BAKE mode, then set the temperature to 350 F and the time to 15 minutes, then press start.
4. When the display shows Add Food then place silicone muffin molds on the cooking tray and place in the vortex plus air fryer oven.
5. Serve and enjoy.

Nutritional Value (Amount per Serving):
Calories 240; Fat 22 g; Carbohydrates 6.8 g; Sugar 0.9 g; Protein 7.8 g; Cholesterol 109 mg

Raspberry Almond Muffins

Preparation Time: 10 minutes; Cooking Time: 35 minutes; Serve: 6

Ingredients:
- 2 eggs
- 4 oz raspberries
- 1 tsp baking powder
- 5 oz almond flour
- 2 tbsp coconut oil
- 2 tbsp Swerve

Directions:
1. In a medium bowl, mix together almond meal and baking powder.
2. Add Swerve, eggs, and oil and stir until just combined. Add raspberries and fold well.
3. Pour batter into the 6 silicone muffin molds.

4. Select BAKE mode, then set the temperature to 350 F and the time to 35 minutes, then press start.
5. When the display shows Add Food then place silicone muffin molds on the cooking tray and place in the vortex plus air fryer oven.
6. Serve and enjoy.

Nutritional Value (Amount per Serving):
Calories 206; Fat 17 g; Carbohydrates 8 g; Sugar 1.8 g; Protein 7.1 g; Cholesterol 55 mg

Cinnamon Apple Bars

Preparation Time: 10 minutes; Cooking Time: 45 minutes; Serve: 8

Ingredients:
- 1/4 cup dried apples
- 1/4 cup coconut butter, softened
- 1 cup pecans
- 1 cup of water
- 1 tsp vanilla
- 2 tbsp swerve
- 1 1/2 tsp baking powder
- 1 1/2 tsp cinnamon
- 1 tbsp ground flax seed

Directions:
1. Add all ingredients into the blender and blend until smooth.
2. Pour blended mixture into the greased baking dish.
3. Select BAKE mode, then set the temperature to 350 F and the time to 45 minutes, then press start.
4. When the display shows Add Food then place the baking dish in the vortex plus air fryer oven.
5. Slice and serve.

Nutritional Value (Amount per Serving):
Calories 165; Fat 15 g; Carbohydrates 6 g; Sugar 1 g; Protein 2 g; Cholesterol 0 mg

Moist Chocolate Cake

Preparation Time: 10 minutes; Cooking Time: 14 minutes; Serve: 8

Ingredients:
- 3 eggs
- 1/3 cup almond milk
- 2 1/4 tsp baking powder
- 1/4 cup cocoa powder
- 1 1/2 cups almond flour
- 1 1/2 tsp vanilla
- 1/3 cup erythritol
- Pinch of salt

Directions:
1. Add all ingredients into the mixing bowl and mix until well combined.
2. Pour batter into the greased 8-inch cake pan.
3. Select BAKE mode, then set the temperature to 350 F and the time to 14 minutes, then press start.
4. When the display shows Add Food then place the cake pan in the vortex plus air fryer oven.
5. Slice and serve.

Nutritional Value (Amount per Serving):
Calories 176; Fat 14 g; Carbohydrates 7 g; Sugar 1 g; Protein 7 g; Cholesterol 61 mg

Delicious Vanilla Cake

Preparation Time: 10 minutes; Cooking Time: 40 minutes; Serve: 8

Ingredients:
- 6 egg whites
- 1/2 cup Swerve
- 1/4 cup sour cream
- 1 tsp vanilla

- 1/4 cup coconut oil, melted
- 1 tsp baking powder
- 1/4 cup coconut flour
- 1 cup almond flour
- Pinch of salt

Directions:
1. In a bowl, whisk together vanilla and coconut oil. Add sour cream and whisk until combined.
2. Add sweetener and egg whites one by one and beat until combined.
3. Stir in flours, baking powder, and salt and blend until well combined.
4. Pour batter into the greased loaf pan.
5. Select BAKE mode, then set the temperature to 350 F and the time to 30-40 minutes, then press start.
6. When the display shows Add Food then place the loaf pan in the vortex plus air fryer oven.
7. Slice and serve.

Nutritional Value (Amount per Serving):
Calories 171; Fat 15 g; Carbohydrates 4 g; Sugar 0.8 g; Protein 6 g; Cholesterol 3 mg

Berry Cobbler

Preparation Time: 10 minutes; Cooking Time: 10 minutes; Serve: 6
Ingredients:
- 1 egg, lightly beaten
- 1 cup raspberries, sliced
- 2 tsp swerve
- 1 tbsp butter, melted
- 1 cup almond flour
- 1/2 tsp vanilla

Directions:
1. Add sliced raspberries into the air fryer baking dish.
2. Sprinkle sweetener over berries.
3. Mix together almond flour, vanilla, and butter in the bowl.
4. Add egg in almond flour mixture and stir well to combine.
5. Spread almond flour mixture over sliced raspberries.
6. Select AIRFRY mode, then set the temperature to 360 F and the time to 10 minutes, then press start.
7. When the display shows Add Food then place the baking dish in the vortex plus air fryer oven.
8. Serve and enjoy.

Nutritional Value (Amount per Serving):
Calories 148; Fat 12 g; Carbohydrates 7 g; Sugar 1.7 g; Protein 5.2 g; Cholesterol 32 mg

Coffee Cookies

Preparation Time: 10 minutes; Cooking Time: 15 minutes; Serve: 12
Ingredients:
- 2 eggs, lightly beaten
- 1/4 cup erythritol
- 1/4 cup brewed espresso
- 1 cup almond flour
- 1/2 cup ghee, melted
- 2 tsp baking powder
- 1/2 tbsp cinnamon

Directions:
1. Add all ingredients into the bowl and mix until well combined.
2. Make small cookies from mixture and place onto the parchment-lined cooking tray.
3. Select BAKE mode, then set the temperature to 350 F and the time to 15 minutes, then press start.

4. When the display shows Add Food then place the cooking tray in the vortex plus air fryer oven.
   5. Serve and enjoy.

Nutritional Value (Amount per Serving):
Calories 141; Fat 13.9 g; Carbohydrates 6.8 g; Sugar 0.4 g; Protein 3 g; Cholesterol 49 mg

Spiced Apples

Preparation Time: 10 minutes; Cooking Time: 10 minutes; Serve: 6

Ingredients:
- 4 small apples, sliced
- 1/2 cup Swerve
- 2 tbsp coconut oil, melted
- 1 tsp apple pie spice

Directions:
1. Add apple slices in a bowl and sprinkle sweetener, apple pie spice, and coconut oil over apple and toss to coat.
2. Transfer apple slices in the baking dish.
3. Select AIRFRY mode, then set the temperature to 350 F and the time to 10 minutes, then press start.
4. When the display shows Add Food then place the baking dish in the vortex plus air fryer oven.
5. Serve and enjoy.

Nutritional Value (Amount per Serving):
Calories 40; Fat 4 g; Carbohydrates 0.5 g; Sugar 0 g; Protein 0 g; Cholesterol 0 mg

Chocolate Macaroon

Preparation Time: 10 minutes; Cooking Time: 20 minutes; Serve: 20

Ingredients:
- 2 eggs
- 1/4 cup coconut oil
- 1/2 tsp baking powder
- 1/4 cup unsweetened cocoa powder
- 3 tbsp coconut flour
- 1 cup almond flour
- 1/3 cup unsweetened coconut, shredded
- 1/3 cup erythritol
- 1 tsp vanilla
- Pinch of salt

Directions:
1. Add all ingredients into the mixing bowl and mix until well combined.
2. Make small balls from mixture and place onto the parchment-lined cooking tray.
3. Select BAKE mode, then set the temperature to 350 F and the time to 15-20 minutes, then press start.
4. When the display shows Add Food then place the cooking tray in the vortex plus air fryer oven.
5. Serve and enjoy.

Nutritional Value (Amount per Serving):
Calories 79; Fat 7 g; Carbohydrates 6 g; Sugar 0.5 g; Protein 2.3 g; Cholesterol 16 mg

Pumpkin Pie

Preparation Time: 10 minutes; Cooking Time: 30 minutes; Serve: 4

Ingredients:
- 3 eggs
- 1/2 cup pumpkin puree
- 1/2 cup cream
- 1/2 cup unsweetened almond milk
- 1/2 tsp cinnamon
- 1 tsp vanilla
- 1/4 cup Swerve

Directions:
1. In a large bowl, add all ingredients and whisk until smooth.
2. Pour pie mixture into the greased baking dish.
3. Select BAKE mode, then set the temperature to 350 F and the time to 30 minutes, then press start.
4. When the display shows Add Food then place the baking dish in the vortex plus air fryer oven.
5. Slice and serve.

Nutritional Value (Amount per Serving):
Calories 86; Fat 5.5 g; Carbohydrates 4.4 g; Sugar 2 g; Protein 4.9 g; Cholesterol 128 mg

Hazelnut Cookies

Preparation Time: 10 minutes; Cooking Time: 10 minutes; Serve: 16
Ingredients:
- 3/4 cup hazelnut flour
- 1/3 cup Swerve
- 1/2 cup almond flour
- 20 drops liquid stevia
- 6 tbsp butter, softened

Directions:
1. Add all ingredients into the mixing bowl and mix until a soft dough is forms.
2. Make small balls from dough and place onto the parchment-lined cooking tray. Flatten each ball using a fork.
3. Select BAKE mode, then set the temperature to 350 F and the time to 10 minutes, then press start.
4. When the display shows Add Food then place the cooking tray in the vortex plus air fryer oven.
5. Serve and enjoy.

Nutritional Value (Amount per Serving):
Calories 92; Fat 9 g; Carbohydrates 1.7 g; Sugar 0.3 g; Protein 1.6 g; Cholesterol 11 mg

Pumpkin Butter Cookies

Preparation Time: 10 minutes; Cooking Time: 20 minutes; Serve: 27
Ingredients:
- 1 egg
- 1 tsp vanilla
- 1/2 cup butter
- 1/2 cup pumpkin puree
- 2 cups almond flour
- 1 tsp liquid stevia
- 1/2 tsp pumpkin pie spice

Directions:
1. Add all ingredients into the mixing bowl and mix until well combined.
2. Make small balls from mixture and place onto the parchment-lined cooking tray. Lightly flatten the balls using a fork.
3. Select BAKE mode, then set the temperature to 300 F and the time to 20 minutes, then press start.
4. When the display shows Add Food then place the cooking tray in the vortex plus air fryer oven.
5. Serve and enjoy.

Nutritional Value (Amount per Serving):
Calories 82; Fat 7 g; Carbohydrates 2 g; Sugar 0.5 g; Protein 2.1 g; Cholesterol 15 mg

Almond Butter Coconut Cookies

Preparation Time: 10 minutes; Cooking Time: 12 minutes; Serve: 10

Ingredients:
- 1 egg
- 1/4 cup coconut butter
- 9 oz almond butter
- 1/4 cup Swerve
- Pinch of salt

Directions:
1. Add all ingredients into the food processor and process until well combined.
2. Make small balls from mixture and place onto the parchment-lined cooking tray.
3. Select BAKE mode, then set the temperature to 320 F and the time to 12 minutes, then press start.
4. When the display shows Add Food then place the cooking tray in the vortex plus air fryer oven.
5. Serve and enjoy.

Nutritional Value (Amount per Serving):
Calories 132; Fat 12 g; Carbohydrates 4.2 g; Sugar 1 g; Protein 4 g; Cholesterol 16 mg

Almond Flaxseed Muffins

Preparation Time: 10 minutes; Cooking Time: 20 minutes; Serve: 9

Ingredients:
- 4 eggs, lightly beaten
- 1/2 cup erythritol
- 1 cup almond flour
- 1 cup ground flaxseed
- 1/2 cup butter, melted
- 1 tbsp cinnamon
- 1 tsp nutmeg
- 1 tsp baking powder
- Pinch of salt

Directions:
1. Add all ingredients into the mixing bowl and beat until well combined.
2. Divide mixture into the 9 silicone muffin molds.
3. Select BAKE mode, then set the temperature to 350 F and the time to 20 minutes, then press start.
4. When the display shows Add Food then place silicone muffin molds on the cooking tray and place in the vortex plus air fryer oven.
5. Serve and enjoy.

Nutritional Value (Amount per Serving):
Calories 259; Fat 22 g; Carbohydrates 7 g; Sugar 0.9 g; Protein 7 g; Cholesterol 100 mg

Delicious Apple Muffins

Preparation Time: 10 minutes; Cooking Time: 20 minutes; Serve: 36

Ingredients:
- 4 eggs
- 2 tbsp olive oil
- 2 tbsp Swerve
- 1/4 cup heavy cream
- 1/2 cup apple, peeled and diced
- 1 cup almond flour
- 1/2 tsp baking soda
- 1 tsp baking powder
- 1 tbsp ground cinnamon

Directions:
1. Add all ingredients except apple into the mixing bowl and mix until well combined. Add chopped apple and stir well.
2. Divide mixture into the 6 silicone muffin molds.
3. Select BAKE mode, then set the temperature to 325 F and the time to 20 minutes, then press start.
4. When the display shows Add Food then place silicone muffin molds on the cooking tray and place in the vortex plus air fryer oven.

5. Serve and enjoy.

Nutritional Value (Amount per Serving):
Calories 37; Fat 3 g; Carbohydrates 1.5 g; Sugar 0.5 g; Protein 1.3 g; Cholesterol 19 mg

Choco Chip Peanut Butter Muffins

Preparation Time: 10 minutes; Cooking Time: 25 minutes; Serve: 8

Ingredients:
- 2 eggs
- 1/3 cup unsweetened coconut milk
- 1/3 cup peanut butter
- 1/3 cup Swerve
- 1 tsp baking powder
- 1/3 cup unsweetened chocolate chips

Directions:
1. In a mixing bowl, mix together all dry ingredients. Add milk and peanut butter and stir to combine.
2. Add eggs and stir until smooth. Add chocolate chips and fold well.
3. Divide mixture into the 8 silicone muffin molds.
4. Select BAKE mode, then set the temperature to 350 F and the time to 25 minutes, then press start.
5. When the display shows Add Food then place silicone muffin molds on the cooking tray and place in the vortex plus air fryer oven.
6. Serve and enjoy.

Nutritional Value (Amount per Serving):
Calories 169; Fat 14 g; Carbohydrates 5 g; Sugar 1 g; Protein 5 g; Cholesterol 41 mg

Chapter 9: Dehydrated Recipes

Crisp Green Bean Chips

Preparation Time: 10 minutes; Cooking Time: 8 hours; Serve: 4
Ingredients:
- 2 1/2 lbs green beans, frozen & thawed
- 2 1/2 tbsp coconut oil, melted
- 1/2 tsp garlic powder
- 1/2 tsp onion powder
- 2 tsp salt

Directions:
1. Add green beans into the large bowl. Pour melted oil over green beans and sprinkle with garlic powder, onion powder, and salt and mix well.
2. Arrange green beans onto the cooking tray and place the cooking tray in vortex plus air fryer oven.
3. Select DEHYDRATE mode, then set the temperature to 135 F and the time to 8 hours, then press start.
4. Store green beans in an airtight container.

Nutritional Value (Amount per Serving):
Calories 105; Fat 8.5 g; Carbohydrates 6.3 g; Sugar 3.1 g; Protein 1.5 g; Cholesterol 0 mg

Zucchini Chips

Preparation Time: 10 minutes; Cooking Time: 10 hours; Serve: 4
Ingredients:
- 4 cups zucchini slices
- 1/2 tsp crushed red pepper flakes
- 1/2 tbsp onion powder
- 1/2 tbsp garlic powder
- 1 tbsp dried parsley
- 1 tbsp dried basil
- 1 tbsp dried oregano
- 2 tbsp olive oil
- 2 tbsp balsamic vinegar
- 1/2 tsp black pepper
- 1/2 tsp salt

Directions:
1. Add sliced zucchini and remaining ingredients into the mixing bowl and toss until well coated.
2. Arrange zucchini slices onto the cooking tray and place the cooking tray in vortex plus air fryer oven.
3. Select DEHYDRATE mode, then set the temperature to 120 F and the time to 10 hours, then press start.
4. Store zucchini chips in an airtight container.

Nutritional Value (Amount per Serving):
Calories 91; Fat 7.4 g; Carbohydrates 6.4 g; Sugar 2.6 g; Protein 1.9 g; Cholesterol 0 mg

Healthy Cashew Almond Crackers

Preparation Time: 10 minutes; Cooking Time: 9 hours; Serve: 12
Ingredients:
- 1 cup ground almonds
- 1 cup ground cashews
- 1/2 cup water
- 1/3 cup ground flax
- 3/4 tsp dried garlic
- 2 tsp rosemary
- Salt

Directions:
1. Add all ingredients except into the large bowl and mix well.
2. Spread mixture onto the parchment-lined cooking tray, about 1/3-inch thick.
3. Place the cooking tray in vortex plus air fryer oven.

4. Select DEHYDRATE mode, then set the temperature to 140 F and the time to 1 hour, then press start.
5. After a one-hour change temperature to 115 F and the timer to 8 hours.
6. Cut into pieces and serve.

Nutritional Value (Amount per Serving):
Calories 113; Fat 9 g; Carbohydrates 5.5 g; Sugar 1 g; Protein 4 g; Cholesterol 0 mg

Walnut Crackers

Preparation Time: 10 minutes; Cooking Time: 9 hours; Serve: 12

Ingredients:
- 2 cup walnuts, soak in water for overnight
- 1 tsp oregano
- 1/4 cup olives, sliced
- 1/3 cup sun-dried tomatoes, chopped
- 1/4 cup water
- 1/2 cup ground flax
- Salt

Directions:
1. Add walnuts in the food processor and process until ground finely.
2. Separately blend together olives and sun-dried tomatoes.
3. Mix together ground walnuts, blended olives & sun-dried tomatoes, ground flax, water, and salt until dough is formed.
4. Spread dough onto the parchment-lined cooking tray, about 1/4-inch thick.
5. Place the cooking tray in vortex plus air fryer oven.
6. Select DEHYDRATE mode, then set the temperature to 140 F and the time to 1 hour, then press start.
7. After a one-hour change temperature to 115 F and the timer to 8 hours.
8. Cut into pieces and serve.

Nutritional Value (Amount per Serving):
Calories 153; Fat 14.1 g; Carbohydrates 3.8 g; Sugar 0.4 g; Protein 6.1 g; Cholesterol 0 mg

Parmesan Zucchini Chips

Preparation Time: 10 minutes; Cooking Time: 10 hours; Serve: 4

Ingredients:
- 4 cups zucchini slices
- 1 tsp vinegar
- 1/8 tsp garlic powder
- 1 oz parmesan cheese, grated
- 1/8 tsp salt

Directions:
1. Add zucchini slices and remaining ingredients into the mixing bowl and toss well.
2. Arrange zucchini slices onto the cooking tray and place the cooking tray in vortex plus air fryer oven.
3. Select DEHYDRATE mode, then set the temperature to 135 F and the time to 10 hours, then press start.
4. Store zucchini chips in an airtight container.

Nutritional Value (Amount per Serving):
Calories 41; Fat 1.7 g; Carbohydrates 4.1 g; Sugar 2 g; Protein 3.7 g; Cholesterol 5 mg

Delicious BBQ Zucchini Chips

Preparation Time: 10 minutes; Cooking Time: 10 hours; Serve: 4

Ingredients:
- 4 cups zucchini slices
- 3 tbsp BBQ sauce, sugar-free

Directions:

1. Add zucchini slices into the large bowl. Pour BBQ sauce over zucchini slices and toss to coat.
2. Arrange zucchini slices onto the cooking tray and place the cooking tray in vortex plus air fryer oven.
3. Select DEHYDRATE mode, then set the temperature to 135 F and the time to 10 hours, then press start.
4. Store zucchini chips in an airtight container.

Nutritional Value (Amount per Serving):
Calories 36; Fat 0.2 g; Carbohydrates 8 g; Sugar 5 g; Protein 1.4 g; Cholesterol 0 mg

Spicy Cucumber Chips

Preparation Time: 10 minutes; Cooking Time: 6 hours; Serve: 4
Ingredients:
- 1 large cucumber, sliced
- 1 tsp dehydrated onions, minced
- 1/2 tsp paprika
- 1/4 tsp garlic powder
- 1/4 tsp onion powder
- 2 tbsp cheddar cheese, shredded
- 2 tbsp parmesan cheese, grated
- 1/8 tsp chipotle chili powder
- 1/8 tsp pepper
- 1/4 tsp salt

Directions:
1. Add cucumber slices into the mixing bowl, mix together remaining ingredients and sprinkle over cucumber slices and toss well.
2. Arrange cucumber slices onto the cooking tray and place the cooking tray in vortex plus air fryer oven.
3. Select DEHYDRATE mode, then set the temperature to 135 F and the time to 6 hours, then press start.
4. Store cucumber chips in an airtight container.

Nutritional Value (Amount per Serving):
Calories 38; Fat 1.9 g; Carbohydrates 3.7 g; Sugar 1.6 g; Protein 2.4 g; Cholesterol 6 mg

Dehydrated Sweet Peppers

Preparation Time: 10 minutes; Cooking Time: 10 hours; Serve: 4
Ingredients:
- 15 sweet peppers, wash, halve, de-seed & cut into strips

Directions:
1. Arrange sweet peppers onto the cooking tray and place the cooking tray in vortex plus air fryer oven.
2. Select DEHYDRATE mode, then set the temperature to 135 F and the time to 10-12 hours, then press start.
3. Store sweet peppers in an airtight container.

Nutritional Value (Amount per Serving):
Calories 5; Fat 0 g; Carbohydrates 1.1 g; Sugar 0.8 g; Protein 0.2 g; Cholesterol 0 mg

Dehydrated Strawberries

Preparation Time: 10 minutes; Cooking Time: 10 hours; Serve: 4
Ingredients:
- 2 cups fresh strawberries, wash, cut stems, & cut into slices

Directions:
1. Arrange strawberry slices onto the cooking tray and place the cooking tray in vortex plus air fryer oven.

2. Select DEHYDRATE mode, then set the temperature to 135 F and the time to 10 hours, then press start.
3. Store strawberry slices in an airtight container.

Nutritional Value (Amount per Serving):
Calories 23; Fat 0.2 g; Carbohydrates 5.5 g; Sugar 3.5 g; Protein 0.5 g; Cholesterol 0 mg

Healthy Beet Chips

Preparation Time: 10 minutes; Cooking Time: 8 hours; Serve: 4
Ingredients:
- 4 medium beets, peel and sliced
- 1 tbsp salt

Directions:
1. Arrange beet slices onto the cooking tray and sprinkle with salt then place the cooking tray in vortex plus air fryer oven.
2. Select DEHYDRATE mode, then set the temperature to 135 F and the time to 8-10 hours, then press start.
3. Store beet slices in an airtight container.

Nutritional Value (Amount per Serving):
Calories 44; Fat 0.2 g; Carbohydrates 10 g; Sugar 8 g; Protein 1.7 g; Cholesterol 0 mg

Broccoli Chips

Preparation Time: 10 minutes; Cooking Time: 10 hours; Serve: 4
Ingredients:
- 1 lb broccoli florets
- 1 tsp onion powder
- 1 garlic clove
- 1/2 cup vegetable broth
- 1/4 cup hemp seeds
- 2 tbsp nutritional yeast
- 2 tbsp tamari sauce

Directions:
1. Add broccoli florets into the mixing bowl.
2. Add remaining ingredients into the blender and blend until smooth.
3. Pour blended mixture over broccoli florets and mix well.
4. Arrange broccoli florets onto the parchment-lined cooking tray and place the cooking tray in vortex plus air fryer oven.
5. Select DEHYDRATE mode, then set the temperature to 115 F and the time to 10-12 hours, then press start.
6. Store broccoli chips in an airtight container.

Nutritional Value (Amount per Serving):
Calories 111; Fat 4.3 g; Carbohydrates 12.2 g; Sugar 2.2 g; Protein 9.7 g; Cholesterol 0 mg

Dried Cauliflower

Preparation Time: 10 minutes; Cooking Time: 8 hours; Serve: 3
Ingredients:
- 1 large cauliflower head, wash & cut into florets
- 1 tbsp chives, chopped
- 2 tbsp tahini
- 1/4 cup dried tomatoes
- 1 cup tomatoes, chopped
- 1/2 lemon juice
- 1/4 tsp chili powder
- Salt

Directions:
1. Add cauliflower florets into the mixing bowl.
2. Add remaining ingredients into the blender and blend until smooth.
3. Pour blended mixture over cauliflower florets and mix well.

4. Arrange cauliflower florets onto the parchment-lined cooking tray and place the cooking tray in vortex plus air fryer oven.
5. Select DEHYDRATE mode, then set the temperature to 105 F and the time to 6-8 hours, then press start.
6. Store cauliflower in an airtight container.

Nutritional Value (Amount per Serving):
Calories 60; Fat 4.6 g; Carbohydrates 3.9 g; Sugar 2.2 g; Protein 1.8 g; Cholesterol 0 mg

Pork Jerky

Preparation Time: 10 minutes; Cooking Time: 5 hours; Serve: 4

Ingredients:
- 1 lb pork loin, cut into thin slices
- 1/2 tsp garlic powder
- 1 tsp sesame oil
- 1 tbsp chili garlic sauce
- 1 tbsp Worcestershire sauce
- 1/3 cup soy sauce
- 1/4 tsp salt
- 1 tsp black pepper
- 1/2 tsp onion powder

Directions:
1. Add all ingredients except pork slices into the large bowl and mix well.
2. Add pork slices in the bowl and mix until well coated, cover, and place in the refrigerator overnight.
3. Arrange marinated pork slices onto the parchment-lined cooking tray and place the cooking tray in vortex plus air fryer oven.
4. Select DEHYDRATE mode, then set the temperature to 160 F and the time to 5 hours, then press start.
5. Store pork jerky in an airtight container.

Nutritional Value (Amount per Serving):
Calories 303; Fat 17 g; Carbohydrates 3.2 g; Sugar 1.3 g; Protein 32.5 g; Cholesterol 91 mg

Beef Jerky

Preparation Time: 10 minutes; Cooking Time: 8 hours; Serve: 6

Ingredients:
- 2 lbs flank steak, cut into thin slices
- 3 tbsp ranch seasoning
- 3/4 cup Worcestershire sauce
- 3/4 cup soy sauce
- 1/4 tsp cayenne pepper
- 1 tsp liquid smoke
- 1 1/2 tbsp red pepper flakes

Directions:
1. Add all ingredients into the large bowl and mix well, cover and place in the refrigerator overnight.
2. Arrange marinated meat slices onto the parchment-lined cooking tray and place the cooking tray in vortex plus air fryer oven.
3. Select DEHYDRATE mode, then set the temperature to 145 F and the time to 8 hours, then press start.
4. Store beef jerky in an airtight container.

Nutritional Value (Amount per Serving):
Calories 360; Fat 12.8 g; Carbohydrates 9.2 g; Sugar 6.7 g; Protein 44.2 g; Cholesterol 83 mg

Easy Chicken Jerky

Preparation Time: 10 minutes; Cooking Time: 7 hours; Serve: 4

Ingredients:

- 1 lb chicken tenders, boneless, skinless and cut into 1/4-inch strips
- 1/2 tsp garlic powder
- 1 tsp lemon juice
- 1/2 cup soy sauce
- 1/4 tsp ground ginger
- 1/4 tsp black pepper

Directions:
1. Add all ingredients except chicken into the zip-lock bag.
2. Add chicken strips and seal bag and shake until chicken is well coated. Place in refrigerator for 1 hour.
3. Arrange marinated chicken slices onto the parchment-lined cooking tray and place the cooking tray in vortex plus air fryer oven.
4. Select DEHYDRATE mode, then set the temperature to 145 F and the time to 7 hours, then press start.
5. Store chicken jerky in an airtight container.

Nutritional Value (Amount per Serving):
Calories 235; Fat 8.5 g; Carbohydrates 2.9 g; Sugar 0.7 g; Protein 34.9 g; Cholesterol 101 mg

Spicy Pork Jerky

Preparation Time: 10 minutes; Cooking Time: 5 hours; Serve: 4
Ingredients:
- 1 lb pork lean meat, sliced thinly
- 1 tsp chili powder
- 1 tsp paprika
- 1/2 tsp garlic powder
- 1/4 tsp pepper
- 1/2 tsp oregano
- 1 tsp salt

Directions:
1. Add meat slices and remaining ingredients into the zip-lock bag, seal bag, and place in the refrigerator overnight.
2. Arrange marinated meat slices onto the parchment-lined cooking tray and place the cooking tray in vortex plus air fryer oven.
3. Select DEHYDRATE mode, then set the temperature to 160 F and the time to 5 hours, then press start.
4. Store pork jerky in an airtight container.

Nutritional Value (Amount per Serving):
Calories 168; Fat 4.2 g; Carbohydrates 1.1 g; Sugar 0.2 g; Protein 29.9 g; Cholesterol 83 mg

Lamb Jerky

Preparation Time: 10 minutes; Cooking Time: 6 hours; Serve: 6
Ingredients:
- 2 lbs boneless lamb, slice into thin strips
- 1 tsp onion powder
- 3 tbsp Worcestershire sauce
- 1/3 cup soy sauce
- 1/2 tsp black pepper
- 1 tbsp oregano
- 1 tsp garlic powder

Directions:
1. Add lamb slices and remaining ingredients into the zip-lock bag, seal bag, and place in the refrigerator overnight.
2. Arrange marinated lamb slices onto the parchment-lined cooking tray and place the cooking tray in vortex plus air fryer oven.
3. Select DEHYDRATE mode, then set the temperature to 145 F and the time to 6 hours, then press start.
4. Store lamb jerky in an airtight container.

Nutritional Value (Amount per Serving):

Calories 302; Fat 11.2 g; Carbohydrates 3.8 g; Sugar 2 g; Protein 43.6 g; Cholesterol 136 mg

Simple Tofu Jerky

Preparation Time: 10 minutes; Cooking Time: 4 hours; Serve: 4
Ingredients:
- 1 block tofu, pressed & cut into slices
- 2 tbsp sriracha
- 2 tbsp Worcestershire sauce

Directions:
1. Add tofu slices and remaining ingredients into the zip-lock bag, seal bag, and place in the refrigerator overnight.
2. Arrange tofu slices onto the parchment-lined cooking tray and place the cooking tray in vortex plus air fryer oven.
3. Select DEHYDRATE mode, then set the temperature to 145 F and the time to 4 hours, then press start.
4. Store tofu jerky in an airtight container.

Nutritional Value (Amount per Serving):
Calories 31; Fat 1 g; Carbohydrates 3.4 g; Sugar 1.6 g; Protein 1.9 g; Cholesterol 0 mg

Eggplant Chips

Preparation Time: 10 minutes; Cooking Time: 4 hours; Serve: 4
Ingredients:
- 1 eggplant, cut into ¼ inch thick slices
- 1/4 tsp garlic powder
- 1 tsp paprika
- 1/4 tsp onion powder

Directions:
1. Add all ingredients into the bowl and toss well.
2. Arrange eggplant slices onto the parchment-lined cooking tray and place the cooking tray in vortex plus air fryer oven.
3. Select DEHYDRATE mode, then set the temperature to 145 F and the time to 4 hours, then press start.
4. Store eggplant chips in an airtight container.

Nutritional Value (Amount per Serving):
Calories 31; Fat 0.3 g; Carbohydrates 7.3 g; Sugar 3.6 g; Protein 1.3 g; Cholesterol 0 mg

Squash Chips

Preparation Time: 10 minutes; Cooking Time: 12 hours; Serve: 6
Ingredients:
- 1 yellow squash, cut into 1/8-inch thick slices
- 2 tsp olive oil
- 2 tbsp vinegar
- Salt

Directions:
1. Add all ingredients into the large bowl and toss well.
2. Arrange squash slices onto the parchment-lined cooking tray and place the cooking tray in vortex plus air fryer oven.
3. Select DEHYDRATE mode, then set the temperature to 115 F and the time to 12 hours, then press start.
4. Store squash chips in an airtight container.

Nutritional Value (Amount per Serving):
Calories 20; Fat 1.6 g; Carbohydrates 1.1 g; Sugar 0.6 g; Protein 0.4 g; Cholesterol 0 mg

Avocado Chips

Preparation Time: 10 minutes; Cooking Time: 10 hours; Serve: 6

Ingredients:
- 4 avocados, halved, pitted & cut into slices
- 1/4 tsp cayenne
- 1/2 lemon juice
- 1/4 tsp sea salt

Directions:
1. Arrange avocado slices onto the parchment-lined cooking tray and place the cooking tray in vortex plus air fryer oven.
2. Drizzle lemon juice over avocado slices and sprinkle with cayenne and salt.
3. Select DEHYDRATE mode, then set the temperature to 160 F and the time to 10 hours, then press start.
4. Store avocado chips in an airtight container.

Nutritional Value (Amount per Serving):
Calories 275; Fat 26.2 g; Carbohydrates 11.7 g; Sugar 0.8 g; Protein 2.6 g; Cholesterol 0 mg

Dehydrated Almonds

Preparation Time: 10 minutes; Cooking Time: 12 hours; Serve: 6

Ingredients:
- 2 cups almonds, soak in water for overnight
- 1 tsp chili powder
- 1 tbsp olive oil
- 3/4 tsp kosher salt

Directions:
1. Add all ingredients into the bowl and toss well.
2. Arrange almonds onto the parchment-lined cooking tray and place the cooking tray in vortex plus air fryer oven.
3. Select DEHYDRATE mode, then set the temperature to 125 F and the time to 12 hours, then press start.
4. Store almonds in an airtight container.

Nutritional Value (Amount per Serving):
Calories 205; Fat 18.2 g; Carbohydrates 7 g; Sugar 1.4 g; Protein 6.8 g; Cholesterol 0 mg

Snap Pea Chips

Preparation Time: 10 minutes; Cooking Time: 8 hours; Serve: 4

Ingredients:
- 2 cups snap peas
- 2 tsp olive oil
- Salt

Directions:
1. Toss snap peas with oil and salt.
2. Arrange snap peas onto the parchment-lined cooking tray and place the cooking tray in vortex plus air fryer oven.
3. Select DEHYDRATE mode, then set the temperature to 135 F and the time to 8 hours, then press start.
4. Store snap peas in an airtight container.

Nutritional Value (Amount per Serving):
Calories 79; Fat 2.6 g; Carbohydrates 10.5 g; Sugar 4.1 g; Protein 3.9 g; Cholesterol 0 mg

Mushroom Chips

Preparation Time: 10 minutes; Cooking Time: 5 hours; Serve: 4

Ingredients:

- 1 cup mushrooms, clean & cut into 1/8-inch thick slices
- 1/4 tbsp fresh lemon juice
- Salt

Directions:
1. Toss mushrooms with lemon juice, and salt into the bowl.
2. Arrange mushroom slices onto the parchment-lined cooking tray and place the cooking tray in vortex plus air fryer oven.
3. Select DEHYDRATE mode, then set the temperature to 160 F and the time to 5 hours, then press start.
4. Store mushroom chips in an airtight container.

Nutritional Value (Amount per Serving):
Calories 4; Fat 0.1 g; Carbohydrates 0.6 g; Sugar 0.3 g; Protein 0.6 g; Cholesterol 0 mg

Marinated Eggplant Slices

Preparation Time: 10 minutes; Cooking Time: 12 hours; Serve: 4

Ingredients:
- 1 eggplant, sliced
- 1/2 cup vinegar
- 1/2 cup olive oil
- 1 tsp paprika
- 1/2 tsp black pepper
- 1 garlic clove, minced
- 1/2 tsp sea salt

Directions:
1. Add eggplant slices and remaining ingredients into the zip-lock bag, seal bag, and place in the refrigerator for 2 hours.
2. Arrange marinated eggplant slices onto the parchment-lined cooking tray and place the cooking tray in vortex plus air fryer oven.
3. Select DEHYDRATE mode, then set the temperature to 115 F and the time to 12 hours, then press start.
4. Store eggplant slices in an airtight container.

Nutritional Value (Amount per Serving):
Calories 254; Fat 25.5 g; Carbohydrates 7.7 g; Sugar 3.6 g; Protein 1.3 g; Cholesterol 0 mg

Easy Kale Chips

Preparation Time: 10 minutes; Cooking Time: 4 hours; Serve: 2

Ingredients:
- 1 kale heads, clean & cut into pieces
- 1/2 tbsp fresh lemon juice
- 1 1/2 tbsp nutritional yeast
- 1 tbsp olive oil
- 1/2 tsp garlic powder
- 1 tsp sea salt

Directions:
1. Add kale and remaining ingredients into the bowl and mix well.
2. Arrange kale pieces onto the parchment-lined cooking tray and place the cooking tray in vortex plus air fryer oven.
3. Select DEHYDRATE mode, then set the temperature to 145 F and the time to 4 hours, then press start.
4. Store kale chips in an airtight container.

Nutritional Value (Amount per Serving):
Calories 111; Fat 7.5 g; Carbohydrates 8.5 g; Sugar 0.3 g; Protein 4.9 g; Cholesterol 0 mg

Parsnips Chips

Preparation Time: 10 minutes; Cooking Time: 6 hours; Serve: 2

Ingredients:

- 1 parsnip, cut into 1/4-inch thick slices
- Pepper
- Salt

Directions:
1. Season parsnip slices with pepper and salt.
2. Arrange parsnip slices onto the parchment-lined cooking tray and place the cooking tray in vortex plus air fryer oven.
3. Select DEHYDRATE mode, then set the temperature to 125 F and the time to 6 hours, then press start.
4. Store parsnip chips in an airtight container.

Nutritional Value (Amount per Serving):
Calories 4; Fat 0 g; Carbohydrates 0.9 g; Sugar 0.2 g; Protein 0.1 g; Cholesterol 0 mg

Turkey Jerky

Preparation Time: 10 minutes; Cooking Time: 5 hours; Serve: 4

Ingredients:
- 1 lb turkey meat, cut into thin slices
- 1/3 cup Worcestershire sauce
- 2 tbsp soy sauce
- 2 tsp garlic powder
- 1 tbsp onion powder
- 1 tsp salt

Directions:
1. Add turkey slices and remaining ingredients into the zip-lock bag, seal bag, and place in the refrigerator overnight.
2. Arrange turkey slices onto the parchment-lined cooking tray and place the cooking tray in vortex plus air fryer oven.
3. Select DEHYDRATE mode, then set the temperature to 160 F and the time to 5 hours, then press start.
4. Store turkey jerky in an airtight container.

Nutritional Value (Amount per Serving):
Calories 228; Fat 5.7 g; Carbohydrates 7 g; Sugar 5.1 g; Protein 34.1 g; Cholesterol 86 mg

Lemon Slices

Preparation Time: 10 minutes; Cooking Time: 10 hours; Serve: 4

Ingredients:
- 4 lemons, wash and cut into 1/4-inch thick slices

Directions:
1. Arrange lemon slices onto the parchment-lined cooking tray and place the cooking tray in vortex plus air fryer oven.
2. Select DEHYDRATE mode, then set the temperature to 125 F and the time to 10 hours, then press start.
3. Store lemon slices in an airtight container.

Nutritional Value (Amount per Serving):
Calories 17; Fat 0.2 g; Carbohydrates 5.4 g; Sugar 1.5 g; Protein 0.6 g; Cholesterol 0 mg

Dehydrated Bell Peppers

Preparation Time: 10 minutes; Cooking Time: 12 hours; Serve: 4

Ingredients:
- 2 green bell peppers
- 1 red bell pepper
- 1 yellow bell pepper

Directions:
1. Cut bell peppers in half, remove seeds & cut into 1/2-inch pieces.

2. Arrange bell pepper pieces onto the parchment-lined cooking tray and place the cooking tray in vortex plus air fryer oven.
3. Select DEHYDRATE mode, then set the temperature to 135 F and the time to 12 hours, then press start.
4. Store bell peppers in an airtight container.

Nutritional Value (Amount per Serving):
Calories 38; Fat 0.3 g; Carbohydrates 9 g; Sugar 6 g; Protein 1.2 g; Cholesterol 0 mg

Chapter 10: 30-Day Meal Plan

Day 1
Breakfast-Spinach Egg Muffins
Lunch-Delicious Baked Tilapia
Dinner-Cajun Pork Chops

Day 2
Breakfast-Cheesy Egg Bites
Lunch-Delicious Turkey Cutlets
Dinner-Steak Tips with Mushrooms

Day 3
Breakfast-Spinach Zucchini Egg Casserole
Lunch-Baked Catfish
Dinner-Juicy Lime Jalapeno Steak

Day 4
Breakfast-Healthy Zucchini Muffins
Lunch-Baked Parmesan Chicken Breasts
Dinner-Mushroom Broccoli Steak Bites

Day 5
Breakfast-Mushroom Cheese Quiche
Lunch-Easy Parmesan Tilapia
Dinner-Rib eye Steaks

Day 6
Breakfast-Sausage Omelet
Lunch-Juicy & Crispy Chicken Drumsticks
Dinner-Juicy Air Fryer Steak

Day 7
Breakfast-Breakfast Egg Bake
Lunch-Garlic Butter Cod
Dinner-Delicious Blackened Pork Tenderloin

Day 8
Breakfast-Artichoke Spinach Egg Bake
Lunch-Breaded Chicken Tenders
Dinner-Simple Herbed Beef Tips

Day 9
Breakfast-Italian Egg Muffins
Lunch-Baked Parmesan Cod
Dinner-Flavorful Cheese Casserole

Day 10
Breakfast-Jalapeno Bacon Egg Cups
Lunch-Crispy Chicken Thighs
Dinner-Spicy Jalapeno Sliders

Day 11
Breakfast-Veggie Cheese Egg Bake
Lunch-Lemon Parmesan Cod
Dinner-Flavorful Lamb Chops

Day 12
Breakfast-Broccoli Egg Muffins
Lunch-Lemon Thyme Chicken
Dinner-Juicy Pork Tenderloin

Day 13
Breakfast-Ham Egg Casserole
Lunch-Lemon Pepper Sea Bass
Dinner-Super Delicious Ranch Pork Chops

Day 14
Breakfast-Tomato Basil Egg Bake
Lunch-Simple Baked Chicken Breasts
Dinner-Flavorful Bone-in Pork Chops

Day 15
Breakfast-Healthy Asparagus Quiche
Lunch-Shrimp with Cherry Tomatoes
Dinner-Flavorful Baked Pork Chops

Day 16
Breakfast-Spinach Egg Muffins
Lunch-Delicious Baked Tilapia
Dinner-Cajun Pork Chops

Day 17
Breakfast-Cheesy Egg Bites
Lunch-Delicious Turkey Cutlets
Dinner-Steak Tips with Mushrooms

Day 18
Breakfast-Spinach Zucchini Egg Casserole
Lunch-Baked Catfish
Dinner-Juicy Lime Jalapeno Steak
Day 19
Breakfast-Healthy Zucchini Muffins
Lunch-Baked Parmesan Chicken Breasts
Dinner-Mushroom Broccoli Steak Bites
Day 20
Breakfast-Mushroom Cheese Quiche
Lunch-Easy Parmesan Tilapia
Dinner-Rib eye Steaks
Day 21
Breakfast-Sausage Omelet
Lunch-Juicy & Crispy Chicken Drumsticks
Dinner-Juicy Air Fryer Steak
Day 22
Breakfast-Breakfast Egg Bake
Lunch-Garlic Butter Cod
Dinner-Delicious Blackened Pork Tenderloin
Day 23
Breakfast-Artichoke Spinach Egg Bake
Lunch-Breaded Chicken Tenders
Dinner-Simple Herbed Beef Tips
Day 24
Breakfast-Italian Egg Muffins
Lunch-Baked Parmesan Cod
Dinner-Flavorful Cheese Casserole
Day 25
Breakfast-Jalapeno Bacon Egg Cups
Lunch-Crispy Chicken Thighs
Dinner-Spicy Jalapeno Sliders
Day 26
Breakfast-Veggie Cheese Egg Bake
Lunch-Lemon Parmesan Cod
Dinner-Flavorful Lamb Chops
Day 27
Breakfast-Broccoli Egg Muffins
Lunch-Lemon Thyme Chicken
Dinner-Juicy Pork Tenderloin
Day 28
Breakfast-Ham Egg Casserole
Lunch-Lemon Pepper Sea Bass
Dinner-Super Delicious Ranch Pork Chops
Day 29
Breakfast-Tomato Basil Egg Bake
Lunch-Simple Baked Chicken Breasts
Dinner-Flavorful Bone-in Pork Chops
Day 30
Breakfast-Healthy Asparagus Quiche
Lunch-Shrimp with Cherry Tomatoes
Dinner-Flavorful Baked Pork Chops

Conclusion

The instant vortex air fryer oven is a multi-tasking cooking appliance that helps you for grilling, roasting, baking, broiling, reheating your leftover food, and dehydrating food vegetables and meat. To do all these tasks you never need to buy separate appliances. Your instant vortex air fryer oven is capable to handle all these tasks. This will make your cooking simple, easy, and smart way.

In this book, we have used a unique combination of a healthy cooking appliance known as a vortex air fryer oven and a healthy diet plan known as the keto diet. Most of the peoples follow the keto diet for weight loss purpose. Keto diet changes your daily eating habit towards healthy eating food. The diet comes with long term health benefits. The book contains healthy keto recipes from breakfast to desserts. All the healthy and delicious recipes are done into an instant vortex air fryer oven. The recipes written in this book are unique and written into an easily understandable form. All the recipes are written in this book comes with their exact preparation and cooking time with their nutritional values.

www.ingramcontent.com/pod-product-compliance
Lightning Source LLC
Chambersburg PA
CBHW080224100526
44583CB00020BA/2578